The Ethics of
Reality TV

The Ethics of Reality TV

A Philosophical Examination

EDITED BY

WENDY N. WYATT AND

KRISTIE BUNTON

continuum

Continuum International Publishing Group
80 Maiden Lane, New York, NY 10038
The Tower Building, 11 York Road, London SE1 7NX

www.continuumbooks.com

Library of Congress Cataloging-in-Publication Data
A catalog record for this book is available from the Library of Congress.

ISBN: HB: 978-1-4411-9381-0
PB: 978-1-4411-8903-5

Typeset by Fakenham Prepress Solutions, Fakenham, Norfolk NR21 8NN
Printed and bound in the United States of America

Contents

Editors' Note

We think one of the strengths of this book is that it features contributors from around the world who explore a television genre that is an international phenomenon. As part of this phenomenon, reality producers tweak their shows to appeal to distinct customs or language in each country where a program will air. So the British version of what became *American Idol* in the USA contained distinctive British elements that were eliminated from the US version. In analysing this international television genre, we think our readers will benefit from hearing authors discuss reality television in their own distinctive voices. One of our chapters, for instance, probes the ethical duties of television producers to respect the cultural and ethical values of viewers in the countries where those mostly European producers are importing reality shows to non-Western viewers. So if our book's analysis suggests respect dictates ethical authenticity, we think its words should, too. Therefore, readers will encounter both "amongst" and "among" and "whilst" and "while" depending on where the author lives. We think preserving regional language is the most authentic and respectful way to treat authors – and readers – in a collection that raises ethical issues.

Foreword: The Morality of Amoral TV

James Poniewozik

The easy answer to the question: "Is reality TV ethical?" is "of course not." For starters, reality TV shows – like fictional TV, or any TV series produced commercially – are products. They are a response to economic conditions (the desire among networks, for instance, to fill hours of TV cheaply and to put on shows that will draw an audience). In this sense, it's as pointless to ask whether reality TV – or any TV genre – is "ethical" as to ask whether running shoes or indexed mutual funds are ethical. That is, sure, they may have ethical effects, but ethics generally don't enter into their creation.

It's also worth noting that asking "is reality TV ethical?" is about as answerable a question as: "Are books ethical?" Reality TV can encompass anything from teen-pregnancy shows to cooking competitions to shows about addiction to documentary serials to travel and home-design series – everything from Morgan Spurlock's *30 Days* to ABC's *101 Ways to Leave a Game Show*. Arguably, the most widely agreed on definition of "reality TV" is "non-fiction television of which I personally disapprove."

The broader sense of the question really falls more along the lines of: "Does reality TV make us bad people?" Does it send bad messages, does it encourage immorality, does it coarsen social standards, is there shame attached into making, participating in and watching it? Here, the common and quick answer is, "of course" – and the makers of reality TV are the last to discourage it.

There is, after all, no more common way to sell a reality show than by suggesting that TV has once again Finally Gone Too Far This Time, or by inviting fans to jeer against an Ultimate Bad Guy, like Simon Cowell or Gordon Ramsay. If there is one thing that reality TV fans generally agree on, it's that they should be ashamed of themselves for watching it.

All of which is to say that to discuss the ethics of reality TV as a yes-or-no, black-and-white question is the most common way of treating the issue, and the least useful. On the other hand, if you consider that reality TV – like any product or narrative – *has* ethics, and ask what those ethics are, the question is much more intriguing, and the results more complicated and surprising.

Maybe the most important distinction is between the ethics *of* reality TV and the ethics *in* reality TV. The former is a question of whether reality TV shows are made honestly, for instance, or whether they treat their participants in a morally responsible manner. The second is a question of whether they communicate a sense of ethics in their narratives and whether they assume, or even prompt, an ethical response from their audience.

The former is important, but in a more narrow sense. There are plenty of examples of disingenuousness in reality TV: there's misleading editing to create conflict and suspense, and there's "frankenbyting," the trick of splicing together quotes from different contexts to make participants say what the producers need them to. (This does not mean, by the way, that audiences are oblivious to the manipulation; half the spectator sport of watching many reality shows, for instance, is second-guessing the editing and misdirection.) More egregiously, reality shows can create dangerous situations or at least encourage them, whether by plying house-guests with booze or making entertainment out of addiction or extreme weight-loss competitions.

But reality show participants are still a relatively small segment of the workforce; whether your reality programming is "ethical" in this sense is probably a lesser question – in terms of absolute human effects – than, say, whether the restaurants you get takeout from are ethical toward their employees.

The reality TV audience is a much bigger group, and the messages this audience receives from reality TV are much more complex, as are the ways in which viewers receive and interpret them. When it comes to the messages embedded in their narratives and the reactions they assume on the part of the audience, many supposedly depraved reality shows are, in fact, among the most moralizing series on TV.

A classic case-in-point is the ur-reality competition on broadcast TV, *Survivor*. Superficially, its premise is amoral in the extreme: You lie, manipulate and betray your teammates to win. Self-preservation is the prime value – "Outwit, Outplay, Outlast" – and, as many finalists have argued to the Tribal Council, it is its own justification: It's "playing the game," and therefore acceptable and admirable.

But that analysis only examines *Survivor* as a game. It's more than that: it's a spectator sport, viewed by millions of people, and the series depends upon those people to have a strong moral investment in and reaction to the story in order to stay involved. Each season involves heated arguments – on and off-screen – about what it really means to "deserve" to win. Seasons are often structured as moral experiments (tribes have been divided by gender, age and race or ethnicity) or as morality plays (e.g. the "Heroes vs. villains" season). The show has long recognized not just the winners of seasons but "fan favorites," a nod to the idea that the audience will sympathize with players they believed to have lost honorably. *Survivor*, in other words, assumes that you, the audience member, have an independent system of moral values that is most likely different from the one rewarded by the game, and that that conflict is at least part of what makes the season engaging.

That a work of pop culture should make that kind of assumption shouldn't surprise us – and when it comes to "higher" genres like fiction, it doesn't. If *Mad Men* or *Boardwalk Empire* depicts sexism, or violence, or self-destructive behavior, it's nuanced story-telling. But if a reality show does the same thing, it's immoral, misanthropic or bigoted. We assume that the audiences of HBO or FX dramas (or for that matter, readers of *Crime and Punishment* or *Lolita*) can empathize with the protagonists without wanting to emulate them; we assume they can maintain a critical distance from the narratives and perceive ironies between the characters' words and their actions. Why? Because we assume that someone who watches *Breaking Bad* is smarter, more mature – better – than someone who watches *Jersey Shore*. Scratch a criticism of reality TV, and often enough you'll find a criticism of the reality-TV audience.

Often too, its provocative premise is 90 percent of the battle for a reality show. Some celebrate fame for its own sake (*Keeping Up With the Kardashians*), others valorize the kind of blue-collar workers who rarely show up on sitcoms anymore (*Deadliest Catch*). Many are based on offensive or morally questionable premises – *Joe Millionaire*, for instance, or *Toddlers and Tiaras* – but they also require a strong and diverse response to create the arguments that keep the shows alive. Mike Darnell and Lauren Zalaznick may not be the Swifts and Twains of our age, but much effective reality TV is really satire boiled down to one extreme gesture. It takes a commonplace piety and skewers it: that team spirit is the key to winning (*Survivor*), that everyone has a special talent (*American Idol*, in particular the audition rounds), that success goes to the deserving (*The Real Housewives of Pretty Much Anywhere*).

Whether reality TV is good TV – that is another question, with as many answers as there are shows. The concept of goodness, however, is alive and well, and the subject of eager debate, among the reality audience. The viewers of reality TV are among the first to cite the genre as evidence that our culture is going to hell. But the controversy, argument and snark that reality TV inspires are vital proof that we have not arrived there yet.

Introduction: Reality TV Matters

Wendy N. Wyatt and Kristie Bunton

Popular Culture and Reality TV Demand Ethical Analysis

The Ethics of Reality TV is a book about popular culture, and – not surprisingly – we think pop culture should be taken seriously. Why? Consider the following reasons.

First, popular culture is, well, popular. It attracts mass audiences like no other kind of culture. In his study of a favorite pop culture text, *American Idol*, Christopher Bell noted that the show draws more than 25 million viewers per episode. This is equal to the combined populations of Colorado, Maryland, Missouri, Minnesota and Wisconsin, and it exceeds the population of Australia.[1] For the first time in 2010, "worldwide viewers watched more reality TV and entertainment shows than dramas and TV series,"[2] and reality shows consistently dominate ratings. In the summer of 2010, for example, 15 of the top 20 highest-rated American programs (for viewers 18 to 49 years old) were reality shows.[3] We think any cultural product with this kind attention-getting power should be taken seriously.

Second, pop culture can and should be accepted and appreciated as "real" culture. Some of the first scholars to study pop culture saw it as "low" culture with little value. In the late 1930s, for example, Frankfurt School theorist Max Horkheimer declared: "What today is called popular entertainment is actually demands evoked, manipulated, and, by implication, deteriorated by the cultural industries. It has little to do with art, least of all where it pretends to be such."[4] Although the Frankfurt School made important contributions to our understanding of communication, this wholesale rejection of pop culture takes an elitist perspective (even as Frankfurt School theorists fought against elitism) that we reject. Instead, we think any cultural artifact – whether it represents "high" culture, "low" culture, or something in between – should be taken seriously because it tells us something about the actual culture in which we live.

Third, pop culture is, or can be, entertaining. But it isn't *just* entertainment. It is ideologically, socially and economically oriented, and it is "an extension of the people from whom it springs and for whom it is created."[5] In other words, popular culture can tell us a lot about ourselves. As Jeffrey Bineham noted, the texts and artifacts of popular culture "are constantly telling us how to think, how to dress, how to talk, what vocations are significant, and what we should do politically and economically; in sum, they tell us who to be."[6] We think any message with this kind of power to illuminate and influence us should be taken seriously.

Finally, pop culture has ethical implications. As the ten chapters in this book will show, the texts of reality TV are ethically laden, and they matter in ways that have real influence on our ethical lives. Popular culture works to shape the minds and souls of those of us who consume it. Therefore, the claim that reality TV is "just entertainment" or "nothing more than low culture" is really just a way of avoiding serious consideration of an increasingly important form of communication, and it's a way of letting reality TV off the ethical hook. Reality television – like all communication – helps shape the way we view and interact with the world, helps make that world meaningful, and even helps construct that world. As James Carey so eloquently stated: "Communication is a symbolic process whereby reality is produced, maintained, repaired and transformed."[7] When we watch reality TV, we are taking part in a ritual that – strange as it may sound – helps bring reality to life. Yes, reality TV may be showing us the reality around us, but it's also helping us create our reality. After all, as Carey said, reality itself is "a vast production, a staged creation – something humanly produced and humanly maintained" through communication.[8] Clearly, anything with the power to construct reality should be taken seriously.

Reality TV is Complicated

In this book, therefore, we seriously consider reality television and the ethical questions it raises. We deliberately avoid condemning reality television. That's too ethically lazy to do, and even if it weren't, reality TV is far too complex to justify a blanket condemnation. In the Foreword to this book, *Time* magazine television critic James Poniewozik wrote "to discuss the ethics of reality television as a yes-or-no, black-and-white question is the most common way of treating this issue, and the least useful." He went on to say: "On the other hand, if you consider that reality TV – like any product or narrative – *has* ethics, and ask what those ethics are, the question is much more intriguing, and the results more complicated and surprising."

We think that's exactly what this book will show: that the ethical analysis of reality television is complicated and surprising.

While we recognize that there is a reality TV *genre*, we think it's unwise to evaluate all of the ethical issues that reality TV raises on the level of genre alone. Reality television is a complex, broad and evolving genre that resists easy definition. Most of us recognize as reality TV the contest shows such as *Project Runway*, *The Amazing Race* and *American Idol*, but we can see those shows have little in common with family-oriented narratives like *Jon and Kate Plus 8*, *19 Kids and Counting* or *Little People, Big World*, which we know are not similar to shows about offbeat occupations like *Pawn Stars*, *Ice Road Truckers* or *Cake Boss*. If we try to compare the self-improvement shows like *What Not to Wear*, *Shedding for the Wedding* and *Biggest Loser* with the philanthropy shows like *Extreme Makeover: Home Edition*, *Three Wishes* or *Secret Millionaire*, we easily see how hard it can be to decide exactly what makes something a reality show. This book demonstrates an important point: reality television as a genre is complicated and cannot be analyzed as if it were a monolithic programming category.

As if the complexity created by a genre that encompasses such a broad variety of program types were not enough, complexity is further created within individual reality programs. That complexity arises because the programs use different techniques and emphasize different approaches. Some reality shows are nearly fiction. They are manipulated and edited in ways that twist the very reality they purport to present. At times, the "real" events they depict seem orchestrated with a heavier hand than the most melodramatic of soap operas. (*The Bachelor*, with its exaggerated dates and sensationalized relationships that never culminate in an actual marriage, is a ready example of such a fictionalized reality show.) Some reality shows are nearly journalism or documentary. They tell stories in a straightforward way about the lives of real people that traditional television news outlets have failed to show us and that socially responsible journalists ought to present to the communities they serve. (The informational look at a polygamous family provided by *Sister Wives* is an example.)

Furthermore, complexity among reality TV shows varies from season to season and participant to participant. In the UK, for instance, the 2007 season of *Celebrity Big Brother* generated a firestorm of public criticism, international news coverage, advertiser defection and government disapproval when participants, stirred up by the boorish reality celebrity Jade Goody, repeatedly made racist remarks about the manners, accent and appearance of their fellow participant, the Indian actress Shilpa Shetty. Despite this obvious lapse into ethically unacceptable stereotyping and exploitation by the program, all seasons of *Celebrity Big Brother* cannot automatically be classified as unethical. Each season and each participant requires ethical analysis. Any reality program and its participants can be simultaneously ethical and unethical, just as any television news story or daily soap opera can be. Media texts, including reality TV, are marked by complexity that demands thoughtful ethical scrutiny.

Because reality TV is complex in all these ways, the ethical questions probed in this book apply differently to different reality programs and partici-pants. For example, the questions Madeleine Esch poses in her chapter about privacy can be applied differently to reality celebrity Bethenny Frankel when viewing her as a participant in *The Real Housewives of New York City*, as the title figure in *Bethenny Getting Married*, as a new parent in *Bethenny Ever After*, or as a contestant in *Dancing with the Stars*. That's just one ethical topic applied to one perennial reality participant.

We also think the complexity of reality TV demands that the chapters in this book not be read in isolation from one another. Reading only Bastiaan Vanacker's chapter on commercialization or Deni Elliott's chapter on democracy building, for example, gives only part of the picture. A sophisticated under-standing of the ethics of reality TV requires a wide-ranging understanding. In other words, the whole is greater than the sum of the individual parts. Reading this book as a coherent whole and comparing the chapters with one another will help build the broad understanding needed for a mature analysis of reality TV's ethics. For instance, Mira Desai's chapter on imposing cultural values and Gareth Palmer's on community are significant on their own, but a richer understanding of the issues emerges from comparing the two.

We think we've covered some of the most important ethical issues in this book, but we're sure there are others – those that the genre has already uncovered and those that new shows will inevitably bring to the surface. Our hope is that this book will help foster thoughtful analysis of existing and newly emerging ethical issues as well as encourage sophisticated consumption (and, ideally, creation) of reality TV. We'll come back to that idea at the end of the book, after our chapters have posed what we think are the crucial questions about the ethics of reality television. But now, let's get to the questions.

Notes

1 Christopher A. Bell, *American Idolatry: Celebrity, Commodity and Reality Television* (Jefferson, NC and London: McFarland, 2010).

2 Pascale Paoli-Lebailly, "Reality TV, Entertainment Viewing Surpasses Drama in 2010," *Rapid TV News*, 28 March 2001. www.rapidtvnews.com.

3 Bill Carter, "Tired of Reality TV but Still Tuning In," *New York Times*, 13 September 2010, B4.

4 Max Horkheimer, "Art and Mass Culture." In *Critical Theory: Selected Essays*, trans. Matthew J. O'Connell (New York: Continuum Publishing Company, 1999) 288.

5 Bell, *American Idolatry*, 16.

6 Jeffrey L. Bineham, "The Construction of Ethical Codes in the Discourse and Criticism of Popular Culture." In *Communication Ethics, Media & Popular Culture*, Phyllis M. Japp, Mark Meister and Debra K. Japp (eds) (New York: Peter Lang 2007) 14.

7 James W. Carey, *Communication as Culture: Essays on Media and Society*, rev. edn (New York: Routledge, 2009) 23.

8 Ibid., 24.

1

Flourishing: Reality TV and a Life of Ethical Excellence

Christopher Meyers

All the best stories are true.[1]

Or better yet: all the best stories *tell truths*. Good stories often capture and convey aspects of us and our moral lives far beyond what logical analysis could ever hope to touch.[2] The best stories, thus, are inherently normative: they can make our lives better, both through what they teach us and in how they enrich our lives with their beauty.

Stories, even the best ones – the technically best, the rhetorically best, the emotively best – can also, of course, make our lives much worse. They can create or exacerbate bigotry and xenophobia. They can dumb us down. They can scare us into inaction or, worse, into taking dreadful action – recall General Colin Powell's great story before the United Nations Security Council in 2003, which provided the Bush Administration's (purported) justification for invading Iraq.

Stories can be told through a wide range of media – oral narratives, plays, songs, novels, newspaper accounts, film and reality TV – and there is no inherent moral difference among them. Theatre can be exploitive and demeaning – consider myriad live sex shows – or raise us to the heights of a William Shakespeare, Eugene O'Neill or Tony Kushner. Television, similarly, can appeal to our basest instincts (think *Temptation Island*, *The Swan* and *Joe Millionaire*) or challenge us intellectually, emotionally and politically (think *The Wire*, *All in the Family* and *West Wing*).

The task given to me with this chapter is to try to determine whether watching reality TV is consistent with a life of ethical excellence or areté.[3] For reality TV to be so consistent, it has to satisfy three criteria: (i) it has to contribute to (or at least not undercut) the elements that contribute to excellence; (ii) it cannot cause undue harm; and (iii) it cannot treat persons with disrespect. My conclusion: reality TV is *not inconsistent* with areté; that is, reality TV, in its current form at least, does not significantly violate either of the central ethical conditions (avoid harm and respect persons), nor – assuming one has balance in one's life – does it essentially corrupt any of the elements. In fact, I take the conclusion a step further: Some reality TV actually *contributes* to an ethical life in the same way other good narratives do, namely, by directly promoting three of the elements: learning, sociality and pleasurable play.

Excellence, however, certainly falls along a continuum with respect both to a life's overall flourishing and to the individual elements that contribute to it. Thus, while some shows detract from areté – either by promoting conditions that diminish flourishing or by treating others as mere means – as long as, again, there is sufficient balance, watching even those shows does not wholly corrupt one's excellence.

Reality TV does not corrupt one's excellence because our lives are always in development, moving (one hopes) toward a more excellent state and because very few reality shows will completely fall on one end of the continuum or the other – *Pawn Stars* is no *Iron Chef America*, but at least it is better than *Jersey Shore*,[4] which also has at least *some* redeeming features. The bulk of reality shows reside in the middle, partly contributing to and partly detracting from a flourishing life. Hence, one more time, balance: "It is better to rise from life as from a banquet neither thirsty nor drunken."[5]

That reality shows fall on a continuum of flourishing features is part of the reason I think my analysis here has only modest practical import. I do not suggest, for example, that those shows that fall below some mid-point moral criterion should be subjected to social censure, or at least no censure beyond that provided by a marketplace that can choose to shun them. Rather, I see the argument's primary value as contributing to efforts to increase media literacy, a principal research goal of at least one of this book's editors:[6] The better evaluative tools we have, the better choices we can make and the better we can be at guiding others, especially parents, to make good viewing choices.

Those familiar with the Western tradition in moral theory will recognize I do not rely on a single theoretician. Rather, I use a method of moral reasoning[7] that incorporates the insights from the three major camps: (i) Immanuel Kant's respect for the inherent value of moral rules, especially, here, his "Kingdom of Ends" formulation of the categorical imperative (never treat persons as a mere means, or tool, for the benefit of others, but always as absolutely valuable "ends in themselves"); (ii) John Stuart Mill's utilitarian exhortation to act so as to promote the greatest aggregate pleasure, particularly higher or intellectual pleasure; and (iii) Aristotle's virtue theory with its call to each of us to develop our character, to strive for moral and intellectual excellence.

One last introductory point is that how one *characterizes* "reality television" certainly influences the analysis. Should, for example, *Keeping Up with the Kardashians* (a show celebrating the antics of a family famous, seemingly, for being famous) be included in the same conceptual category as, say, *Mythbusters* (which humorously uses a scientific method to test the plausibility of various urban and Hollywood myths)? Both are non-fiction television programs that ostensibly reflect unfiltered, if not unedited, reality and neither relies on professional actors. They are otherwise, however, far apart in content, structure and quality.

Whereas one might wish for an analytic or conceptual definition of reality TV, one that would provide a neat method for clear distinctions, the subject matter simply makes that implausible; the range of types of shows is too wide (and is being expanded almost weekly). My definition, thus, is sociological or descriptive;[8] it appeals to how people – producers, critics, journalists, participants and viewers – refer to it. Namely: *Reality TV is at least largely unscripted, normally relies on untrained actors, and purports to provide a narrative of ordinary life.* This liberal definition also avoids the straw person of focusing only on the worst; a more inclusive definition – keeping *Mythbusters*[9] alongside *Kardashians* – captures the diverse mix and complexity of the genre. The more inclusive definition is thus both fairer and, it turns out, more sympathetic to reality TV. Within the array of programs that qualify, some morally enhance while others demean, and persons' lives are made ethically better when they partake of the former and avoid the latter, or at least when they more frequently do so.

Getting to this conclusion requires some foundational work. First, I provide an argument for the relative values of higher and lower pleasures; second, I claim that persons have a duty to strive for arête; and third, I give a brief description of the full set of elements that contribute to areté, with a discussion of how they must in turn be guided by character and practical wisdom. With these elements in place, I then return to show that reality TV can promote some of those conditions, while not fully contradicting any. The last step is to test watching reality TV against the ethical conditions (avoid harm and respect persons), from which I conclude, again, that done in moderation, reality TV is not inconsistent with an excellent life.

Higher and Lower Pleasures

In line with the utilitarian tradition, I take all pleasure to be good, as long as it does not violate the ethical conditions. However, as Mill makes clear, *some pleasures are better than others*; namely, the higher, intellectual, pleasures are better than the lower, the physical. The higher pleasures are exemplified in many of the elements that make up areté, and they help create the mental capacities necessary for practical wisdom, via which appreciation of those elements is made possible. In short, they are the features that distinguish persons from other animals.

The argument for this (admittedly elitist) view comes from well-known passages in Mill's *Utilitarianism*:

> Human beings have faculties more elevated than the animal appetites, and when once made conscious of them, do not regard anything as happiness which does not include their gratification... It is quite compatible with the principle of utility to recognise the fact that some kinds of pleasure are more desirable and more valuable than others... If I am asked, what I mean by difference of quality in pleasures, or what makes one pleasure more valuable than another... there is but one possible answer. Of two pleasures, if there be one to which all or almost all who have experience of both give a decided preference, irrespective of any feeling of moral obligation to prefer it, that is the more desirable pleasure... [Thus] it is better to be a human being dissatisfied than a pig satisfied; better to be Socrates dissatisfied than a fool satisfied. And if the fool, or the pig, are of a different opinion, it is because they only know their own side of the question.[10]

Much of reality TV gets its appeal through stimulation of the lower pleasures, through erotic titillation, voyeurism and a vicarious amusement with characters' sexual, alcoholic and violent antics. Contrast this with activities that stimulate physical *and* mental pleasure – say a great meal with fine, smart friends. Paraphrasing Mill's argument, those who know and appreciate both kinds of pleasure, those who are essentially experts on the subject, know the latter to be a better pleasure, "and if the fool, or the pig, are of a different opinion, it is because they only know their own side of the question." Further, even if for whatever reason one does not immediately experience the intellectual pleasures as better, one's capacity for flourishing has been enhanced, as per the argument above.

I am *not* saying, mind you, that physical pleasures are inherently degrading or debased; life would not be as rich, as excellent, without great sex, good wine and hot fudge sundaes. But a life devoted only, or even mainly, to the physical is incomplete.

A Normative Approach to Flourishing

Mill expands upon the "higher pleasures" argument in *On Liberty*, where he shows how human enhancement, "development," occurs through the exercise of such intellectual activities. These produce, he says, "different experiments of living," in which,

> the human faculties of perception, judgment, discriminative feeling, mental activity, and even moral preference, are exercised only in making a choice. He who does anything because it is the custom, makes no choice. He gains no practice either in discerning or in desiring what is best... It is not by wearing down into uniformity all that is individual in themselves, but by cultivating it and calling it forth, within the limits imposed by the rights and interests of others, that human beings become a noble and beautiful object of contemplation... Having said that individuality is the same thing with development, and that it is only the cultivation of individuality which produces, or can produce, well-developed human beings, I might here close the argument: for what more or better can be said of any condition of human affairs, than that it brings human beings themselves nearer to the best thing they can be?[11]

Despite these eloquent exhortations to self-cultivation, Mill's moral theory provides at best a weak duty of self-improvement: personal development makes us better people, more interesting, and better able thereby to push society forward. But we have every right to choose to be "ape-like," mere imitators of others.[12] The most that can be said is that the processes by which development emerges – "He must use observation to see, reasoning and judgment to foresee, activity to gather materials for decision, discrimination to decide, and when he has decided, firmness and self-control to hold to his deliberate decision"[13] – are also the tools by which we develop the wisdom and judgment needed to more accurately determine which options, in any given scenario, are more likely to produce aggregate pleasure.

I thus add to Mill's arguments W. D. Ross's dictum that we in fact have a strong *prima facie* duty of self-improvement: "Some [duties] rest on the fact that we can improve our own condition in respect of virtue or of intelligence."[14] From this combination I get my theoretical starting point: persons should strive to enhance their lives so as to achieve areté. Our lives are better, richer, fuller and we *thrive* more, when we develop our physical and mental capacities to their greater potential.

Without this normative conception of flourishing, the moral analysis of reality TV, or of any form of entertainment for that matter, would be pretty straightforward: as long as some, *any*, people enjoy it, as long as no one is significantly harmed by it, and as long as it does not treat others as mere means, it is morally good. I argue, however, that we also have a duty to strive for more excellent lives, to (again quoting Ross) "improve our own condition in respect of [among other things] virtue or of intelligence." Doing so not only provides us with (higher) pleasure, but it also endows us with the discernment to more wisely improve our moral relations with others and to thereby improve society.

Now, the harm and respect caveats are potentially major obstacles to ethically approving of reality TV. As I will argue below, however, even though many shows violate one or both of these conditions, none appear to do so in a way that would make the shows unethical. But that conclusion does not settle the question. The character approach outlined here stresses that a full understanding of our moral lives requires going beyond such impact on others; we need also to evaluate how watching reality TV contributes to or detracts from our own characters.

Flourishing Characterized

What, then, are the conditions that produce flourishing lives? I provide the full list for a number of reasons. First, the elements are open to interpretation, with such evaluation potentially affecting the subsequent conclusions about areté and reality TV. My version is based on Aristotle's, on contemporary literature on happiness, and on wise friends' and colleagues' comments. Any given reader, however, might disagree with my reasoning. Second, such disagreement should emerge only after careful reflection on what makes for a life of excellence – a worthy exercise in its own right. Third, even if the reader were to fully embrace my list, she or he might disagree with the relationship between the various elements and reality TV, again potentially producing a different overall conclusion.

That said, I move through the full list pretty quickly, later coming back to a much more developed analysis of the three most relevant to the discussion at hand: learning, sociality and playing. I also divide them into what philosophers call necessary, sufficient and enhancing conditions, i.e. respectively, those that must be present for excellence, those that are not necessary, but on their own satisfy all the elements, and those that are neither necessary nor sufficient, but can enhance persons' lives in often profound ways. Furthermore, with all these conditions, there is an assumption of adequate material circumstances and good fortune. In short, one cannot engage in any of what follows unless one has a roof over one's head, food in one's mouth (and in one's children's), and at least minimal health. By the same token, one has to have adequate luck:

> For there is required [for happiness], as we said, not only complete virtue but also a complete life, since many changes occur in life, and all manner of chances, and the most prosperous may fall into great misfortunes in old age, as is told of Priam in the Trojan Cycle; and one who has experienced such chances and has ended wretchedly no one calls happy.[15]

Necessary Conditions

- *Social relations*: having friends to share good conversation, good food and drink; to play with; to support and to be supported by.

- *Challenge and achievement*: establishing goals, or being thrust into a taxing circumstance, and working hard to overcome the obstacles and to succeed.[16]

- *Learning*: being committed to enhancing one's knowledge and skills, whether done formally or informally.

- *Contemplation*: thinking more about life's meaning and value than about political ambition or about how to procure a wider flat-screen television.

- *Play*: engaging in physical play, intellectual play, emotional play, sexual play – done pleasurably, freely and for its own sake, with no goal of producing a secondary outcome (though it often does enhance, and thus overlap with, social relations).

Sufficient Conditions

- *Work*: being engaged by work, *real* work, that challenges, makes us better, teaches us, and connects us with others; i.e. it satisfies each of the necessary elements. Because, however, for most humans, work is instrumental only (assuming it is even available) – i.e. it is a *means* to, rather than a *reason* for, living – the type of work described here cannot be a necessary condition.

● *Family*: reveling in the great love, joy, pride and sorrow that come with family relations. Those relations are often amply rich with intellectual and character-enhancing components, and can thereby be a sufficient criterion. They cannot, however, be a necessary one because one can achieve all those components through friendships.[17]

Enriching elements

● *Spirituality*: embracing that there is much beyond our narrow frame of reference, whether that is obtained through a religious reality, or experienced in the wonders of artistic expression, or appreciated through the sublimity of nature grasped while knee deep in a trout stream.[18] Because such experiences need not include a social element and are generally not perceived as playful, spirituality is not a sufficient condition, even if it often challenges, teaches and motivates contemplation.

● *Resources*: having a minimal level is, as discussed above, a necessary condition; beyond that, resources – particularly money – provide opportunities, opportunities for more contemplation, more play, more learning and more access to great art and trout streams. Money alone cannot make one happy,[19] but it can sure as heck make getting there easier and more fun.

A life of excellence and flourishing, thus, is one lived actively and fully; it is rich with ongoing educational opportunities, challenges (including challenging work), critical contemplation and play; and it is filled with fine companions. These elements, though, must also be *guided by* two other conditions: character and practical wisdom.

Character means being *committed to* an honourable existence; that is, being habituated to virtue, to seeking and living by the mean between excess and deficiency, as dictated by the circumstances attached to the individual and the situation, and as expressed in a life of honesty, benevolence, non-malevolence, respecting others, courage, fidelity, perseverance, fairness and personal accountability.

Practical wisdom, or *phronesis*, is the discerning judgment gained through rational reflection upon experience and the teaching of others. Such judgment helps one to better choose from among the many competing options in life (including watching reality TV), to evaluate what is in fact the mean between extremes in given cases (*how much* reality TV should one watch?), and to more accurately predict the consequences of one's choices (what gets left undone while one watches?). While the acquisition of practical wisdom is never complete – one can always gain new insights from new experiences and critical reflection – on Aristotle's account, one cannot be virtuous, and thus one cannot flourish, unless one has some (undefined and probably indefinable) minimum.

All this once again reinforces the point that none of the elements of areté is reducible to an either/or. Rather, one can be more or less virtuous and wise, and, through them, more or less social, playful, etc. An excellent life is always in development: Assuming one has the right kind of commitment, has adequate material conditions, is sufficiently fortunate, and has at least a minimal level of practical wisdom, one's life is continually progressing. That commitment entails hard work, a striving for ever more wisdom and better habituated virtue.

Reality TV and a Flourishing Life

The requirement for the hard work needed for continuing development might seem to force the conclusion that reality TV is inconsistent with an excellent life. While it is obviously pure speculation, my reading of Aristotle and Mill is that they would both reach that conclusion, given their respective arguments about education (already detailed, above) and given the distinction they each draw between animals and humans – animals cannot, they say, be happy because they cannot contemplate and because they cannot be active and free choosers. Aristotle makes this clear in his discussion of why contemplation is necessary for excellence: "The other animals have no share in happiness, being completely deprived of [rationally critical] activity. For while the whole life of the gods is blessed, and that of men too in so far as some likeness of such activity belongs to them, none of the other animals is happy, since they in no way share in contemplation."[20] Watching reality TV, Aristotle and Mill would likely say, is equivalent to an animal's level of cognition. It thus fails the test of contemplation and thus is inconsistent with an excellent life.

That conclusion seems to me *too* elitist. Most devotees of particular shows and characters (and certainly all those preoccupied by them) are critically and actively engaged with the story line – with how their favorite characters work to overcome obstacles, with how antagonists make favorites' lives more difficult, with the struggles of characters' love lives.[21] While that level of critical engagement is obviously limited, it is certainly beyond that of animals and, to my mind, meets the minimal condition necessary for contemplation. Thus, watching reality TV – assuming the ethical conditions – is not inconsistent with an excellent life.

Reality TV as Enhancing Areté

That tepid conclusion – that reality TV is not inconsistent with excellence – in fact does not go far enough. Some watching of some reality TV can *enhance* excellence, in particular through the conditions of learning, sociality and play. In this section I thus give more detailed accounts of each and show their link to reality TV.[22]

Learning

The "lifelong learning" movement has become almost a cliché, but its roots are found in philosophically sophisticated notions of moral maturity, character development and an ethical life. Examples abound,[23] but I will stick with this paper's two main theoretical sources. In Aristotle's case, we get the argument that young children are not capable of genuine reasoning;[24] they need to have their intellectual skills refined through teaching and practice and their moral virtues developed through role-modelling and habituation. In other words, education is indispensible to both the intellectual and moral virtues that are necessary for a developed character.

Similarly, and given his own upbringing[25] no surprise, Mill was adamant about the importance of learning for personal development and cultivation of one's fullest self.[26] For instance, in *On Liberty* – a book putatively dedicated to urging that people should largely be left to their own devices – he stresses education's importance throughout: In the Introduction he (disturbingly) concludes "despotism is a legitimate mode of government in dealing with barbarians," given their uneducated and "backward" condition;[27] in Chapter 3, he discusses the demanding tools[28] needed for proper reasoning (tools available only after extensive education); and in Chapter 5, he both insists that free persons can have their liberty properly constrained when they are uninformed about a particular concern or threat,[29] and that education should be compulsory.[30]

If, as suggested above, our lives are always in development, if we are never fully "cultivated," then we should never stop learning. It is clear some reality TV *is* educational, if often in a playful way. Instances range from nature shows, to cooking competitions, to home improvement programs. One of my favorites is *Mythbusters*, where one can learn everything from the fact that elephants really are afraid of mice, to the plausible idea that torpedoes were used in the thirteenth century, to the notion that it's safe to yodel in avalanche-prone country. In short, reality TV plainly can motivate learning and it thereby provides a key element of excellence.

Sociality

Aristotle's familiar characterization of humans as political (and rational) animals was meant to stress our social nature; we cannot be complete as humans, let alone achieve areté, without social relations. The view is also now widely accepted in psychological literature on happiness, as summarized by Luigino Bruno:

> There has been increasing appreciation within psychology of the funda-mental importance of supportive interpersonal relationships for well-being and happiness. This dimension is so important that some theorists have defined 'relatedness' as a basic human need that is *essential* for well-being. In particular within the so-called 'eudaimonic' approach, many authors see a *universal* association between the quality of relationships and subjective well-being.[31]

When they are richly connected with others, people are happier (both disposi-tionally and as part of a deeper contentment), less lonely and feel a greater satisfaction in life. This is why sociality is a necessary condition of a flour-ishing life, and, as noted above, watching reality TV has become, for many, a very social activity. As of this writing, 10,816,947 people have "liked" *Jersey Shore*'s Facebook page, through which they also "friend" one another and "converse" over the show's minutiae. Through all this they "come together," cementing old and creating new friendships. The scare quotes indicate how these social activities diverge from their pre-network equivalents, but, however different, the activities are still unquestionably social.

The sociality created by reality TV is in fact like that created through being sports fans. Complete strangers feel wholly connected to one another only because they are rooting for the same team (and are alienated from, even hostile to, the opposition's players and fans). While such sociality may lack the richness and active contemplation of deep friendships,[32] assuming other, richer, interpersonal relations exist in our lives, there is no plausible exclusion of reality TV as a potentially important contributor to the sociality needed for flourishing.

Playing

Again, Aristotle: "To amuse oneself in order that one may exert oneself... seems right; for amusement is a sort of relaxation, and we need relaxation because we cannot work continuously. Relaxation, then, is not an end; for it is taken for the sake of activity."[33] As with all features of flourishing, balance is crucial; too much playing disrupts the efforts needed for achievement of the other conditions, but some activity done simply for the fun of it, with no external purpose, makes life better. I break from Aristotle in that I do not think "amusement" need be done (only) so "that one may exert oneself... for the sake of activity." Rather, play is an end in itself – fun for fun's sake – but also a means to other goods, including learning, connecting with nature, enhancing relationships and making for more productive work.

But precisely because play is not otherwise productive, it is all the more critical that participation in it not violate the central ethical conditions. Play done at others' expense, that intentionally hurts others, or is achieved only by demeaning others, is still *conceptually* play, but because it is done viciously, it reduces the player's virtue and thereby detracts from a flourishing life. As I will argue below, some reality TV seems to rely upon the humiliation of others. Play done only, or even primarily, with that as its goal is thus not consistent with contributing to flourishing.

Avoiding Harm and Respect for Others

So, watching even the more crass versions of reality TV is not inconsistent with an ethical life; some shows can even contribute to it, assuming a balanced life and assuming, in all cases, the principles of harm avoidance and respect are not violated. Violation of these ethical conditions would defeat any flourishing enhancement.

But that caveat is also messy. How much harm is too much? How disrespectfully must persons be treated? What would count as genuine balance? There is no cookie-cutter answer to any of these questions, but the easiest is the balance question because its answer will always be contextual, dictated by the individual's circumstances, capacities and opportunities. That is, the answer will be, can only be, revealed through a practically wise analysis of that individual and her or his context. Someone who is leading a reasonably active, virtuous, socially rich life can no doubt "afford" some brain-dead reality TV time, just as that person can afford time watching *How I Met Your Mother*, or pouring over baseball stats, or reading trashy books. The person without such a life probably has bigger things to worry about than her or his fascination with some reality TV show or star.

On the harm question, reality TV shows cannot cause their *participants* significant physical, emotional or economic harm, unless they genuinely consent to that threat because any associated flourishing afforded to viewers would be built on the backs – maybe quite literally – of those participants. I will expand on the "genuine consent" criterion in the respect argument, below; by "significant," I mean such harm that a reasonable group of persons (e.g. a jury) would deem to be profound enough as to warrant compensation, for instance in the form of restitution.

The question of harm to viewers is much more problematic. While there is plenty of noise on the topic, [34] genuine scholarship showing a *causal* relationship between reality TV and individual or social harms is pretty thin. If such a connection can in fact be established, one would, I assume, appeal to a standard process of moral reasoning to determine whether the harms are significant enough to warrant the sorts of restrictions already in place for shows with age-inappropriate sexuality or violence (e.g. time of day and cable versus broadcast).

On the respect question, much of reality TV clearly uses persons as a means. Many shows entice people to bare their worst behaviours and character flaws to millions through such enticements as a potential mate, fame or fortune and viewers clearly revel in these participants' misdeeds and misfortunes. That is, participants are distinctly used both for producers' profit and for viewers' entertainment. Even talent competition shows like *American Idol* have a built-in tension between humiliating some participants and revelling in the achievements and skill of others.

But recall Kant's dictum is against using persons as *mere* means. He recognized that we justly use one another all the time; our relationships *typically* include some transactional aspect. For example, we use a grocery check-out clerk to purchase our goods or a bank teller to manage our financial transactions; students use faculty to learn and faculty use students for a paycheck; romantic partners use one another for intimacy, sexual gratification and financial stability. These relationships, however, do not violate the dictum as long as all participants *genuinely consent* to the activity. That is, we use persons as *mere* means when they are either coerced into the transaction, when they do not have adequate information to be able to freely choose, or when they could not coherently consent. [35]

Much of the concern over reality TV is that it uses people in such a degrading manner that it is hard to imagine how they *could have* genuinely consented. How could one freely choose to debase oneself so, to submit oneself to the humiliation offered up by someone like Simon Cowell?[36] But such denigration exists across the reality TV spectrum. For example, Jennifer L. Pozner discusses a contestant on *The Bachelor*:[37]

> a vegetarian [who] described eating meat for the first time in 12 years just because Andrew Firestone (star of "The Bachelor's" third season) fed it to her. 'My stomach will never be the same,' she said, grateful for the crumbs. After she got the heave-ho, she batted her big brown eyes at the camera and moaned: 'You wanna see a girl that's crushed, you got her.'[38]

Pozner's general thesis, in fact, is that much of reality TV's structure is built around the humiliation of women.

So, again, how *could one* freely choose to be so humiliated? The answer is it does not matter how you or I feel about participating in the activity. As this book's chapter on exploitation also notes, as long as reality participants know what they are getting into and they are not coerced, their participation is freely undertaken. That the humiliating structure *is* so apparent speaks to participants' being adequately informed,[39] and since enticement cannot be reasonably seen as coercion, participation is sufficiently voluntary. In other words, even if the vast majority of us might think the choices degrading, the mere means standard is not violated.

From the perspective of the *viewer*, however, getting pleasure from the humiliation of others can never admit of a virtuous mean:

> Not every action nor every passion admits of a mean; for some have names that already imply badness, e.g. spite, shamelessness, envy and in the case of actions adultery, theft, murder; for all of these and suchlike things imply by their names that they are themselves bad and not the excesses or deficiencies of them. It is not possible, then, ever to be right with regard to them; one must always be wrong.[40]

I do not, though, know of any shows where humiliation is the entire focus; even those that promote it, also depend on glee at other characters' eventual successes. Or even the same person's – recall Susan Boyle's appearance on the British reality TV show, *Britain's Got Talent*. The audience began with some pretty foul shout-outs about her plain appearance, a reaction that quickly turned to avid appreciation for her amazing voice.

For whatever reason, reality producers seemingly assume their audience wants some such humiliation, as it is a common element in otherwise good shows – see, for example, *Pawn Stars*' treatment of Chumlee, who is often the subject of putdowns. Again, the structure of most reality TV programs depends on the tension between humiliation and praise, which places the burden on the virtuous viewer, who can, and should, essentially "work around" those ethical problems, focusing on the playful or educational or social aspects of a show while also being repulsed by the humiliation.[41]

We thus have the full argument for this chapter's thesis: reality TV is not only consistent with an ethical life; some watching of some of it can enhance one's life. This conclusion, though, should not be read as an exhortation to run to the nearest couch and grab the remote. Even in those cases where reality TV does enhance, it does not do so in a unique way; all its contributions to flourishing can no doubt be obtained, by most of us,[42] in other, more effective ways. But as an occasional break? As long as that occurs within an otherwise balanced life, I see no justified proscription.

Notes

1   David Shields, *Reality Hunger: A Manifesto* (New York: Alfred A. Knopf, 2010), 52.

2   Shields, *Reality Hunger.* "In our hunger for all things true, we make the facts irrelevant... [Truth] is that which had been made luminous, undeniably authentic by having been found and taken up, always at a cost, from deeper, more shared levels of the life we all really live" (pp. 86, 47). For a deeper illumination of this point see Martha C. Nussbaum, *Love's Knowledge: Essays on Philosophy and Literature* (New York: Oxford University Press, 1990).

3   "Areté," for the ancient Greeks, was sometimes synonymous with the rich, extended, flourishing life ("eudaimonia") that represented humans' fullest individual achievement, and sometimes presented as one of the *conditions* of eudaimonia. For simplicity's sake, I will use "areté," "excellence," "flourishing," as different terms for a life lived to its best and fullest, i.e. for a eudaimonic life.

4   *Pawn Stars* portrays a family-run pawn shop in Las Vegas and includes considerable historical commentary (driven by the items customers bring in); *Iron Chef America* is a cooking competition in which master chefs are given an hour to turn the "mystery ingredient" into five gourmet plates; and *Jersey Shore* is an MTV product that follows eight strangers brought together in a single house in New Jersey, with particular attention paid to melodrama and sexuality.

5   This well-known quotation is routinely attributed to Aristotle (see, for example, http://philosophical-quotes.com/657.html), but I could not find its original source; either way, it is an eloquent expression of the need for balance.

6 Wendy N. Wyatt, "The Ethical Obligations of News Consumers," in *Journalism Ethics: A Philosophical Approach*, ed. Christopher Meyers (New York: Oxford University Press, 2010) 283–95.

7 For a fuller account of that method, see Christopher Meyers, "*Re*-Appreciating W. D Ross: Naturalizing Prima Facie Duties and a Proposed Method," *Journal of Mass Media Ethics* 26, no. 4 (2011, 316–31).

8 For an explanation of the differences between conceptual and descriptive definitions, see Michael Davis, "Why Journalism is a Profession," in Meyers, *Journalism Ethics,* 91–102.

9 I characterize *Mythbusters* (and similarly structured shows, e.g. *Pawn Stars, Dancing with the Stars, American Pickers)* as unscripted because, even though the voiceover is clearly scripted and the general approach to the "experiments" is planned out, more than half of the televised portion is spontaneous activity and reactions.

10 John Stuart Mill, "Utilitarianism," in *Classics of Political and Moral Philosophy*, ed. Steven M. Cahn (New York: Oxford University Press, 2002), 896–9. Mill no doubt relied on Aristotle's similar arguments here. See, for example, Book I, Section 3 of *Nicomachean Ethics*: "Now each man judges well the things he knows, and of these he is a good judge. And so the man who has been educated in a subject is a good judge of that subject, and the man who has received an all-round education is a good judge in general. Hence a young man is not a proper hearer of lectures on political science; for he is inexperienced in the actions that occur in life… And it makes no difference whether he is young in years or youthful in character; the defect does not depend on time, but on his living." [I use the W. D. Ross translation (Oxford: Clarendon Press, 1908), in part because it is available online. See: http://classics.mit.edu/Aristotle/nicomachaen. html]

11 John Stuart Mill, *On Liberty*, ed. Currin V. Shields (Indianapolis, IN: Bobbs-Merrill, 1956), 68, 71, 76–7.

12 Mill, *On Liberty*, 69.

13 Ibid.

14 William David Ross, *The Right and The Good* (Indianapolis, IN: Hackett Publishing, 1988), 21. Kant also, if somewhat confusingly, appeals to an *imperfect* duty of self-improvement. See H. J. Paton, *The Moral Law* (London: Hutchinson and Co, 1972), 84ff.

15 Aristotle, *Nicomachean Ethics*, I.9.

16 As Abigail Adams, wife of John Adams and mother to John Quincy Adams put it (in a 1780 letter to her son): "It is not in the still calm of life, or the repose of a pacific station, that great characters are formed. The habits of a vigorous mind are formed in contending with difficulties. Great necessities call out great virtues." See Abigail Adams, "Quotes," GoodReads Inc., 2001. http://www.goodreads.com/author/quotes/1479.Abigail_Adams

17 Kant, for example, lived most of his adult life largely separate from family (until his sister came to live with him in his final years). He lived, though, a rich social life, as, essentially, the life of the party. See Manfred Kuehn, *Kant: A Biography* (Cambridge: Cambridge University Press, 2002).

18 See Immanuel Kant, *Observations on the Beautiful and the Sublime*, trans. John T. Goldthwait (Berkeley: University of California Press, 2004), in which he describes an overwhelming sense of terror at the power of nature, tempered against the realization of the transcendent capacity of human reason.

19 Luigino Bruno, "The Happiness of Sociality. Economics and Eudaimonia: A Necessary Encounter," *Rationality and Society* 22 (2010): 383–406.

20 Aristotle, *Nicomachean Ethics*, X. 8. See also Mill's references to "barbarians" and to "ape-like" imitation, cited in footnotes [26 and 10] respectively.

21 I am grateful to Richard Collins for this argument.

22 My sense is the other elements are not promoted through reality TV, but I again encourage the reader to reflect on this.

23 Three are Bertrand Russell, *Education and the Good Life* (New York: W. W. Norton & Co, 1970); Martha Nussbaum, *Cultivating Humanity: A Classical Defense of Reform in Liberal Education* (Cambridge, MA: Cambridge University Press, 1997); and Amy Gutman, *Democratic Education,* rev. edn (Princeton, NJ: Princeton University Press, 1999).

24 Aristotle also, infamously, thought the same of women and slaves (i.e. conquered non-Greeks): "For the slave has no deliberative faculty at all; the woman has, but it is without authority, and the [male] child has, but it is immature." Aristotle, *Politics*, I. 13, trans. Benjamin Jowett (Chelmsford, MA: Courier Dover Publications, 2000). Available at The Internet Classics Archive (online). http://classics.mit.edu/Aristotle/politics.html

25 See John Stuart Mill, *Autobiography*, Bartleby.com: Harvard Classics (online). http://www.bartleby.com/25/1/.

26 See also Robin Haack, "Education and the Good Life," *Philosophy* 56 (1981): 289–302.

27 John Stuart Mill, *On Liberty*, 14. Here he also says, "for the same reason we may leave out of consideration those backward states of society in which the race itself may be considered as in its nonage."

28 The tools include using "observation to see, reasoning and judgment to foresee, activity to gather materials for decision, discrimination to decide, and… firmness and self-control to hold to his deliberate decision." Mill, *On Liberty*, 71.

29 See the "bridge-walker" example in Mill, On *Liberty*, 117.

30 "Consider, for example, the case of education. Is it not almost a self-evident axiom that the state should require and compel education, up to a certain standard, of every human being who is born its citizen?" Mill, *On Libery*, 128. Mill makes a similar point, this time directed at parents, in *Principles of Political Economy*, 7th edn, Book V, Chapter 11, William J. Ashley ed. (London: Longmans, Green and Co., 1909). Available at http://www.econlib.org/library/Mill/mlP73.html.

31 Bruno, "The Happiness of Sociality," 394–5.

32 Because of that relative superficiality, the activities may promote unreflective loyalty, even fanaticism. See Noam Chomsky: "For one thing, [spectator sports] are a great way to build up chauvinism – you start by developing these totally irrational loyalties early in life, and they translate very nicely to other areas. [Such loyalties are] training for subordination to power, and for chauvinism." Noam Chomsky, Peter Rounds Mitchell and John Schoeffel, *Understanding Power: The Indispensable Chomsky* (New York: The New Press, 2002) 100.

33 Aristotle, *Nicomachean Ethics*, VII. 6.

34 See, for example, "Is Reality TV Harmful?" *BBC News* online. 1 September 2004. http://news.bbc.co.uk/2/hi/talking_point/3607482.stm.

35 For example, it would be incoherent to choose to be enslaved, since one cannot freely choose to forfeit one's freedom.

36 Cowell was the producer of *American Idol* and one of its earliest, and by far, harshest judges.

37 *The Bachelor* is one of many similar shows in which multiple people vie for the hand of the show's star.

38 Jennifer Pozner, *Reality Bites Back: The Troubling Truth about Guilty Pleasure TV* (Berkeley: Seal Press, 2010) 54.

39 One might be able to plausibly argue that participants in early reality TV shows did not have enough information to genuinely consent. Given how ubiquitous the shows are now, however, anyone who agrees to participate surely knows what he or she is getting into.

40 Aristotle, *Nicomachean Ethics*, II. 6.

41 One could also, of course, encourage the producers to at least reduce that element or, if it gets bad enough, simply stop watching.

42 An exception would be persons who are significantly disabled and incapable of, for example, active physical interaction with others.

2

Stereotypes: Reality TV as Both Creator and Confronter

Kristie Bunton

Introduction

Since 2002, television viewers have enjoyed episodes of the ABC network's reality dating contest, *The Bachelor*, in which provocatively styled young women prance before a hunky man supposedly seeking true love. As any *Bachelor* season unfolded, viewers saw nearly interchangeable "bachelorettes" gather around the patio of the bachelor's mansion for a nightly cocktail party at which they vied for time alone with the eligible man. Viewers could expect to see an innocent Southern belle, an outdoorsy brunette, and a vixen intent on mowing down her competition to capture the man. Viewers also could expect to see the bachelor progress from woman to woman, stopping between cuddles to tell the cameras – and the viewers – how "well" he was getting to know the "real" Ashley or Jenna, and how he remained committed to finding his ideal wife. Each episode ended with a ceremony at which the bachelor bestowed roses on women he wanted to pursue and the program's host asked rejected women to depart immediately.

In January 2011, ABC restored Brad Womack to the bachelor mansion. He was infamous as the only bachelor ever to reject every contestant presented to him. After explaining the therapeutic "work" he'd since done to become ready for love and apologizing to the two finalists he had humiliated three years before, Womack was whisked out to the mansion's entrance. There 30 new women, eager for his attention, paraded before him. He kissed or squeezed each Barbie-like beauty, and the fourteenth *Bachelor* contest was under way.

Are women and men this desperate to marry? Most young women don't serve themselves up as readily available sex objects to chauvinists like Womack, do they? How can viewers be entertained by reality television's repeated presentations of rigidly defined, outdated gender roles? Reality television must be guilty of stereotyping.

Yes, and no. However many stereotypes some reality television programs present, all reality television is not the same. Reality is a broad genre that includes everything from *Bachelor*-style dating contests to talent contests such as *American Idol*, real estate series such as *House Hunters*, soap opera-style squabbles such as *Jersey Shore*, shows about offbeat occupations such as *Cake Boss*, and shows about unusual families such as *Sister Wives*. The stereotypes these reality programs suggest are not all the same, nor are they equally harmful to reality show participants or viewers. To flatly say reality television unethically stereotypes people is to stereotype reality television. It is more accurate to say some reality television unethically stereotypes some people, while some reality television challenges some stereotypes.

For instance, during January 2011, while ABC's *The Bachelor* persistently presented outdated gender role stereotypes, the network's *Extreme Makeover: Home Edition* quietly countered them. The show, which since its 2003 debut has selected worthy families and built them new homes in a week, visited Savannah, Georgia, to help Carmen and Jim Simpson, who struggled to care for a child with a severe physical condition. The Simpsons wanted to "pay forward" the program's generosity, so they offered the show a list of other deserving people. They described a friend who couldn't afford a diamond engagement ring. The program provided a ring, and during a clothing drive where the show addressed the Simpsons' desire to collect coats for needy people, this bachelor eagerly asked his intended to marry him. She said yes. They hugged, kissed and celebrated. By *Bachelor* standards, this couple weighed too much and wore discount-store clothes, and they stood in a community hall full of donations. But this program demonstrated that pudgy, plain people enjoy romance, too.

The next week, while the bachelor and his all-white bevvy of beauties again cavorted on lavish dates, *Extreme Makeover: Home Edition* debunked more stereotypes. The show's big orange bus rolled to Augusta, Georgia, where viewers met Earnie Graham, whose home repair had abruptly ended with her brother's death. But rather than hear a sob story about single parenting, viewers saw an African-American mother and two children who were happy and involved in their community, with nary a mention of an absent father. Because of Graham's devoted Girl Scouts volunteer work, the show invited an all-female crew to demolish her old house. Armed with sledge hammers and axes, these women attacked the house – and drove the crane swinging the wrecking ball, too. This family and these construction workers provided a notable contrast to the passive beauties languishing on the bachelor's couch.

One network. One month. Two equally long-running reality shows. The message for viewers? Mixed. *The Bachelor* stereotyped pretty people, while *Extreme Makeover: Home Edition* embraced ordinary people. Clearly, reality television is a complex source of messages about the identities of contemporary people, and some of those messages foster stereotypes, while others do not. Reality television is a polysemic text open to multiple interpretations, and the stereotypes it contains deserve ethical analysis.

The Ethical Critique of Reality TV Stereotypes

Reality television's use of stereotypes suggests two primary ethical questions: (i) do reality producers have a duty not to cast and edit their shows in ways that foster stereotypes? (ii) do reality viewers have a duty not to accept the stereotypes some reality programs contain?

To answer these questions, an application of duty-based ethical principles seems appropriate, and any duty-based analysis begins with the foundational work of eighteenth-century German philosopher Immanuel Kant. For Kant, ethical decisions must be rooted in a person's good will, which is the only thing that is always and uniquely a moral good. "A good will is not good because of what it effects or accomplishes – because of its fitness for attaining some proposed end: it is good through its willing alone – that is, good in itself."[1] Decisions cannot be motivated by self-interest or by possible consequences, but by the good will that dictates performing ethical duty – the same ethical duty in all cases. This principle of acting universally to fulfil duty is widely known as Kant's categorical imperative: "Act as if the maxim of your action were to become through your will a universal law of nature."[2] In the act of performing a universal duty, people – described by Kant as "rational beings" who are "an object of reverence" – must be respected as ends in themselves. This corollary to Kant's categorical imperative is thus: "Act in such a way that you always treat humanity, whether in your own person or in the person of any other, never simply as a means, but always at the same time as an end."[3]

Two twentieth-century philosophers enhance the duty-based principles ideas of Kant. First, Scottish philosopher W. D. Ross suggests that seven prima facie duties, rather than one universal duty, may be applied to decide an ethical question. These self-evident duties are fidelity (keeping promises), reparation (righting wrongs), gratitude (repaying benefits by conveying benefits to others), non-maleficence (doing no harm), justice (fairly distributing burdens and benefits), beneficence (doing good to others) and self-improvement (fostering one's own wisdom and goodness). In any situation, one of the duties will rise to the level of "absolute obligation" and trump the others, thus dictating the ethical decision.[4] Second, US political philosopher John Rawls adds the important principle that an ethical outcome is one derived from the duty of protecting the interests of the most vulnerable stakeholder in a situation.[5]

Whether created by program producers or enjoyed by viewers, stereotypes on reality television cannot survive the scrutiny of these duty-based ethical principles. Producers and viewers can hardly be motivated by good will in the Kantian sense when they actively foster false impressions of groups of people for ratings or profit, or when they are entertained by the misrepresentation of others. Nor can creating stereotypes or being entertained by them be universalized; no rational person would suggest that stereotypes be employed in every media message. As well, no ethical argument can be made for using people as means to an end – whether that end is the profit and recognition that may accrue to producers or the entertainment that may be afforded to viewers – through stereotyping.

Furthermore, creating stereotypes or being entertained by them cannot be said to fulfill the prima facie duties set out by W. D. Ross. In fact, using stereotypes does wrong, creates harm and unfairly burdens the people who are objects of stereotyping, as well as promotes a failure of self-improvement in the people who create or are entertained by the stereotypes. Finally, the most vulnerable stakeholder in the reality television stereotyping situation would seem to be the person who shares the identity characteristics of those who are stereotyped by the program but who has not volunteered to participate in a program that depicts those characteristics stereotypically. Taking into account the interests of that person would dictate not using the stereotypes, which undermine the ability of people to act autonomously when others apply media-depicted stereotypes to them.

That ethical critique, then, can be used to assess how reality television and its viewers foster or debunk stereotypes.

Reality TV Creates a New Cast of Characters

Rather than simply offer stereotypes, reality television often provides enter-taining messages about who comprises our communities and how they behave. In April 2009, when Susan Boyle stepped to the *Britain's Got Talent* microphone, the acerbic judge Simon Cowell wasn't the only person who had to change his mind about who's got talent. Thanks to a YouTube video, millions of people worldwide saw a dowdy Scottish villager who possessed a soaring voice that would sell millions of albums over the next two years.

As it did in vaulting Boyle onto the world stage, reality television erases lines between what is public and private and who is ordinary or celebrity.[6] For example, in a society that pressures parents to be perfect, reality TV viewers don't have to worry theirs are the only children who throw bedtime tantrums. *Supernanny* viewers see ordinary parents failing to put their children to bed calmly and on time. This dose of parenting reality is no small thing. For decades television has provided an unrealistic stream of images about families, perpetuating a false nostalgia for what family historian Stephanie Coontz calls a "way we never were."[7] *Supernanny*, by comparison, suggests it's acceptable for parents to recognize they need help learning to raise their children.

Whether depicting struggling parents or shy Scottish singers, reality television often presents people who have been ignored by mainstream entertainment. Reality television sometimes has been more diverse and used more real lives and language than has fictional television.[8] "Whether its subject is kids from New Jersey, adolescent mothers or commercial fisherman, reality TV has discovered new faces, new idioms, new modes of being."[9]

For instance, after its 1992 debut, MTV's *The Real World* was lauded for being among the first US television shows to fairly depict a gay man. The 1994 series shattered gay stereotypes by including Pedro Zamora, who "grabbed the show's spotlight and educated its young viewers about what it was like to live with AIDS."[10]

Similarly, the fashion reality show *Project Runway* also has challenged stereotypes about sexual orientation, race and ethnicity. The show's would-be fashion designers and its judges don't particularly care about anyone else's identity characteristics. They care whether a contestant can produce creative clothing. Thus, the show presents a diverse world rarely seen on mainstream fictional television.[11]

On *19 Kids and Counting*, viewers glimpse another world rarely shown on fictional television: that of an evangelical Christian family. Viewers may smile at the antics of all the children who crowd Jim Bob and Michelle Duggar's Arkansas house, but the show never encourages viewers to make fun of the family. Rather, the show neutrally presents the Duggars' religious and patriotic values, and offers viewers information about a community often treated as fodder for jokes. Similarly, *Sister Wives* offers a straightforward look into the rarely seen world of polygamy by featuring Kody Brown, his four wives and 16 children.

Meanwhile, *What Not to Wear* uses humor to feature women of all ages whose wardrobes are laughably unfashionable. It's true that the show's fashion experts insist the women assemble a formulaic new wardrobe by shopping at stores with which the program has sponsorship arrangements, but those experts never suggest the women diet, exercise excessively, or have plastic surgery. Whether plump or petite, the women are treated to flattering clothing, hairstyles and makeup. Yes, *What Not to Wear* plays on the belief that all women clamor to be made over, but at least the program shows all women, not just stick-thin bachelorettes.

These examples suggest reality television programs are capable of incorporating a Kantian respect for persons in general and for persons who might be different from television viewers. No matter how different or similar a person's characteristics to those of the viewer, all people are nevertheless worthy of respect just because they are human.

Reality TV Casts and Edits for Stereotypes

Despite these encouraging presentations of ordinary, under-represented people, reality television programs also have presented and reinforced stereotypes of gender, race, sexual orientation, religion, socioeconomic class and other identity characteristics. Media activist Jennifer Pozner suggests these stereotypes are "endemic, even necessary"[12] to some reality shows.

Pozner and other critics say the stereotyping begins with casting, when reality producers deliberately choose participants for stock roles.[13] For instance, producers of *The Real World* have been accused of casting predictable characters such as the naïve, small-town, white person and the street-savvy, urban, African American person who will inevitably clash before becoming fast friends. Thus, critics say *The Real World* has suggested through casting and editing that racism is a recurring characteristic of rural conservatives but never of urban liberals and that racism can be overcome simply by developing friendships across racial lines.[14]

Reality television may not provide stereotypical lines for actors to deliver, as would a scripted show, but producers do influence participants' behavior on these "unscripted" shows. Producers feed ideas to participants before recording on-camera monologues, and producers reward or punish particular behaviors by giving participants basic supplies or extra treats. Contestants confined to the *Big Brother* house or marooned on the *Survivor* island care a lot about items the shows' producers distribute, and thus contestants quickly figure out which of their actions get more goodies. Too, because producers control post-production editing of the programs, they can heighten the drama by emphasizing stereotypes that clash.[15]

Sex-role stereotypes are among the most frequent reality television stereotypes, and *The Bachelor* is as good – or bad – an example as any. Critics suggest the show perpetuates stereotypes of the man as all-powerful sexual predator and the woman as gold digger disguised as helpless damsel.[16] *The Bachelor* is not alone in this regard. Most reality dating shows present a patriarchal man and a delicate princess awaiting his rescue. These depictions represent outdated ideas about gender that stem from hundreds of years' worth of depictions of women and men. Visual imagery in Western society at least since the Renaissance has presented women as passive sexualized objects artfully displayed for the male gaze.[17] *The Bachelor* formula is no different. A parade of almost identical long-haired, tautly toned and exceedingly thin yet large-breasted women is arrayed before one man. The bachelor dictates the dating activities while the "bachelorettes" – and yes, these girlish women are labeled with this diminutive title – provocatively display themselves to attract his attention. This is hardly assertive twenty-first-century womanhood. Instead, it perpetuates an outdated princess myth, in which "the mythmaking machines of media and marketing persistently tie ideal femininity and attractiveness to a very specific mode of sexuality, one that involves exhibitionism and a submissive appeal to the male gaze, without any consideration of the girl's own interests, ideas, or sense of well-being."[18] Furthermore, the "bachelorette" women epitomize a stereotypical ideal female body that is "both slender and voluptuous" – and therefore "practically a physical impossibility" without plastic surgery. [19]

Dating contest shows such as *The Bachelor* don't just stereotype women. They also present a "limiting vision of masculinity."[20] The bachelor must be tall and chiseled in the masculinity as muscularity mode, and he is encouraged to be sexually voracious. He is expected to be physically intimate with every contestant in his season-long hunt. That the woman he ultimately selects will be submissive goes without saying. No *Bachelor* aspires to be a house husband or full-time father. No, ma'am. This man will take care of his little woman. No matter that Americans' views about marriage are changing dramatically today. In the world of *The Bachelor*, marriage is organized along traditionally rigid gender lines.[21] (Of course, that presumes *The Bachelor* actually marries his princess. Few ever have.)

To be fair, pause for a moment to assess *The Bachelorette*. Some viewers have suggested the spinoff program counters sex-role stereotypes by placing the woman in *The Bachelor*'s position of power to select a mate. Those viewers are wrong. As Pozner points out, the spin-off fails in several ways to meaningfully reverse stereotypical roles. First, the woman cast as *The Bachelorette* must have been publicly rejected by a bachelor who didn't pick her at the end of his series; a bachelor, by comparison, is selected to star in the series on his own merits. Second, women who compete for *The Bachelor*'s attention routinely are presented as cat-fighting competitors, while men who vie for *The Bachelorette* "are usually shown palling around with one another, chugging beer and male-bonding over *The Bachelorette*'s hot bod."[22] Third, while *The Bachelor* is encouraged to become physically intimate with as many female contestants as possible during his series, *The Bachelorette* has been chided on her own program, as well as on talk shows and by bloggers, for even the slightest of physical intimacies, as in an instance in which the program host asked a *Bachelorette* to justify kissing more than one man during the multi-week series. Finally, when men are dumped by *The Bachelorette*, they typically are asked about their career plans; one contestant even ended up being offered a job on an entertainment news show. Women who are spurned by *The Bachelor*, by contrast, are shown weeping broken-heartedly as they are driven away from the mansion.[23] In sum, then, *The Bachelorette* may be starring in her own reality series, but she remains a passive, sexualized princess, while the men she dates remain powerful and aggressive. So much for turning the stereotyping tables.

Reality programs such as *The Bachelor* and *The Bachelorette* that cast for sex-role stereotypes or edit events to emphasize stereotypical conflict, fail the Kantian ethical test of respecting persons as worthwhile ends in themselves. Furthermore, the persistent use of these outmoded stereotypes promotes the failure of any self-improvement of the sort that W. D. Ross said was a duty of the ethical person. A reasonable viewer hardly can be improved by spending time watching shallow, old-fashioned stereotypes.

Reality TV Perpetuates Symbolic Annihilation

At least *Bachelor* and *Bachelorette* viewers have experience interacting with the opposite sex and can competently compare the shows' stereotypes to those experiences. Where reality TV stereotypes become more troubling is in connection to race and ethnicity, where many viewers lack experience interacting with people of differing backgrounds. By their total absence, *The Bachelor* suggests people of color don't matter. The powerful, desirable male has always been white, and the fraction of female contestants who have been anything other than white were usually rejected early in the season.[24] *The Bachelor* presents a curiously white world to viewers in a country where one in seven new marriages is inter-racial or interethnic, where mixed-race people represent one of the fastest growing demographic segments, and where citizens recently elected a president of mixed race.[25]

The Bachelor typifies the concept of symbolic annihilation. Symbolic annihilation suggests groups of people who are not presented or who are severely under-represented by television may be mentally erased from viewers' thoughts and therefore dismissed as unimportant to the larger culture. For years, racial and ethnic minority groups have been among the people most frequently symbolically annihilated by television. Complicating their symbolic annihilation is their stereotyping. When these same under-represented minority group members are presented on television, they have frequently been misrepresented, or stereotyped.

Certainly this occurs on reality television. "As reality shows are some of the only places viewers regularly see people of color on TV, their imagery takes on greater significance," Pozner writes.[26] Mainstream broadcast networks do not include people of racial or ethnic minority status on their dating shows, thus perpetuating as "reality" a "white beauty yardstick" to which people of color literally can never measure up, even "in a country that, statistically speaking, is getting darker all the time."[27] Cable networks, which target smaller, more specific audience groups, feature people of color on dating reality shows but often in stereotypical ways. Pozner argues, for instance, that VH1's *Flavor of Love* revived damaging racist stereotypes of African Americans nearly 100 years after minstrel shows perpetrated them. The show arrayed 20 young, single African American women in front of the has-been rapper Flavor Flav, who was at least 25 years their senior. He then literally objectified the women by replacing their given names with nicknames, usually chosen to relate to their body parts, and slapping those labels on their breasts or buttocks. He furthered the racist stereotyping by requiring contestants to cook fried chicken and clean disgusting household messes. Yet the *Flavor of Love* women fought over this man who lacked any obvious qualities that would make him a *Bachelor*-like prize.[28]

In their backbiting and outrageousness, the "flavorettes" – and yes, the show called them this – epitomized the "crazy black woman" stereotype applied to other African American women on reality television contests. After participating on *The Apprentice*, Omarosa Manigault-Stallworth became the best known "crazy black woman" on reality television, but one pops up each season on *America's Next Top Model*.[29] In the case of the "flavorettes," the "crazy black woman" behaviour resulted in a spin-off show – *Flavor of Love Girls: Charm School* – designed to class them up.[30] In a television world that features few realistic, complex African American female characters, this kind of racist stereotyping is clearly unethical.

Racist stereotyping is unethical when it happens to men of color, too. Flavor Flav is a caricature of the shiftless black man, as is Teeny, the unemployed, freeloading brother of *American Idol* singer Fantasia, whose life and family featured in the VH1 reality show *Fantasia for Real* that debuted late in 2010.[31] *The Real World* has been criticized for stereotyping African American men as sexually violent.[32] *Washington Post* television writer Paul Farhi suggests most reality programs consistently stereotype African American men as "the Bad Black Guy." This stereotype is magnified by the symbolic annihilation of African American men. Because so many white men are seen on reality television, they get to be courageous, smart, ignorant, silly, sexy or funny. "You'd never make the same assumption about African American men, for the simple reason that it's hard to see diversity when there's only one black man per show. The rigid tokenism of reality programs – call it the 'one black guy at a time' rule – magnifies the behaviour of the BBG, giving him metaphoric power," Farhi writes.[33] In the rare instance a reality show includes two African American men, it has been accused of stereotyping one as the "integrated" or "acceptable" black man and the other as the "hood" or "unacceptable" black man.[34]

Clearly, racist stereotypes perpetuated by reality producers and consumed by viewers fail the Kantian tests of good will and respect for persons. These pernicious stereotypes also fail Ross' duties not to harm people, to fairly distribute burdens and benefits, to do good to others, and to foster one's own wisdom and goodness. Additionally, these stereotypes unfairly burden the people about whom viewers may assume the stereotypes they've seen on television are accurate. Those people likely qualify as the most vulnerable stakeholders Rawls suggested are deserving of ethical consideration.

Why Stereotypes on Reality TV Matter

Fictional television entertainment stereotypes people by identity character-istics in each of the same potentially harmful ways reality television does, and so does non-fictional television news. So why does stereotyping on reality television particularly merit examination?

First, people watch a lot of reality television. In 2010, the typical US television viewer saw 34 hours of television a week. Many viewers, especially those under age 50, spent many of those hours on reality programs. In 2010, no fictional entertainment program ranked in the ten highest-rated programs among all US television viewers, but one reality program – *Undercover Boss* – did.[35] US television networks aired almost 600 different prime-time reality programs between 2000 and 2010,[36] and some observers contend reality is the most popular television genre in the world.[37] Stereotypes on reality television are consumed by millions of viewers.

Second, "reality" is a powerful label that raises the expectation of accuracy among viewers.[38] "Even though many people who watch it say, 'Oh, I know it's sort of made up', there's something about the fact that it's called reality that somehow still gives it a different sense of credibility that people aren't willing to give a sitcom or a drama," notes media literacy expert Andrea Quijada.[39] Stereotypes seem more troubling when they're labelled "real."[40]

Third, reality programs too often use a single character to represent a racial or ethnic minority community. This combination of symbolic annihilation and misrepresentation can mislead viewers. *Washington Post* columnist Clarence Page points out that "when viewers are fed a steady diet of stereotypes, stereotypes create a reality all their own," especially in a society where racial division persists.[41]

Finally, and most importantly, stereotypes on reality television matter because they can be a potent agent of social learning. Television "plays a significant role in how audiences shape their racially stratified and gendered world," providing "a means for members of different social, cultural and ethnic groups to learn about each other."[42] Reality television conveys stereotypes about those groups. Whether those stereotypes are believable is not of as much concern as the fact that even unrealistic stereotypes may influence viewers' perceptions.[43] Social psychology studies conclude that people activate stereotypes automatically and quickly, often without even being conscious of doing so.[44] Furthermore, social psychologists find that people who are asked to generate stereotypes about groups of people easily produce significantly more negative stereotypes than positive ones, and that people are much more likely to automatically invoke negative stereotypes about people or communities they don't know.[45]

The problem is that stereotypes don't just describe identity characteristics. They exploit and prescribe those characteristics in judgemental ways. While it is a natural cognitive function to compress complex ideas to manage what would otherwise be a cognitive overload, that compression – which becomes the stereotype – is not neutral. It is distorted, magnifying some characteristics and minimizing others. "Stereotypes usually fail to reflect the richness of the subculture and ignore the realities from which the images come."[46] Stereotypes reflect value judgements, letting the holder of the stereotype exploit the traits of some people in a group to judge other people in that group. In this way, stereotyped people are judged by the values laden in the stereotype, and others will begin to expect those people will behave as the stereotype dictates.

An Ethical Approach to Reality TV Stereotypes

Rather than judging one another based on stereotypes, people could learn from one another by sharing their stories. The philosopher Kwame Anthony Appiah suggests that "evaluating stories together is one of the central human ways of learning to align our responses to the world."[47] Indeed, Appiah proposes that the central ethical responsibility people have to one another as fellow inhabitants of a planet that is home to six billion other people is simply getting used to one another. He writes: "I am urging that we should learn about people in other places, take an interest in their civilizations, their arguments, their errors, their achievements, not because that will bring us to agreement, but because it will help us get used to one another."[48] He encourages people to engage in cross-cultural conversations that will show them what they share with one another. After all, he concludes, "when the stranger is no longer imaginary, but real and present, sharing a human social life, you may like or dislike him, you may agree or disagree; but if it is what you both want, you can make sense of each other in the end."[49] For Appiah, this kind of cross-cultural understanding is an ethical duty.

Appiah's idea of cross-cultural inquiry as an ethical duty is not new and likely is influenced by his understanding of the ancient Greeks. As philosopher Martha Nussbaum points out, the Greeks argued that "we should not allow differences of nationality or class or ethnic membership or even gender to erect barriers between us and our fellow human beings."[50] Immanuel Kant's duty-based ethical principles that emphasize respect for persons as moral beings also were profoundly influenced by the Greeks and their idea of cross-cultural inquiry. We respect one another as morally worthwhile when we attempt to understand one another, Kant might say.

Obviously, in a complex world, people cannot conduct cross-cultural inquiry by sitting down and talking to every person who possesses characteristics different from theirs. But most of those people can watch television, which is perhaps the most powerful storyteller on planet Earth. When reality television viewers see previously ignored communities of people depicted in an evenhanded manner – think of the evangelical Duggar family of *19 Kids and Counting* or the polygamist Brown family of *Sister Wives* – they are offered a chance to engage in a kind of cross-cultural inquiry. Viewers can get used to the idea that all families are not arranged just like their own. A different family arrangement may not be worse; it may just be different. Reaching even that simple conclusion may be worthwhile for people in today's diverse world.

Ethically sensitive reality television viewers cannot control the stereotypes program producers include in their shows, but those viewers can respond with a "turn it off and talk back" strategy that fosters cross-cultural inquiry for others. Simply put, viewers first can refuse to watch reality programs that abound with ethically questionable stereotypes. Second, ethically savvy viewers who are confronted with stereotypes can point out and challenge them on the many message boards, chat rooms and blogs frequented by both fellow viewers and program producers. Similarly, those same savvy viewers can praise reality television programs that avoid stereotypes and instead offer worthwhile glimpses into the lives and characteristics of previously under-represented communities. Perhaps then reality television will give viewers more *19 Kids* or *Sister Wives* and fewer bachelors and bachelorettes.

Notes

1 Immanuel Kant, *Groundwork on the Metaphysics of Morals*, H. J. Patton, trans. (New York: Harper Torchbooks, 1964) 62.

2 Kant, *Groundwork on the Metaphysics of Morals*, 89.

3 Ibid., 96.

4 W. D. Ross, *The Right and the Good* (Indianapolis, IN: Hackett Publishing, 1988).

5 John Rawls, *A Theory of Justice*, rev. edn (Cambridge, MA: Belknap Press, 1999).

6 Anita Biressi and Heather Nunn, *Reality TV: Realism and Revelation* (London: Wallflower Press, 2005) 2.

7 Stephanie Coontz, *The Way We Never Were: American Families and the Nostalgia Trap* (New York: Basic Books, 2000).

8 Biressi and Nunn, *Reality TV*, 26.

9 Virginia Heffernan, "Mining Reality," *The New York Times Opinionator*, 3 April 2011. http://opinionator.blogs.nytimes.com/2011/04/03/mining-reality/?pagemode=print.

10 Maryann Haggerty, "Reality TV: Is It Harmless Entertainment or a Cultural Threat?" *CQ Researcher* 20: 29 (2010) 684.

11 Heather Hendershot, "Belabored Reality: Making It Work on The Simple Life and Project Runway," in *Reality TV: Remaking Television Culture*, Susan

Murray and Laurie Ouellette (eds) (New York: New York University Press, 2009) 255; Jennifer L. Pozner, *Reality Bites Back: The Troubling Truth about Guilty Pleasure TV* (Berkeley: Seal Press, 2010) 140–1.

12 Pozner, *Reality Bites Back*, 47.

13 Biressi and Nunn, *Reality TV*, 28; Pozner, *Reality Bites Back*, 27.

14 Jon Kraszewski, "Country Hicks and Urban Cliques: Mediating Race, Reality, and Liberalism on MTV's The Real World," in *Reality TV: Remaking Television Culture*, Susan Murray and Laurie Ouellette (eds) (New York: New York University Press, 2009) 208.

15 James Poniewozik, "How Reality TV Fakes It," *Time*, 29 January 2006. www. time.com; Mark Andrejevic, *Reality TV: The Work of Being Watched* (Lanham, MD: Rowman & Littlefield Publishers, Inc., 2004) 103–5.

16 Annette Hill, *Reality TV: Audiences and Popular Factual Television* (New York: Routledge, 2005) 118–19; Pozner, *Reality Bites Back*, 36–41; Jonathan Gray, "Cinderella Burps: Gender, Performativity, and the Dating Show," in *Reality TV: Remaking Television Culture*, Susan Murray and Laurie Ouellette (eds) (New York: New York University Press, 2009) 261–3.

17 Gigi M. Durham, *The Lolita Effect* (New York: The Overlook Press, 2008) 77–9, 166.

18 Durham, *The Lolita Effect*, 84.

19 Ibid., 98.

20 Pozner, *Reality Bites Back*, 46.

21 Ibid., 249.

22 Ibid., 245.

23 Ibid., 244–6.

24 Susan J. Douglas, *The Rise of Enlightened Sexism: How Pop Culture Took Us from Girl Power to Girls Gone Wild* (New York: St Martin's Press, 2010) 208; and Pozner, *Reality Bites Back*, 163–4.

25 Pozner, *Reality Bites Back,*165; and Susan Saulny, "Black? White? Asian? More Young Americans Choose All of the Above," *The New York Times*, 30 January 2011, 1.

26 Pozner, *Reality Bites Back*, 94.

27 Jeff Yang and Angelo Ragaza, "The Beauty Machine," in *Facing Difference: Race, Gender and Mass Media*, Shirley Biagi and Marilyn Kern-Foxworth (eds) (Thousand Oaks, CA: Pine Forge Press, 1997) 11–12.

28 Pozner, *Reality Bites Back,* 180–3.

29 Kerrie Murphy, "Irritating Regardless of Race, Colour or Creed," *Weekend Australian*, 14 October 2006, 34; Pozner, *Reality Bites Back;* and Teresa Wiltz, "The Evil Sista of Reality Television; Shows Trot Out Old Stereotypes to Spice Up Stagnant Story Lines," *The Washington Post*, 25 February 2004, C01.

30 Pozner, *Reality Bites Back*, 188.

31 Brian Lowry, "Stereotypes: Reality TV's Dirty Little Secret," *Variety*, 11–17 January 2010, 16.

32 Kraszewski, "Country Hicks and Urban Cliques," 218; Katrina E. Bell-Jordan, "Black. White. And a Survivor of The Real World: Constructions of Race on Reality TV," *Critical Studies in Media Communications* 25, no. 4 (2008): 364.

33 Paul Farhi, "Reality TV Broadcasts 'Bad Black Guy' Stereotype," *The Washington Post*, 20 February 2001, C01.

34 Bell-Jordan, "Black. White. And a Survivor," 360.

35 Brian Stelter, "TV Viewing Continues to Edge Up," *The New York Times*, 2 January 2011. www.nytimes.com.

36 Eric Deggans, "So-Called 'Reality TV' Really Just a Ploy to Grab Young Viewers," *St Petersburg Times*, 10 December 2010, 2E.

37 Mark P. Orbe, "Representations of Race in Reality TV: Watch and Discuss," *Critical Studies in Media Communication* 25, no. 4 (2008): 345.

38 Biressi and Nunn, *Reality TV*, 3.

39 Haggerty, "Reality TV," 692.

40 Guy Adams, "Italian Americans Outraged at Reality TV 'Slur,'" *The Independent* (London), 26 December 2009, 30.

41 Clarence Page, "Warped Reality on the Screen," *The Washington Times*, 23 February 2001, A16

42 Shannon B. Campbell, Steven S. Giannino, Chrystal R. China and Christopher S. Harris, "I Love New York: Does New York Love Me?" *Journal of International Women's Studies* 10, no. 2 (2008): 20.

43 Mark C. Hopson, "'Now Watch Me Dance': Responding to Critical Observations, Constructions, and Performances of Race on Reality Television," *Critical Studies in Media Communication* 25, no. 4 (2008): 441.

44 Charles Stangor, "The Study of Stereotyping, Prejudice, and Discrimination Within Social Psychology: A Quick History of Theory and Research," in *Handbook of Prejudice, Stereotyping, and Discrimination*, Todd D. Nelson ed. (New York: Psychology Press, Taylor & Francis Group, 2009) 9.

45 Stangor, "The Study of Stereotyping," 9–10.

46 Angela Cooke-Jackson and Elizabeth K. Hansen, "Appalachian Culture and Reality TV: The Ethical Dilemma of Stereotyping Others," *Journal of Mass Media Ethics* 23, no. 3 (2008): 186.

47 Kwame Anthony Appiah, *Cosmopolitanism: Ethics in a World of Strangers* (New York: W. W. Norton, 2006) 29.

48 Appiah, *Cosmopolitanism*, 78.

49 Ibid., 99.

50 Martha C. Nussbaum, *Cultivating Humanity: A Classical Defense of Reform in Liberal Education* (Cambridge: Harvard University Press, 1997) 58–9.

3

Privacy: What Has Reality TV Got to Hide?

Madeleine Shufeldt Esch

One day in 2010, Bethenny Frankel woke up, threw on some clothes, fitted her infant daughter into a baby carrier on her chest, leashed her dog and set out for a morning stroll to the neighborhood convenience store. When she exited the shop, she spotted a paparazzo with his camera and she promptly hid behind strangers walking down the street. She explained to the burly man sheltering her: "I don't want them to get me and my baby [on camera]." She was not wearing makeup and had dressed rather sloppily. Moreover, as a new mother, she likely wanted to protect her child from intrusions – but the irony here is that Frankel was already being followed by television cameras, as she has been for much of the past five years. First she was a contestant on *The Apprentice: Martha Stewart*, then more famously she appeared as one of the *Real Housewives of New York City* and as star of *Bethenny Getting Married?* (Both on Bravo). This morning errand scene would become part of Season 2, Episode 3 in her most recent series, *Bethenny Ever After*, and yet, despite making a television brand of her personal life and seeking celebrity status, Frankel still wanted privacy.

Through the profusion of reality shows over the past decade, viewers can now follow the private lives of families of all shapes and sizes – from Frankel welcoming her first child to Michelle and Jim Bob Duggar of *19*

Kids and Counting (TLC) welcoming their nineteenth. The intimacies of courtship, weddings and childbirth can be screened alongside the bickering of frenemies, the partying of twenty-somethings, and the mid-life crises of urban professionals. As viewers, we can peek into private hospital rooms, judicial chambers and therapists' offices when we tire of makeovers, home renovations and talent competitions. Few areas of what was once called "private life" aren't featured somewhere in the reality television line-up. Powering these reality television tell-all moments are the ordinary folks eager to sign up for their chance at 15 minutes of fame – even if that means letting camera crews into their homes or baring their souls for a national television audience.

The boundaries of what we consider too private to televise may be eroding. In the early years of the reality boom, a *Time* magazine/CNN poll found that the majority of adults surveyed would be averse to participating in the more revealing varieties of reality television, but roughly a quarter of those surveyed would be willing – at least hypothetically – to be filmed for a reality television show wearing pajamas (31 percent), kissing a significant other (24 percent), crying (26 percent) or fighting (25 percent). The limits of our exhibitionism would seem to have eroded to sexual intercourse (5 percent) and nudity (8 percent)[1]

By 2008, reality television fans would welcome a show with the promise of nudity at its core in the makeover program *How to Look Good Naked* (Lifetime). As promised in the title, this format stripped participants down to their bare essentials (or at least bra and panties) as the camera zoomed in on self-perceived physical imperfections. With a stated mission to improve women's self-esteem, episodes regularly delved into a woman's health or psychological history to establish a back-story. Despite all these revelations, the series gestured toward protecting the privacy of its participants. In an episode featuring an insecure young woman living with heart disease, a life-size cardboard cutout of her was shown for strangers to evaluate. Host Carson Kressley explained jauntily: "We chopped off your head to protect your identity!" Later, a photo of her wearing only bra and panties was enlarged to billboard size and displayed in downtown Los Angeles. This time, host Kressley said sarcastically: "I would hate to go too far!"[2] How far is too far, really?

With so many willing victims/participants, is "privacy" even a relevant concern? Do reality television producers have an ethical obligation to safeguard the privacy of their subjects even when apparently rational individuals invite the cameras into their living rooms?

I will answer yes on both counts and further suggest that viewers, too, need to keep a critical eye open, turning away from programs that shamelessly invade privacy to satisfy prurient interests and thinking carefully about why we maintain and value our own privacy.

Privacy as a Legal and Moral Right

Ferdinand Schoeman opens his book *Privacy and Social Freedom* with this caveat: "Often it is suggested that the best way to begin a discussion of a volatile and controversial concept like privacy is with a definition. However, given the socially hyperactive role that privacy plays in contemporary controversies regarding the evolving contours of personhood, there may be some benefit in not striving for verbal precision before this evolution is further played out."[3] Verbal precision is difficult, so I will likewise set aside some of these definitional discussions except to briefly distinguish between the legal and moral concerns of privacy.

Legal Protections of Privacy

First, it is useful to acknowledge that privacy is not a right enshrined in the US Constitution or the Bill of Rights, but the courts have consistently recognized certain grounds that constitute invasion of privacy – particularly by the media. That is, the right of freedom of the press is checked by considerations for individual privacy, particularly in these four areas: "intrusion, public disclosure of private and embarrassing facts, false light, and misappropriation of a person's name or image without permission."[4] These four categories were first outlined in 1890 by Samuel Warren and Louis Brandeis (who would later become a Supreme Court justice)[5]. The eminent legal scholars examined existing case law and "concluded that such cases were in reality based upon a broader principle which was entitled to separate recognition. This principle they called the right to privacy."[6]

This framework has been directly applied to reality television in a variety of instances. For example, in 1998, the producers of a show called *On Scene: Emergency Response* were sued in California courts for recording an accident scene and the victim's conversations with EMS workers without the victim's permission. At that time, the judge viewed reality television producers as journalists, writing in the decision: "No constitutional precedent or principle of which we are aware gives a reporter general license to intrude in an objectively offensive manner into private places, conversations or matters merely because the reporter thinks he or she may thereby find something that will warrant publication or broadcast."[7] To avoid such lawsuits (and their potential to encroach upon freedom of the press), reality television producers now assiduously procure signed legal release forms from would-be participants.[8] The informed consent process works well to indemnify reality television producers, their companies and their networks from any legal liability for breach of privacy.

Even the simplest reality television formats rely on legal consent to pursue what might otherwise be construed as invasion of privacy by the courts. For example, one can't submit a hilarious video clip to the long-running bloopers show *America's Funniest Home Videos* (ABC) without waiving certain legal rights. Many of the videos featured on *AFV* show people caught in moments they may wish they could forget; through the broadcast, what might once have been their private humiliation is made public, taken out of context, replayed repeatedly, and generally mocked. Even in a 30-second clip with no names used and little context provided (most *AFV* entries are accompanied by the host's witty, but often fictional, narration) there is the potential for invasion of privacy on the grounds of intrusion or disclosure of embarrassing facts. Given this, the producers of *AFV* require a lengthy release form relinquishing a wide array of rights including the unlimited use of and profit from a person's "name, voice, likeness, biographical information, appearance and performance...."[9]

Furthermore, and more relevant to my immediate purposes here, those who would submit a video also give up "claims for breach of contract, infliction of emotional distress, defamation, false light, common law or statutory misappropriation, invasion or other violations of any actual or purported right of privacy and/or publicity...."[10] This language is not at all unusual in reality television contracts.[11] While many shows do not make their contractual agreements so readily available online, if a show with minimal privacy risks such as *AFV* has a document totaling 17 single-spaced pages, one can only imagine the intricacies of contracts for more elaborate and potentially invasive reality formats. Furthermore, while such documents may satisfy the lawyers, this legalistic approach barely scrapes the surface of ethical obligations that media producers may face to value the privacy of those who come before the camera's lens.

Privacy in Media Ethics

Perhaps surprisingly, privacy per se has not been a frequent focus of media scholars examining reality television. For these scholars, the question has more often been framed in terms of surveillance technologies and the ways in which reality television participants are disciplined and incited to self-improvement through the critiques of expert judges – often based on covertly taped footage.[12] This perspective is definitely worthwhile, but it doesn't get at the root issue of whether reality television constitutes an unethical invasion of privacy. On the other hand, the issue of privacy has been productively taken up by media ethicists studying journalistic reporting.

For journalists, the key question is how to weigh the public's right to know against an individual's right to privacy. These issues can be particularly sticky with political candidates and elected officials, as well as with topics involving social stigma such as mental illness or sexually transmitted diseases. Candace Cummins Gauthier explores three ethical models for journalists with an eye to assessing how they might make decisions about invasions of privacy.[13] She explains a Kantian model wherein people must be viewed as ends in and of themselves, not used as means to an end; a utilitarian model that considers where the greatest good lies; and a model she labels "transfer of power." Explaining this third model, she writes: "Privacy protects our thoughts, words, relationships, and activities from being used against us. It protects us from the judgments and repressive or punitive reactions of institutions, groups, and individuals. Privacy, understood in this way, serves as a valuable counterweight to the power of others."[14]

If power (as privacy) is taken from individuals and conferred upon the public via journalistic practice, we ought to ask to what use the public will put that wrested power. Gauthier concludes that, following this logic, invasions of privacy may be justifiable when the subject is in a position of power over a given public. For example, in the case of an elected representative, citizens have a reasonable interest in stripping some of his or her privacy in order to maintain a better balance of power and a well-functioning democratic system.

At least two potential problems complicate applying theorizations of journalistic practice to contemporary reality television: (i) whereas newsmakers are often unwilling or unwitting participants in the stories (reporters ferret out skeletons in the closet, a celebrity is involved in an accident, a citizen becomes a crime victim), reality television participants typically are willing participants; and (ii) whereas journalists can readily turn to a utilitarian model or Gauthier's transfer of power theory to support their incursions into private realms (the public needs to know), reality television producers – notwithstanding their frequent protestations to be engaged in serious social documentary – are primarily purveyors of entertainment. This is not to say that ethical considerations need not apply.

On the contrary, in the case of reality television, ethicists face a heavier burden to explain why we should still be concerned about invasions of privacy given the willingness of our neighbors to sacrifice their privacy for our entertainment. The privacy risks borne by reality television participants seem further outweighed by the potential benefits when we recognize that these benefits now regularly include not just fleeting fame but also professional advice, a new wardrobe or home, free medical attention, travel to exotic destinations, career advancement and other forms of philanthropy.[15] Jon Gosselin, father of the Gosselin clan of twins and sextuplets featured in *Jon & Kate Plus 8* (TLC) addressed this point directly in explaining his family's decision to go ahead with a fifth season of the show despite growing concerns about privacy: "I don't like the public life. [But] there's a lot of positives, obviously – the house, an education for our kids, car, whatever. Material things."[16]

Is there something valuable about privacy that shouldn't be trumped by material rewards and/or that isn't made clear in legal release forms?

Why Privacy Matters: Benn's Privacy Framework

Perhaps complete privacy is not inherently valuable or beneficial (social isolation can be a very effective punishment) and the specific realms we deem private are certainly culturally and historically contingent (e.g. cultures vary widely in their views toward nudity). On the other hand, while recognizing those points, we can also posit that some measure of privacy is integral to full personhood and a free society.

Philosopher Stanley Benn writes that understanding privacy as a right means that we find people have a "normative capacity to decide whether to maintain or relax the state of being private."[17] In contemporary Western democracies, we find a certain expectation of privacy in daily life (unless we abuse that right through illegal acts or relinquish some of our privacy voluntarily in the course of seeking publicity), and in Benn's view, that state of assumed privacy is to be cherished. Benn challenges a utilitarian view that would find cause for alarm only if a loss of privacy resulted in an immediate threat or harm. In Benn's view, even if no harm comes to us through being spied upon, observation treats people as objects "not like subjects with sensibilities and aspirations of their own, capable, as mere specimens are not, of reciprocal relations with the observer."[18] Those without recourse to privacy cannot be truly free.

Therefore, in general you have an interest in keeping your affairs unobserved, in living your life discreetly. However, Benn notes that in certain situations this interest may not be well-reasoned or healthy. There is likely to be significant room for disagreement about the benefits of privacy for a given person "since whether he is better off on account of his being private is an evaluative matter, even when it is what he desires."[19] This recognition gives us leave to interrogate the matter of reality TV's all-seeing cameras more deeply. The simple fact that participants have freely agreed to be filmed or have sought the spotlight does not invalidate questions of morality and risk for the producers, the individual participant or for contemporary society as a whole.

Benn distinguishes three types of privacy interests: proprietary, personal or intimate, and what he calls "freedom-based" interests. While his conception of "freedom-based interests" pertains mainly to limitations on state surveillance, the other two categories are immediately relevant to a discussion of reality television. In the following section I'll apply these in turn to some contemporary reality television examples.

Proprietary Interests in Privacy

Let's return to Bethenny Frankel for a moment. Reading the example that begins the chapter, our first impulse might be to label her hypocritical or inauthentic, but her distinction between the camera crew with whom she has a contract and the enterprising photographer with a telephoto lens is a meaningful one. In this case, Frankel's actions demonstrate that privacy can be reduced without being invaded because she has made the rational decision to trade some of her privacy for increased celebrity and remuneration (although the exact details of her contract with Bravo are not public). She derives far less benefit from the paparazzo's photographs because in that instance, she has not consented and has no indication of how these images will be used. He is *invading* her privacy.[20]

Her interest in maintaining a state of privacy free from paparazzi is a *proprietary interest* in privacy. Such interests are often protected by existing property laws, as Warren and Brandeis outlined, including those laws pertaining to intellectual property, trespass and libel.[21] A proprietary interest in privacy is not only about who will profit from the publicity as in the example above, but also about the risk of material or emotional loss when privacy is breached. To expand this discussion, we also need to think about "property in the intangible assets of name, identity, and reputation, which no one else ought to be able to exploit *without permission*."[22] The producers of *Bethenny Ever After* have Frankel's permission to exploit her identity, image and reputation, but the paparazzo does not.

If we think of this level of privacy only in terms of last names or other personally identifiable information, we miss larger more abstract costs of diminished privacy. How else do the "intangible assets" of identity come within the camera's lens on reality television? We might think that participating in a single episode of a reality show couldn't amount to much loss of privacy (not compared with being followed by the cameras for five years, at least), but when a makeover format examines our health records or financial history, there are real material risks to reputation and perhaps employment in addition to embarrassment. These risks are typically not clearly enumerated in legal release forms and may be difficult (if not impossible) to predict even for savvy viewers and rational decision-makers, let alone vulnerable populations whose decision-making ability may be impaired or limited.

Take the case of *Extreme Makeover: Home Edition* (ABC), the philanthropic surprise makeover series. Here the rewards are legendarily elaborate (an entirely new home with stylish decor and state of the art fixtures), but the cost to personal privacy may be great even though the family is off-camera for much of each episode. However, the premise of the show involves a focus on how the nominated family has suffered some misfortune, usually as a result of illness, unemployment, or natural disaster. While the show often makes an effort to present each family as fully human, the message is easily lost in a parade of the downtrodden or deserving poor. Whereas before *EMHE* a family may have been struggling with quiet dignity, after *EMHE*, the whole town, the whole nation, will know the particulars of their insurance/mortgage/unemployment/health woes. For these participants, the loss of privacy is unlikely to lead to a financial loss, but it may well dramatically alter their reputation in the community. Even as they move on in life, perhaps more successfully thanks to the charity they've received, their tale will be replayed in re-runs, on DVDs and via online streaming video. The precise implications of this extended use of their story are hard to predict, even for astute industry-watchers, let alone potential participants facing the decision to sign mind-numbing pages of legalese release forms.

On the popular health-makeover show *The Biggest Loser* (NBC), a dozen or so clinically obese participants compete in a dramatic weight-loss challenge with those who fail to lose weight eliminated over the course of a season. Here, the potential benefit of participation is a healthier body mass index, perhaps better eating habits and a healthier lifestyle overall, thanks to intensive coaching from health and fitness experts. While the fact of their obesity is unlikely to be private information, participants lose privacy regarding their weight, diets, appearance and other health information, and they perhaps lose some measure of their dignity. The risks certainly include embarrassment, as participants are shown in ill-fitting workout gear, struggling with their exercises, giving in to culinary temptation, and so on. However, the bigger concern might be about the loss of privacy regarding their health information, the particularities of which probably should be private. The sort of information conveyed on the show would, in other contexts, be subject to doctor–patient confidentiality. But the revelation of such information could potentially influence participants' employment or their health insurance. While any loss of employment would be tantamount to illegal discrimination in hiring, insurance companies regularly and legally adjust their rates on the basis of health risks. Thus a seemingly minor invasion of privacy (restricted to one arena of life: health) could have very real material consequences.

In academic research, scholars who would study human subjects, for example, in a clinical weight-loss program akin to the *Biggest Loser* approach, face a special onus to have their research plans approved by a university-convened ethics panel, typically called the Institutional Review Board (IRB). The process requires researchers to show that the risks borne by individual participants both in terms of privacy and wellness are outweighed by the potential benefits of the research for either the individuals themselves or society at large. Furthermore, academic researchers must often detail what counseling services they will provide, when and how participants will be able to withdraw from a study, and other measures to protect the interests and privacy of their human subjects. This process is akin to the legal consent forms relied on by television producers, but crucially it also emphasizes explaining risks in terms participants can understand (not legalese) and covers ethical implications, not only legal ones. There is no similar ethical review process for reality television producers, but perhaps there should be.

Personal and Intimate Interests

Following Benn's typology of privacy interests, there is more to consider than the immediate questions of reputation or remuneration encompassed by proprietary interests in maintaining a state of privacy. There is also a relevant interest in maintaining privacy in at least some areas of life in order to maintain healthy personal relationships. We protect our privacy not just for our own sakes but for the sake of our relationships. Jeffrey Rosen writes: "Privacy is necessary for the formation of intimate relationships, allowing us to reveal parts of ourselves to friends, family members, and lovers that we withhold from the rest of the world. It is, therefore, a precondition for friendship, individuality, and even love."[23] If we reveal everything to everyone, there is no possibility of intimacy based on a unique trust between individuals. Reality television – especially the slice-of-life formats that include all areas of the participants' lives – threatens to remove the possibility of intimacy among participants even as a sort of promise of intimate relationship is extended to millions of viewers.

This perspective on privacy relates closely to sociologist Erving Goffman's view that daily interactions are made possible by the maintenance of certain private areas where we prepare for our social roles.[24] We habitually carve out spaces where we can safely put on our makeup, relax and let loose, or privately collaborate with our colleagues; Goffman calls these backstage regions. As may already be evident, Goffman's view is dramaturgical, meaning he applies concepts from the world of theatre, such as performance, role and backstage, to interpret social interactions. We are all, he argues, performing roles and we may perform different roles in different contexts. For example, you are a student at school, a son or daughter at home, a clerk at work. You may also be gregarious with one group of friends and shy with another. Rather than seeing these different roles as duplicitous, Goffman, Benn and others recognize them as essential to a smoothly functioning society. To maintain these separate roles, we engage in practices of "audience segmentation" such that the people for whom we perform in one area are not privy to our other performances. We keep dinner guests out of the messy kitchen and we decline to "friend" our bosses on Facebook to keep separate our roles as host/cook and employee/socialite. Reality TV, by virtue of its national audience and intrusive cameras, makes this audience segmentation and role maintenance impossible.

This shift towards performance uniformity is further exacerbated by the extensive use of "confession cam" segments in many reality television formats. A common trope of reality formats established firmly as early as the first season of MTV's The Real World in 1992, in the confessional segment participants speak directly to camera in a "private" mode about their thoughts and reactions. They may reflect on their own actions or those of others, but like the confessional in the Catholic Church, these revelations are understood to be genuine, unfiltered and unscripted. Unlike a church confessional, these reflections will not be held in confidence and may be edited with other footage to create a dramatic contrast between words and deeds.

When cameras come into the home or when participants agree to live in The Real World house, for example, there is no longer any assurance of those essential backstage spaces. Children growing up in reality television families like the Gosselins will rarely find backstage spaces in which to experiment with their identities and will be defined by a single role everyone has seen them play (sibling) rather than the multiple roles they might perform in a less-televised life. Children may have little proprietary interest in privacy, but they do have a personal interest in privacy – perhaps more so even than adults.

This point has been the subject of considerable debate among fans and critics of Jon & Kate Plus 8 (TLC).[25] Parents Jon and Kate Gosselin are not unaware of these concerns and have weighed the loss of privacy against the material benefits of participation, as expressed in Jon's statement quoted earlier in the chapter. By the beginning of Season 5, the whole family was seeking a bit more privacy. They moved to a bigger house on a large lot not only for additional space but also to keep curious passersby at bay. As they settled into the new house, the Gosselins declared all bedrooms off limits from the cameras. At last, the kids would have their own backstage space and some measure of privacy, but it's worth noting that it took four seasons before this policy was established and it may not be enough.[26]

Reportedly, the kids have expressed to other family members some discomfort with their televised lives. Kate's sister-in-law Jodi Kreider told the *New York Post*, "[The kids] would say, "Aunt Jodi, I don't like the cameras on every vacation with us. I don't like them" … Kids have bad times, bad moments – they cry, and having the camera zoom in on a crying child…. This should not be a form of entertainment." Kreider continued: "Unfortunately, I think it has come down to all about the ratings… And no one is looking at these children, at what they are going through, and the life consequences they are going to have as they get older."[27] While most of us have the luxury of down-playing embarrassing childhood incidents or hiding the photos of our awkward tween years, child stars of reality television will not have this option as they grow up in the spotlight. Thanks to re-runs, DVD box sets, and a multitude of websites, they won't be able to outrun their parents' tabloid-fodder divorce or their own childhood tantrums, experiences that those of us not on reality television usually manage to keep private as we strive to become successful, independent adults.

Privacy and the Consistent Self

While for children and adults alike, personal growth over time may seem to be an obvious goal, the overall ethos of reality television challenges this idea as well. In a recent study examining *The Bachelor* reality competition franchise, Rachel Dubrofsky interrogates the effect of on-camera confession on ideals of mental health.[28] While her research focuses on surveillance more than privacy as such, her argument is germane here. Dubrofsky suggests that while traditional therapeutic discourse focuses on efforts to change or reform the self, reality television has embraced a "therapeutics of self" that prizes consistency rather than change. That is, the "good" characters in reality television don't say one thing to the confession cam and do another in their interactions. They don't change their behavior because of the cameras, and while they may enjoy an on-camera makeover, they don't change their essential identity over the course of the series. In dramaturgical terms, they never drop character; their performance is the same in front and back regions.

Adopting the voice of a reality show participant, Dubrofsky summarizes consistent self-ideal: "I have confessed myself adequately, I have shown my emotions, I have revealed my inner feelings, and I have been (on the show) who I truly am in 'real' life, consistently and unchanged. My reward, if nothing else, is that I am who I am."[29] From a therapeutic standpoint, this shift is problematic because it nullifies ideas of personal and social betterment and results in a sort of relativism that does not critique existing social structures or past personal behaviour. From a privacy standpoint, I would add that this shift is problematic because it suggests that a life well lived should have no need for privacy. After all, what do you have to hide?

Interestingly, Goffman foresaw the same shift. Even as he wrote in 1959, well before the dawn of reality television, he noted the possible emergence of an "anti-dramaturgical social movement, a cult of confession," and he admitted somewhat hesitantly that this might be a natural progression or evolution.[30] In other words, for the past 50 years, privacy has been diminishing in importance as a social value. In the digital age, some observers enthusiastically welcome this more "transparent society" ushered in as more and more information about us floats in cyberspace and reality television confessions become commonplace. Rather than feeling vulnerable in such a society, we might take comfort in the fact that everyone else is just as exposed as we are. This view holds that as long as we each have access to each other's information (citizens can investigate politicians and employers and employees alike can keep tabs on each other), we'll maintain an egalitarian democratic society.

However, Jeffrey Rosen argues that this view not only rejects the Goffmanian norm of audience segmentation but, more problematically, he writes: "The defenders of transparency are confusing secrecy with privacy, even though secrecy is only a small dimension of privacy."[31] Desiring privacy is not tantamount to admitting that we have something to hide.

The deleterious effects of this new climate of openness, not unlike global warming, are gradual and man-made. As we are beginning to see far-reaching environmental effects of climate change, Rosen points out that we are also "beginning to learn how much is being lost in a culture of transparency: the capacity for creativity and eccentricity, for the development of self and soul, for understanding, friendship, and even love."[32] To underscore the value of personal privacy, perhaps a cautionary tale is in order.

A Life Without Privacy

The costs of a life without privacy are great:

> The man who is compelled to live every minute of his life among others and whose every need, thought, desire, fancy or gratification is subject to public scrutiny, has been deprived of his individuality and human dignity. Such an individual merges with the mass. His opinions, being public, tend never to be different; his aspirations, being known, tend always to be conventionally accepted ones; his feelings, being openly exhibited, tend to lose their quality of unique personal warmth and to become the feelings of every man. Such a being, although sentient, is fungible; he is not an individual.[33]

If this sounds hyperbolic, consider how the pitfalls of a life without privacy were elaborately demonstrated in the social experiments of internet-video pioneer Josh Harris. In 2000, he and his girlfriend decided to give up their domestic privacy in nearly every way possible by fitting their apartment with dozens of motion-tracking cameras and microphones hooked to a live internet stream. They spared no expense in fitting cameras even inside the refrigerator and toilet in the interest of granting their audience the fullest possible access to their lives. The project, dubbed "We Live in Public," was just one of Harris's innovative experiments with online video and do-it-yourself programming, but this time he had gone too far. The couple found that their relationship could not thrive without privacy. There was nothing that they shared together that they didn't also share with their online fans. The stress of living in public caused Harris' girlfriend to leave him after a few months. Later, Harris himself suffered a near mental breakdown and ended the project abruptly, disappearing not only from the "We Live in Public" website but from his social life altogether.[34] The subsequent cautionary tale told in a 2009 documentary *We Live in Public* highlights well the essential function of privacy in the maintenance of relationships.

Most reality television participants will have nowhere near the exposure of Harris and will likely not suffer dramatically for their temporary loss of privacy, but the gradual erosion of concern for privacy and the emergent ideal of the "consistent self" should warrant our concern if we want to maintain a free society.

Downsides to Privacy

Complete privacy isn't always desirable, however. In this section, I address two areas where privacy can actually be seen as detrimental to healthy relationships and democratic society. Specifically, I'll consider how reality television might be praised for highlighting situations where privacy is abused or used to maintain social taboos. Rather than undermining the argument in favour of privacy laid out so far, these instances might better be seen as notes of caution. As with so many things, with privacy, a middle ground may be the best situation. Too little privacy leaves us self-conscious or objectified, but too much can be problematic in other ways.

Endangerment and Illegality

Benn's theory holds that privacy may be justifiably breached when it has been abused. Thus, police can obtain search warrants when they have sufficient evidence of a probable crime. In a similar vein, we might see the invasion of privacy inherent in a show like *Intervention* (A&E) as morally justified because the addicts who are the focus on this program rely on their state of privacy to indulge their self-endangering and illegal habits. In this program format, friends and family of addicts nominate their loved ones for a surprise on-camera intervention with an addiction counselor. While the addicts do consent to the filming, they are only told they are participating in a documentary about addiction (arguably a deceptive pretense), and with this understanding, they reveal their crimes as well as often deep emotional scars. The potential benefit of recognizing an addiction and receiving life-saving treatment is a strong argument in favor of the invasion of privacy, but I'm not sure it is strong enough to justify the *televised* intervention. First, a person in the throes of addiction can scarcely be considered a rational decision-maker, particularly when not given full information about the nature of the program. Second, not only has the subject's proprietary interest in privacy been breached, so too has her *personal interest* in privacy been violated because the relationships on display in the television program will be irrevocably altered by her participation.

Taboos and Exclusion

Privacy can enhance freedom or circumscribe it. By staking out areas in which no one should interfere with individual choice, privacy enables us to protect our reputations, create our identities, safeguard our career prospects and build relationships. However, there is also the sense that privacy can circumscribe freedom by "manifest[ing] a rigid and internalized form of social control" – that is, areas of life may be kept private not to allow greater choice but by virtue of social taboo.[35] (Matters of illness, defecation, sex and nudity tend to fall here. The "closeting" of homosexuality is another clear example in our contemporary society.) This distinction may be useful because we can see that diminished privacy of the sort that allows greater freedom would likely cause greater psychological damage than diminished privacy of the sort that maintains taboos or leaves social ills unspeakable. In contemplating the ethics of privacy in reality television, it's important to recognize that giving up some measure of privacy can be a strategy to challenge restrictive ideologies and the injustices of the status quo.

Therefore at least some reality television formats can be seen, not as prurient invasions of privacy perpetrated against innocent unwitting citizens, but as claims by those individuals to fuller inclusion in the social norm. Diminished privacy might also illuminate social ills that often go unspoken – the failures of sex education may be highlighted in *16 and Pregnant* (MTV), the overcrowding of the prison system in *Lockup* (MSNBC). Of the latter series, James Parker opines in *The Atlantic*: "Sensational? Sort of exploitative? Intermittently debasing? Check, check, and check again. But *Lockup* keeps going, into unexpected zones of sympathy and catharsis."[36] Such series may actually have stronger potential benefits for society as a whole than for the individuals who choose to open up their lives on camera. Reality television in this vein can help us see our culture in a fresh light and may inspire political engagement and social change.

Explaining this more critical stance toward privacy, Richard Wasserstrom writes about the powerful sense of shame that can be engendered by an insistence on privacy:

> We've made ourselves vulnerable – or at least far more vulnerable than we need be – by accepting the notion that there are thoughts and actions concerning which we ought to feel ashamed or embarrassed. When we realize that everyone has fantasies, desires, worries about all sorts of supposedly terrible, wicked and shameful things, we ought to see that they are not really things to be ashamed of at all. We regard ourselves as vulnerable because in part we think we are different, if not unique.[37]

In this view, the taboos about what ought to be done in private are sociocultural constructions – often based in outmoded ideas, superstitions or ideology.

Wasserstrom continues that first it may be healthy to recognize these as social constructs; second, that we will be "more secure and at ease in the world" as our attitudes about privacy and taboos change; and third, that "interpersonal relationships will in fact be better if there is less of a concern for privacy."[38] This perspective puts the privacy invasions of a show like *How to Look Good Naked* in a new light as its repeated revelations of women's insecurities about their bodies (and its use of outlandish stunts like semi-naked photos of average women on billboards) may help to chip away at the epidemic of eating disorders and the more intractable cultural association of shame with the female body.

This viewpoint can also help to explain why some individuals would consent to participate in reality television formats that would seem, at first glance, not to be in their best interest. Consider the example of *Sister Wives* (TLC), a slice-of-life reality show that focuses on the Brown family: patriarch Kody, his four wives and their children. By agreeing to reveal their polygamist lifestyle on a weekly television series, they've not only opened up the intimate details of their private life to neighbors and strangers, they've opened themselves up for legal investigations. Why would they agree to participate in such a show, particularly without disguising their names or their location? In this case, by revoking their right to privacy, the Brown family may also be seen as making a claim that this lifestyle need not be closeted.

While I am not eager to defend polygamy, I do see that it must be a strain to live in a society in which you must keep your lifestyle not just private but secret, especially when that lifestyle is based in deeply held religious belief, as the Browns' would seem to be. When "privacy" is forced on a person, that situation limits his autonomy and his personhood. In this way, the incursions of reality television into previously hidden terrain could be seen as a positive force for a more open-minded and diverse society. We might see the same effect in the TLC series *19 Kids and Counting*, which follows a conservative Christian couple raising their 19 biological children. As television viewers are exposed to an ever-wider range of families and lifestyles, the idea of what a "normal" American family looks like is challenged, broadened and perhaps made more inclusive. In these cases, the loss of privacy is outweighed by the potential benefit of a more accepting and tolerant society as a result of seeing that, despite surface differences, large families, same-sex families, differently able families, polygamist families and celebrity families are all just families. (For an amplification of this point, read Chapter 2 on stereotyping and Chapter 9 on democracy, both of which suggest an ethical duty simply to get used to people who appear to be different than we are.)

Conclusion

Certainly the documentary tradition has been a powerful force for social change, but if we are just gawking at freak shows, that's hardly paving the way for a more perfect society. The relative value of any show, I would suggest, largely depends upon production decisions of format, sensitive editing, and how much latitude the participants are given to express their own thoughts and draw their own boundaries. Unfortunately, much of today's reality television does not seem to be interested in these loftier aims. Nor should all reality television be expected to change the world. There's undoubtedly a place for pure, unscripted entertainment. But this can be done more ethically.

Perhaps we should call upon producers of reality television to rethink their reliance on indemnifying legal release agreements in order to recognize privacy as a moral right, not just a legal one. Following the Institutional Research Board model of academia, television production companies could present would-be participants with a list of potential harms or side-effects of diminished privacy as well as counselling resources they might find useful. Production crews could even encourage participants to set their own boundaries (be they physical or temporal, bedrooms or bedtimes). Rather than diminishing the dramatic potential of a series, such a move might actually yield more interesting television if it allowed participants to cultivate more meaningful relationships or become less one-dimensional people through the simple act of respecting their privacy. Yet, these proposals likely seem rather naïve to anyone with a rudimentary understanding of the business of television production.

The good news is that responsibility for ethical decision-making doesn't only lie with television producers and would-be participants/celebrities; it also lies with us as viewers to make considered choices about what reality television programmes we watch. How to decide which series constitute unethical invasions of privacy? It's certainly not always a clear-cut distinction, but it may be useful to consider the following questions:

- Do the participants seem to derive some benefit (material and/or emotional) in exchange for their loss of privacy?

- Does the format of the show suggest that producers have taken steps to protect participants' proprietary interest in privacy? For example, is there a voice-over explaining that subjects agreed to be filmed or that names have been changed to protect privacy? Does the format avoid undue use of information that might damage a person's career prospects, insurability, or reputation?

- Are copies of the legal release forms made available on the show's website so that would-be participants can carefully consider the risks in advance?

- Do the participants seem to have private places or spaces in their lives that aren't caught on camera? Are they allowed to "escape" the cameras when they desire to?

- Does the editing of the show allow for participants to narrate their own experiences (e.g. by allowing them to explain the context or motivation for their actions)? Are these "confessional" segments used to give participants a greater degree of subjectivity rather than to paint them as two-faced or oblivious?

- Does the show invade privacy in order to highlight a lifestyle or social issue that would otherwise be inaccessible, neglected, or misunderstood?

If a given reality television show meets most or all of these criteria, we might deem it an acceptable incursion into otherwise private realms. On the other hand, if a show fails to meet most or all of these criteria, that strongly suggests the show's treatment of participants' privacy is unethical. Those series that respectfully highlight diverse lifestyles, meaningful relationships and personal empowerment should be celebrated; those driven by prurient interests that treat their subjects only as creatures in a zoo should be disdained. Given the explosion of reality formats, we know there are always going to be other viewing options.

Notes

1   Time/CNN. "Time/CNN Poll: What Would You Do?" *Time*, 26 June 2000, 56.

2   "Heather," *How to Look Good Naked*, season 2, episode 8, directed by Becky Smith, aired 9 September 2008 (Los Angeles: RDF USA).

3   Ferdinand David Schoeman, *Privacy and Social Freedom* (New York: Cambridge University Press, 1992) 11.

4   Carole Rich, *Writing and Reporting the News*, 6th edn (New York: Cengage, 2010) 299.

5   Samuel Warren and Louis Brandeis, "The right to privacy [the implicit made explicit]," In *Philosophical Dimensions of Privacy: An Anthology*, Ferdinand Schoeman ed. (New York: Cambridge University Press, 1984) 75–103.

6   William Prosser, "Privacy [A Legal Analysis]." In *Philosophical Dimensions of Privacy: An Anthology*, Ferdinand Schoeman ed. (New York: Cambridge University Press, 1984) 105.

7 Kathryn Mackle Werdegar quoted in Dan Trigoboff, "WhatchaGonna Do? Sue." *Broadcasting & Cable* (8 June 1998): 32.

8 If subjects are unavailable or unwilling to sign consent forms, shows will sometimes instead obscure the identities of those caught on tape, as the long-running real crime reality show *Cops* does when the alleged criminals do not grant their consent.

9 Cara Communications Corporation, "AFV Release Forms," ABC.com. Last modified 20 November 2009. http://abc.go.com/shows/americas-funniest-home-videos/release-forms.

10 Cara Communications, "AVF Release Forms."

11 Debora Halbert, "Who owns your personality: Reality TV and publicity rights," in *Survivor Lessons*, Matt Smith and Andrew Wood (eds) (Jefferson, NC: McFarland, 2003) 37–56.

12 For more on this perspective see: Mark Andrejevic, *Reality TV: The Work of Being Watched* (Boulder, CO: Rowman & Littlefield, 2004) and Deborah Jermyn, "'This Is About Real People!' Video Technology, Actuality and Affect in the Television Crime Appeal," In *Understanding Reality Television*, Su Holmes and Deborah Jermyn (eds) (New York: Routledge, 2004) 173–90.

13 Candace Cummins Gauthier, "Privacy Invasion by the News Media: Three Ethical Models." *Journal of Mass Media Ethics* 17, no. 1 (2002): 20–34.

14 Gauthier, "Privacy Invasion," 26.

15 Laurie Ouellette and James Hay, *Better Living Through Reality TV: Television and Post-Welfare Citizenship* (Malden, MA: Blackwell, 2008).

16 Quoted in Lynette Rice, "Kids, Cameras, Controversy," *Entertainment Weekly*, 22 May 2009. http://www.ew.com/ew/article/0,,20278901,00.html.

17 Stanley Benn, *A Theory of Freedom* (New York: Cambridge University Press, 1988), 266.

18 Benn, *A Theory of Freedom*, 273.

19 Ibid., 266.

20 Of course, in the modern celebrity industry, all publicity is good publicity, but that's a separate point.

21 Benn, *A Theory of Freedom*, 290.

22 Ibid., (emphasis added).

23 Jeffrey Rosen, *The Unwanted Gaze: The Destruction of Privacy in America* (New York: Random House, 2000) 11.

24 Erving Goffman, *The Presentation of Self in Everyday Life* (New York: Doubleday, 1959).

25 The show is now called *Kate Plus 8* after the couple divorced.

26 Lynette Rice, "Jon & Kate Talk to EW about Life in the Fishbowl." *Entertainment Weekly*, 13 May 2009. http://insidetv.ew.com/2009/05/13/kate-gosselin-o/.

27 "Are Jon and Kate Gosselin Exploiting Their Children?" *The New York Post*, 28 May 2009. http://www.foxnews.com/entertainment/2009/05/28/jon-kate-gosselin-exploiting-children/

28 Rachel Dubrofksy, "Therapeutics of the Self: Surveillance in the Service of the Therapeutic," *Television and New Media* 8, no. 4 (2007): 263–84.

29 Dubrofsky, "Therapeutics of the Self," 270.

30 Goffman, *The Presentation of Self in Everyday Life,* 205.

31 Rosen, *The Unwanted Gaze*, 210.

32 Ibid., 223.

33 Edward Bloustein, "Privacy as an Aspect of Human Dignity: An Answer to Dean Prosser," In *Philosophical Dimensions of Privacy: An Anthology*, Ferdinand Schoeman ed. (New York: Cambridge University Press, 1984) 188.

34 *We Live in Public*, directed by Ondi Timoner (Pasadena, CA: Interloper Films, 2009), DVD.

35 Ferdinand Schoeman, *Privacy and Social Freedom* (New York: Cambridge University Press, 1992) 15.

36 James Parker, "Prison Porn," *The Atlantic*, March 2010. http://www.theatlantic.com/magazine/archive/2010/03/prison-porn/7906/.

37 Richard Wasserstrom, "Privacy: Some Arguments and Assumptions." In *Philosophical Dimensions of Privacy: An Anthology*, Ferdinand Schoeman ed. (New York: Cambridge University Press, 1984) 330.

38 Wasserstrom, "Privacy," 331.

4

Cultural Values: Reality TV Manufactures Marriage

Mira K. Desai

With a population of 1.21 billion people, India is competing with China to be the most populous country in the world. India is obsessed with marriage, which is seen as a license to parenthood. In most Indian communities, marriage is defined by the pregnancy of the bride within a year or two of marriage; dating, heterosexual friendships, homosexual relationships and courtship prior to marriage are not accepted norms. For most Indian young people, courtships and weddings have little space for the bride and groom as marriages are mainly arranged by their elders as alliances of lineage and socioeconomics. By some estimates, the proportion of 'arranged' versus 'love' marriages in India is nine to one. Indian society is highly multicultural and diverse, and so are many traditions and customs related to marriage. However, across these traditions and customs, marriage is considered a sacrosanct union between two individuals and their families, and a wedding is a public event where everyone known to both the families is invited.

This chapter elaborates the recent phenomenon of showcasing marriage on reality television shows in India. The chapter examines how reality television is reflecting and influencing changes in courtship and marriage in India, and it argues that reality marriage shows are creating interest in 'pan-Indian' marriages that borrow from different cultural orientations and shift the emphasis in marriages from the collective to the individual. Reality marriage shows have made their presence felt as an economically lucrative, ethically questionable, socially inevitable, politically interesting genre of television programming.

Women, Marriage and Indian Family

Marriage in any given society represents how it defines male–female relationships, sexuality and the institution of family. India is still a rural economy. In 2011, about 69 per cent of its population lived in rural areas[1] and 58 per cent of its labour force made their livelihood from agriculture.[2] Family composition remains 'joint', indicating the couple, their children and grandchildren live together. Occasionally, a family of cousins and three or four generations stay under one roof and share the same kitchen. The norms of behaviour for married couples living in joint families (usually with the husband's parents) are fairly rigid. In certain Hindu communities even today women (mainly young daughters-in-law) are supposed to cover their faces with a veil in front of their elders, and the married couple is not supposed to show physical affection publicly. Children are not encouraged to talk about sexual conduct, which is a matter to be experienced upon marriage. Premarital sex is a taboo.

Amongst Hindus, marriage is supposedly 'for life'. The ideas of divorce or living together without marriage are not well received, irrespective of a family's caste, class or geography. Women have little say about their marriages, and proverbs like 'daughter and cow go wherever they are directed to go' still remain. There are variations across communities about how marriage proposals and negotiations are conducted, with demands, functions and expectations arrived upon by the two families. The most frequent assumption is that the bride's parents have a lesser 'say' than the groom's parents, but that is now changing because of population trends. In 2011, the Indian government observed 'an improvement in the status of women in the country' because there were 940 females for every 1,000 males in India, which was the highest number of females per 1,000 males since 1971, when the number reached a low of 930 females per 1,000 males. (By comparison, in the USA in 2011, there were 1,250 females for every 1,000 males.)[3]

Change in women's status is not rapid, however. Historically, women's status deteriorated after the Vedic period between the fourteenth and nineteenth centuries. *Manu Smriti* (Hindu scripture) mentions women's lives from the cradle to the grave as defined by their roles as daughter, wife and mother under the supervision of father, husband and son. Deterioration in women's status varied through practices such as child marriage, *pardah* (secluding women from men by veiling women or by using curtains, walls or enclosures to separate the sexes), widow abuse, *sati* (immolating a widow after her husband's death), female infanticide, and so on. Even in the twenty-first century, although the situation is changing in urban areas, Indian newspapers and television are not without news stories of young married women being abused by their in-laws, women committing suicides, or working women being raped by company transport drivers. In April 2011 in Mumbai, a commercial capital of India, the news reported two 'suicide' cases in which mothers threw their 5- to 8-year-old children from building roofs before jumping themselves. Initial reports indicated that physical torture, dowry demands and verbal abuse by their in-laws caused the mothers to commit these murder-suicides.[4]

Marriage and Media in India

Amongst many factors that have changed ideas about women's roles, courtship and marriage in India, 'the main factor which brought about change was [the] influence of Western thought', according to Sur.[5] Amongst those Western ideas is the emergence of self-arranged marriage, love-cum-arranged marriage, or even free choice by the prospective partners in marriage. These changes are mainly due to the education of women, exposure to the media, and intra- as well as inter-state migration for study and work by young people. Cinema is practically another religion in India, which is home to a prolific film industry that produces 1,000 films a year, making India the largest film-producing country in the world. Indian film viewers have seen ample examples of inter-religion marriages, as well as divorces mainly amongst Hindi film personalities.

Swayamvar is a term used for the process of choosing a life partner. The Sanskrit term *Swayam* means 'self', and *Var* means 'bride-groom' or the way a number of grooms are introduced to the bride in an elaborate public function usually arranged by the parents. Indian history and the Hindu religion contain many references to the practice of swayamvar to arrange marriages, which are 'an arrangement made between families and a mandatory duty for the boy and the girl, marking the end of their childhood'.[6]

Swayamvar and the media have old associations. The musical play *Sita Swayamvar* by Vishnudas A. Bhave debuted in 1841, and in 1928 the popular theatre personality Gandharva Natya Mandli performed *Swayamva.* Several Hindi films since the 1920s have depicted the practice of swayamvar. Eventually, the century-old Hindi film industry shifted to producing stories of love and romance instead of arranged marriage proposals. Many Hindi films present marriage as the ultimate goal for lovers who struggle to gain sanction from their families and community. Interestingly, whilst romantic love is an accepted theme of media messages in India, sexuality and physically intimate relationships are not a matter of either public display or media depiction. In Hindi films, physical intimacy by the characters is not shown; instead, it is depicted using semantic codes of flowers, birds, fire, rain, or most commonly, a song and dance sequence. These depictions are changing, however, as film censorship becomes more lenient.[7]

Since 1991, Indian audiences have seen their share of global-transnational television, through an explosion of private satellite television channels. The fascination of Indian television with wedding themes began in soap operas and extended to non-fiction formats mainly due to the ratings success of fictional characters' weddings. Fictional serials and soap operas began to showcase weddings in a big way, bringing an end to the then-cluttered television landscape of soap operas themed around mother-in-law and daughter-in-law conflict. Non-fiction television programmes soon followed with the wedding emphasis. When *The Big Fat Indian Wedding* show began on NDTV in May 2008, its producers said the programme showed that 'when it comes to marriages, we Indians believe in the Big Bang theory. Everything is larger than life – the song, the dance, rituals, fireworks, festivity and the huge family tree that descends in strength for this made-in-India extravaganza.'[8] The show brought 'real' weddings, as if they were private marriage videos, into public space, where they were presented by glamorous anchors. All the weddings, which came from across India or featured Indians abroad, were larger than life. Reality wedding shows also brought to Indian audiences scenes of characters flirting with each other, getting physically cozy or even using words that had not been accepted otherwise in the public sphere.

Reality Marriage Shows on Indian Television

The association between marriage and reality television is global. There are shows like *Marry Me,* an Irish television series on RTE One that presents the dream of proposing marriage to a partner without his or her knowledge, or *The Marriage Referee,* an American show on NBC that lets couples present their problems to a celebrity and audience panel who act like sports referees.

WE's *Bridezillas*, TLC's *Say Yes to the Dress*, VH1's *Wedding Wars*, and E!'s controversial *Bridalplasty* are just a few other programmes on a long list that also includes WE's *Rich Bride, Poor Bride*, which showcases the trials and tribulations of pulling off a fancy wedding on a limited budget, and VH1's *My Big Friggin' Wedding*, which documents the drama of five New Jersey couples preparing for their big day.

These programmes have been adapted worldwide. The Indian version of *Perfect Bride*, which was similar to American television's *The Bachelor*, added the groom's mother as a player in her son's selection of a bride. With shows like *Rakhi Ka Swayamvar* (on NDTV Imagine in 2009), *Rahul Dulhaniya Le jayega* (on NDTV Imagine in 2010), *Shaadi 3 Crore Ki* (on Imagine in 2011), and *Band Baja Bride* (on NDTV Good Times in 2011), Indian television paved a real path to the marriage *mandap*, or wedding venue.

Reality television shows, in the form of game shows and singing contests, existed on Indian television for years, but the nature and scope of reality television devoted to courtships and weddings demands attention, as the volume and diversity of these programmes has been overwhelming. Whilst Indian television audiences witnessed talent shows (*Indian Idol*, *Jhalak Dikhlaja*, *India's Got Talent*), game shows (*Antakshari*, *Kaun Banega Crorepati*), and adventure shows (*Khatron ke khiladi*, *Muzhe Is Jangle se bachao*), newer concepts emerged after 2000, including mate-selection shows (*Rakhi ka Swayamvar*, *Perfect Bride*), loyalty testing shows (*Emotional Atyachar*), family exchange shows (*Big Switch*), and relationship testing shows (*Date Trap*, *Love Lock*). Reality courtship and marriage shows have attracted big audiences. Television Audience Measurement (TAM) genre share ratings for Indian reality shows rose from 4.3 per cent to 6.9 per cent in 2009 with numerous shows like *Rakhi Ka Swayamvar*, *Sachch ka Samnna*, *Perfect Bride*, *Iss Jungle Se Mughe Bacchao* and *Pati Patni aur Woh*, and the success of *Swayamvar* showed a new peak in viewership for courtship and marriage reality shows.

Swayamvar Season 1, *Rakhi Ka Swayamvar*, aired in June through August 2009 and featured five couples, including celebrities Rakhi Sawant and Ellesh Parujanwala. In fact, most of the couples were celebrity couples in real life. *Swayamvar* was followed by another show, *Pati Patni Aur Woh* (Husband, Wife and The Other) in October 2009 on the same channel. That programme was intended to extend the success of *Swayamvar* by focusing on the first couple who were supposed to wed through a reality show, Rakhi Sawant and Ellesh Parujanwala. The two became engaged but did not marry and declared the end of their relationship due to 'irreconcilable differences'.

Whilst the first reality TV show wedding never took place and the relationship did not survive, the couple featured in *Swayamvar* Season 2 (Rahul Mahajan and Dimpy Ganguly) did marry. They have become news items for turmoil in their married life, as have another reality show couple, Sara Khan and Ali Merchant, who got married on *Big Boss* Season 4 and later called for quits. As a result, subsequent reality show weddings and the people associated with them (such as *Perfect Bride* couple Rumpa Roy and Hitesh Chauhan) have been publicly pushed to give media statements that their 'marriage will last'.[9]

Reality TV and Consequential Ethics

Considering the influx of reality courtship and marriage shows into the homes of Indian television viewers, it makes sense to ask what ethical effects the programmes may have on viewers. Do the courtship and marriage shows unethically encourage young people to disregard traditional community values about mate selection? Do the shows promote wedding celebrations focused on lavish displays of wealth rather than on emotional and spiritual values associated with marriage and relationships? Do the shows help young women imagine how they might have more of a voice in selecting a groom, or do they give prospective brides an unrealistic view of their role?

To answer such questions, an ethical analysis requires the application of ethical theory, which generally can be placed into three categories: (i) theories of the good, or consequential theories; (ii) theories of the right, or non-consequential theories; and (iii) theories of virtue. 'Consequential theories articulate principles that define goodness and identify actions that promote the good; non-consequential, or deontological, theories articulate principles that say what is just and what is our duty... Virtue theories describe moral character and specify the virtues that individuals need to be ethical.'[10]

The analysis of reality courtship and marriage programmes seems a natural place to apply consequential theories of ethics because most of the questions raised about the programmes' ethical effects are focused on the shows' consequences. Given their popularity and wide viewership, do these reality shows challenge cultural values about marriage in ethically harmful ways? What, if anything, might be some short- and long-term benefits of the shows, not just for individual viewers, but for the Indian society overall?

Ethical Harms of Reality Marriage Shows

Today, reality marriage shows have been well-established as a formula in the clutter of Indian television programming that attracts many viewers.

The shows make 'marriage' an essential ingredient of programming, no matter what the story line requires. As well, they raise ethical harms for Indian viewers, particularly as the shows send messages that conflict with community and family values about courtship and marriage. This section will consider six possible ethical harms.

The Harm of Failing to Reflect Societal Values

Reality wedding shows that present young people involved in romance and courtship, or that depict displays of physical affection, do not reflect the values of a society that frowns on flirting and public physical intimacy. A 2011 field survey of 48 parents and 100 young people from four religious backgrounds in Mumbai suggested some change in values about mate selection, but the survey also suggested the persistence of traditional values. Eighty per cent of the 18- to 24-year-old never-married men and women who were surveyed agreed with their parents that 'moral values' (defined by the survey as 'high moral standards/values, good traditional values and character over looks') were the most important criterion for selecting a mate. Sikh (91 per cent) and Hindu (81 per cent) parents were most likely to select 'moral values' as the top requirement for their child's mate, but Muslim (64 per cent) and Christian (61 per cent) parents also selected it. The young men surveyed selected 'traditional values' as the most important characteristic for a spouse, whilst the young women selected 'character over looks'. Both the male and female respondents were more likely to value 'physical traits' in their potential spouses than their parents were, and the young people were much more likely to favour courtship before marriage; 82 per cent of the young women favoured courtship, whilst 50 per cent of the young men did. Less than half of the Muslim parents (35 per cent), Hindu parents (41 per cent) and Sikh parents (49 per cent) favoured courtship, although 68 per cent of the Christian parents did.[11] By portraying the possibility that anyone can marry anyone else, reality marriage shows may be influencing India's age-old 'preservation of genetic heritage' through 'caste-based arranged marriages'.[12]

The Harm of 'Indianizing' Western Programmes

In fact, many of the reality marriage shows are licensed formats that originated in other countries and have been 'Indianized' to suit what programme producers think are the local tastes. Most of the reality marriage shows emphasize the visual splendour of Indian weddings in terms of clothing, rituals and decorations. The first season of *Swayamvar* featured Rakhi Sawant, an outspoken actress and dancer who had appeared in several films and music videos, and who was prominent from her controversial role on a season of the reality show *Big Boss*. To publicly promote *Swayamvar*, she appeared in suggestive Indian attire that she usually never wore otherwise. The 16 male contenders on the show, who were reduced to three before a final selection, wrote poetry, serenaded her with songs, arm wrestled and even walked on burning coals to show their love for her. In the second season of *Swayamvar*, 16,500 young women applied to be amongst the 15 who were chosen to compete to be the bride of Rahul Mahajan. Although the programme's format was 'modern', it promoted traditional Indian stereotypes for brides-to-be, including that of being a good cook, understanding home remedies and making cow-dung floors, an old practice that persists in rural India where concrete floors are still not the norm.

The Harm of Focusing on Physical and Material Aspects of Weddings

To satisfy the demands of the television medium, reality shows also pay an increased attention to the physical aspects of weddings, insist on a need to 'show' emotions, and make a public display of everything personal. The brides who participate are pushed into undue expectations about their bodies and their appearance. It's 'not just their bodies that are scrutinized; couples who can't afford to pay for a lavish ceremony are also shown constant images that suggest that without a big budget, their weddings simply won't measure up.'[13] In fact, Indian reality shows emphasize the spectacular nature of lavish weddings that most viewers cannot afford to host or attend. In 2011, Imagine TV's *Shaadi 3 crore ki* gave the families of groom Inderpal Singh Sehgal and bride Jasmit Singh Gaba, who expected to spend about 1.5 million rupees (approximately $33,000) for their wedding, a three-crores (about 30 million rupees, or $678,000) wedding. The show gave the couple and their families four weeks to put on a dream wedding and portrayed the ensuing conflicts and tensions over their decisions about how to spend the money. The groom was quoted in Indian media saying, '*Yeh koi mazaak nahin hai, Bilkul real shaadi hai*' (This is no joke, it's a real marriage),[14] to assure viewers and perhaps himself too that to be part of a three-crore 'dream' wedding, his personal life must be on public display.

The Harm of Ignoring Collective Roles and the Sanctity of Marriage

No matter how elaborate and entertaining the mate selection process is when depicted on a reality show, most of the shows don't recognize the fact that many young people's parents still play an important role in selecting their spouses. Nor do the shows recognize the belief in India that marriage is a sacrosanct union. Rather, they present marriages that have not sustained the test of time. The ideas of 'family' and 'marriage' in India are undergoing numerous changes due to globalization. As a result, marriage reality shows reflect some change in conventional processes associated with marriage and showcase the shift of control and decision-making about marriage from a 'collective' endeavour to an 'individual' pursuit. At the same time, the shows promote older stereotypes and often 'bring real drama, hilarity and personal transformations', as one show's announcement put it, to what is supposed to be 'the most sacred relationship' in India.[15]

It has indeed become a joke in India that one can marry on national television. Whilst Hollie McKay notes that reality marriage shows are 'genuinely trying to portray the joys of getting married' in Western contexts,[16] Indian reality marriage shows sometimes have made marriage a joke. The failing relationships of reality marriage show contestants in India actually create a question about whether it is 'worth being married' that young people and their families might consider.

The Indian cricket star Sreesanth was asked if he would be a groom on the third season of *Swayamvar*. He stated: 'I can't make a fool of myself by getting married on a reality TV show. I did not want to become part of a circus'. Interestingly, he also stated: 'I would not mind my marriage being shown on TV. But what I do with my fiancée, how I choose my bride, and what we plan to do after marriage should be a closely guarded secret.'[17] Such media reports on the one hand reflect public skepticism about marriage reality shows, but on the other hand keep public interest in reality marriage shows alive.

The Harm of Commodifying Marriage

Reality shows have, by design, distorted marriage into a commodity that can be sold and attract public attention. *Swayamvar* producers have selected controversial figures as protagonists who will select a mate during the show: Rakhi Sawant, a dancer and performer who has been interviewed widely about her troubled childhood; Rahul Mahajan, the son of an assassinated politician and the ex-husband of a pilot who accused him of domestic violence; and Ratan Rajput, a television soap opera actress whose selection for the third season of *Swayamvar* generated 40,000 enquiries from viewers who wanted the chance to compete for her attention on the show, which called her a 'daughter of the nation'. These selections clearly indicate the channel's intention of gaining mileage out of these figures' 'real' lives for a reality show where 'marriage' is not an institution but a product that can be sold. *Swayamvar* also runs opinion polls, games, audio downloads, text-message alerts and episode previews with advertisements on the channel's website, creating alternate revenue streams for the television channel. At the time of the last episode of *Swayamvar* Season 3, the bride's clothing designer's name was superimposed on the bride during the episode. So, in a way, the marriage reality shows sell everything from hairdressers, footwear, jewellry, beauty clinics, beauty products and clothing to hotels, travel companies and car rentals (that supported the show).

Instead of referring to marriage as a union of two individuals, reality shows turn marriage into a 'show' of beauty, clothing, jewelry, food, industries and economic power, sending the message that both parties need money for marriage. Are marriage reality shows thus imposing Western values on Indian audiences? Whilst audience reception studies have clearly rejected cultural imperialism theory, especially in non-Western countries,[18] a consensus is still not reached. The evidence indicates that Western values are imposed on India through media messages and cultural products.[19] However, there are counter flows that suggest India is one of the countries influencing many of its Asian counterparts, as well as the rest of the world, with its media products. So reality marriage shows may influence not only the Indian social fabric but many other Asian cultures.

The Harm of Reducing Marriage to a Commercial, Pan-Indian Celebration

Present reality marriage shows in India represent a Hindu worldview of a diverse country in which many other religions are also practised. Devdutt Pattanaik notes the complexity of wedding rituals even amongst Hindus from different regions of India by noting:

a Malayali Hindu wedding has today been reduced to the simple act of a man tying a thread around a woman's neck before witnesses from the bride's and groom's family. The ceremony ends in less than a minute, whilst a royal Marwari wedding can extend over several days. Add to this the modern Bollywoodization of everything Indian, and we have hybrid post-modern weddings taking place where champagne is drunk when the *havan* [a Hindu worship ritual involving fire] is being conducted and to mind it is seen as being uncool![20]

One cannot deny the fact that marriage in India is a public event and to an extent involves an entire community, if not country. Mass weddings are also a norm, and they keep happening.[21] Reality marriage programmes have added audience voting to mate selection, taking the element of community involvement to a new extreme. For *Swayamvar*, public voting is a revenue model, as well as a device to hold public attention. Discounting the debate over the ethics of intervening into someone else's life by voting for their marriage partner, public voting on reality marriage shows creates huge commercial opportunities for the mobile telephone companies, the television channels and programme producers. By one estimate, a two-week ad campaign that ran during the reality programme *Kaun Banega Crorepati* (an Indian contest show based loosely on *Who Wants to Be a Millionaire*, which began in the UK) generated so many viewer text messages and calls per day that one mobile telephone service provider did 30 million rupees' worth of business.[22]

These capitalist consumerist media presentations are inevitable, and culture too becomes a commodity in them. *Swayamvar* Season 1 adapted the traditional Hindu *haldi* ritual in which turmeric paste is applied to the bride and groom prior to marriage. The turmeric paste has religious as well as cosmetic significance, as turmeric is considered auspicious and improves skin colour. In place of turmeric, *Swayamvar* bride Rakhi Sawant received 'Fair and Lovely fairness cream' since it was the programme sponsor. The show juxtaposed advertisements of the cream with the ceremony, attempting to replace the age-old ritual with a commercial product.

Swayamvar and many other reality marriage shows give the impression to viewers that marriage is a romantic, cultural extravaganza with little realization that marriage brings responsibilities for both the parties. The programmes also culturally fuse a diverse Indian culture, where the Hindu, Christian, Muslim and Sikh faiths are widely observed, into one dominant view that suggests Hindu customs and rituals prevail. In this way, the programmes typify two of the four antisocial effects of television identified by William J. Brown and Awind Singhal as 'cognitive, affective or behavioural activities considered being socially undesirable by most members of the social system'. Amongst those antisocial effects are negative portrayals of women and children, and unrealistic depictions of interpersonal and social relationships.[23] The reality marriage shows reflect both those negative effects.

Ethical Benefits of Reality Marriage Shows

Despite these harms, is it possible that reality marriage shows also might create ethical benefits for viewers? This section will probe that possibility by identifying three potentially beneficial consequences of the shows.

The Benefit of Presenting Alternatives to Tradition

In a society where marriage conventionally is not an individual choice but a family decision, reality marriage shows bring in a newer dimension. They isolate the individual – often a young woman – from the family and give power to that individual in a public space. Many young women seem to have started exploring this power as an alternative to the otherwise rigid system of arranged marriage. The telecast of the *Band Baaja Bride* wedding reality show presenting a couple from Hubli, Karnataka, clearly showed increasing tensions around this issue between generations. The show was positioned as a makeover programme in which the anchors take viewers through the journey of a real bride who is seeking a 'perfect' wedding day look, from her makeup and hairstyle to her clothing and jewelry. The *Band Baaja Bride* contestant went in for the 'makeover' with the 'permission' of her groom (as revealed by the anchor), but her parents were not happy with the development, so the anchors then mediated the tension on the show itself. The groom kept stating that he liked the bride as she was but 'allowed' her to go for the makeover to make her happy. During the makeover, the bride kept stating that 'my fiancé likes long hair; my in-laws are traditional'. The couple's match was revealed towards the end of the show to be a 'love marriage'. Such a depiction shifts the responsibility of marriage onto an individual from the otherwise known 'family' context. In this way, perhaps reality marriage shows can be serving an ethical purpose for viewers, who become aware of alternatives to the traditional practice. (Of course, presenting marriage as an 'individual' issue within a collective culture may be unrealistic because sustaining that individuality post-marriage is difficult when the society still functions on collective norms and expects women to compromise as they typically move to their husbands' homes and communities after marriage.)

The Benefit of Conveying Unification within Diversity

Reality television weddings, and for that matter television serials that portray marriage, are providing a cultural context about courtship and marriage rituals to Indians, especially diasporas (people who now live away from their country). As a result, there has been renewed interest in rituals and traditional ways of doing things, courtesy of the reality television marriage shows and marriage portrayals in the soap operas. In a society as diverse as India, as the media portrayals become norms, there is also unification within diversity. More and more people may follow the same wedding and marriage practices they've seen on television.

The Benefit of Promoting New Roles for Women

Reality television weddings also have succeeded in providing templates for 'bad marriage' or a 'mockery of marriage', whilst at the same time providing a possibility for women that suggests they have 'right to choose' their spouse or how to conduct their marriage. These ideas have not been a norm otherwise in Indian society. The blog space and news comments about *Swayamvar* clearly suggest how many women, and even men, view bride Rakhi Sawant as a symbol of a woman who has a mind of her own. *Perfect Bride* winner Rumpa Roy was quoted in the media as saying: 'I am a designer working with a leading export house right now. I can use the fame and contacts that I got through this show to progress in my field. Otherwise I am a very camera-shy person and do not wish to star in any more shows.'[24] This seems to indicate how a reality show wedding for her was meant to be a professional opportunity. Women on reality marriage shows do gain some agency, however superficial, as equal partners. Many other women viewers are presented with the worldview that they do not need to suffer in a relationship and instead can assert themselves and take charge of their lives.

Conclusion

This chapter has demonstrated the ethically complicated nature of reality courtship and marriage shows in India. On the one hand, the shows may create harmful consequences, through their failure to reflect traditional cultural and spiritual values, their adoption of Western practices and their commodification of what is still regarded as a collective decision to enter a sanctified union. On the other hand, the shows may create some ethical benefits. For instance, the commodification of marriage as an event showcasing 'culture' on reality television in India may lead to an opening up of 'rigid' caste-based, parent-driven unions to marriages based on the individual's 'right' to choose one's partner. Reality television marriages that give voice to women, however subverted that voice may be, have created questions in the minds of a younger generation of women about the age-old tradition of arranged marriage. Whilst the debate over whether reality show marriages are a joke will continue, there is no doubt that the shows are here for real. They have succeeded in initiating change in the otherwise rigid institution of marriage in India. Time will reveal whether the current chaos of cultural values created by reality marriage shows is helping foster social good or diminishing the age-old institution of marriage.

Notes

1 India Ministry of Home Affairs, 'Census of India 2011: Rural/Urban Distribution of Population', 15 July 2011. http://www.censusindia.gov.in/2011-prov-results/paper2/data_files/india/Rural_Urban_2011.pdf.

2 India.gov.in, 'Sectors: Agriculture', 29 April 2011. http://india.gov.in/sectors/agriculture/index.php.

3 India Ministry of Home Affairs, 'Census of India 2011: Gender Composition of the Population', 8 March 2011. http://www.censusindia.gov.in/2011-prov-results/data_files/india/Final%20PPT%202011_chapter5.pdf.

4 A number of news reports covered these cases. See, for example: Nitasha Natu, 'Mother Pushes 2 Kids, Leaps from 19th Floor', *The Times of India*, 9 March 2011. http://articles.timesofindia.indiatimes.com/2011-03-09/mumbai/28672386_1_gaurav-malad-gupta-family; 'Mumbai Woman Jumps to Death with 6 Year Old Son', NDTV.com, 17 April 2011. http://www.ndtv.com/article/cities/mumbai-woman-jumps-to-death-with-6-year-old-son-99294; Manish K. Pathak, 'Harassed New Mother Jumps to Death; Husband, In-laws Arrested', dailybhaskar.com, 11 May 2011. http://daily.bhaskar.com/article/MAH-MUM-harassed-new-mother-jumps-to-death-2094533.html.

5 A. K. Sur, *Sex and Marriage in India* (Bombay: Allied Publishers, 1973) 152.

6 Devdutt Pattanaik, 'Decoding a Hindu Marriage', 6 February 2011. http://devdutt.com

7 Bharati Dubey, 'An A-grade Idea', *The Times of India*, 7 August 2011, 6.

8 NDTV, 'About The Show', *The Big Fat Indian Wedding*, 2011. http://goodtimes.ndtv.com/GoodTimesShowPage.aspx?ShowID=14

9 '"Our Marriage Will Last" Say Perfect Bride Winners', dnaindia.com, 13 December 2009. http://www.dnaindia.com/entertainment/report_our-marriage-will-last-say-perfect-bride-winners_1323259

10 Stephen J. A. Ward, *Global Journalism Ethics* (Montreal: McGill Queen's University Press, 2010) 25–6.

11 R. Deka, 'Mate Selection Criteria: Comparative Study of Parents and Youth' (unpublished master's thesis, SNDT Women's University, Mumbai, India, 2011).

12 S. B. Ahloowalia, *Invasion of the Genes: Genetic Heritage of India* (New York: Strategic Book Publishing, 2009).

13 Hollie McKay, 'Wedding Themed Reality Shows Make a Mockery of Marriage?' *Fox News*, 14 March 2011. http://www.foxnews.com/entertainment/2011/03/14

14 Divya Pal, 'Jasmeet, Inderpal's Expensive TV Wedding', *Times of India*, 17 March, 2011. http://timesofindia.indiatimes.com/entertainment/tv/Jasmeet-Inderpals-expensive-TV-wedding/articleshow/7717533.cms.

15 Star India PVT, 'Exclusive Sneak Peak of the Show', *Wife Bina Life*, 2011. http://starplus.startv.in/show/Wife_Bina_Life/publicopinion_0_163.aspx

16 Ibid.

17 R. Dubey, 'Who's Gearing for Swayamvar 3?' *Hindustan Times*, 20 March 2010. http://www.hindustantimes.com.

18 See Mira K. Desai and B. C. Agrawal, *Television and Cultural Change: Analysis of Transnational Television in India* (New Delhi: Concept, 2009); G. Wang, Jan Servaes and A. Goonasekera, *The Communications Landscape: Demystifying Media Globalisation* (London: Routledge, 2000).

19 See Vamsee Juluri, 'Music Television and the Invention of Youth Culture in India', *Television and New Media* 3, no. 4 (November 2002): 367–86; P. Sonwalkar, 'India: Making of Little Cultural/Media Imperialism?' *Gazette* 63, no. 6 (2001): 505–19.

20 Pattanaik, 'Decoding a Hindu Marriage'.

21 'Mass Marriage: 251 Couples to Wed in Ballia', *The Times of India*, 6 March 2011. http://articles.timesofindia.indiatimes.com/2011-03-06/varanasi/28659766_1_mass-marriage-hindu-couples-high-profile-wedding.

22 Nazia Vasi, 'KBC Makes Airtel a Crorepati', *The Times of India*, 23 July 2005. http://articles.timesofindia.indiatimes.com/2005-07-23/india/27863981_1_sms-star-tv-indian-idol.

23 W. Brown and A. Singhal, 'Ethical Dilemmas of Prosocial Televison', *Communication Quarterly* 38, no. 3 (Summer 1990): 268–80.

24 '"Our Marriage Will Last" Say Perfect Bride Winners', dnaindia.com.

5

Community: Reality TV Reaching Out

Gareth Palmer

We have reached a point in both the development and study of reality television where its boundaries are beginning to seem limitless. It is increasingly difficult to conceive of factual television formats that do not depend upon the distinctive features of the reality genre. The use of personal testimony, the shaky hand-held camera motions, even the adoption of certain fonts all signify a form that was on the margins in the 1980s but has been completely integrated into the mainstream today. Audience research indicates that even the phrase 'reality television' has been absorbed into younger viewers' understanding of factual forms, thus eliding the boundaries that used to be maintained with those 'discourses of sobriety' by which traditional documentary defined itself.[1] It is this blurring of boundaries and a growing cynicism about various forms of reality television that complicate the question of the genre's value.

One way of considering that value is to look at the ways various types of reality TV have reached out to and sought to construct different forms of community. This might be a productive approach because traditionally speaking, documentary, which provides the origins for reality TV, has been premised on the notion of community – both as subject(s) and as communities of interest. In the following chapter, I will suggest that reality TV can best be understood as an ongoing site of struggle and negotiation where various communities are made and unmade in a complex fusion of producer intentions and meaning making by diverse audiences. This results in a complex picture of the value that reality TV has for different types of communities.

Community and Communitarianism

The term 'community' has widespread appeal; it masks issues like social class and can seem to embrace all members of society. But whilst concerns about the state of the community have long preoccupied writers and politicians – from David Reisman's *The Lonely Crowd* in 1950[2] through to Robert Putnam's *Bowling Alone* in 2001[3] – an interest in what community should mean came into sharp focus in the 1980s as a result of a shift to the political right on both sides of the Atlantic.

The election of two conservatives – Margaret Thatcher in the UK in 1979 and Ronald Reagan in the USA in 1980 – ushered in a monetarist ideology, which gave free reign to the market and its apparent natural mechanism for helping goods and services find their correct level. In significant ways these changes meant the dismantling of the state apparatus. For example, the marketisation of policing meant fewer officers in communities and their replacement by closed-circuit television (CCTV), which serves a surveillance function. Community became re-defined as those identified and categorized under the increasing surveillance of the state – thus as subjects. This change occurred co-terminously with communities that had developed an understanding of their own identities through the auspices of identity politics and were self-defined as never before. On a larger scale, conflicts in the Falkland Islands and Grenada meant people were encouraged to act as a patriotic community in support of their nation. Finally, the new flow of money in share-issues caused by the privatization of companies previously owned by the state and the abundant supply of mortgages meant people could find themselves freshly enfranchised and able to behave as members of the property-owning democracy.

These various understandings of community entailed the abandonment of older definitions. This was noticeable in the new social mobility – which changed geographic, people-based definitions of community – and in the eradication of trade unions and other free-forming associations. Traditional notions of community were dispensed with as old-fashioned and class-bound, whilst new, liberating concepts were embraced as promising a more democratic future. In amongst all these changes, 'community' became a valuable term as it represented a conceptual space into which many people could be interpellated despite some of the obvious contradictions between groupings.

The complexity of these changes and the need to find some form of shared purpose found political articulation in the 1990s through what has been called the communitarian impulse. As an ethic, communitarianism focuses on the public good and poses the question: what can community members do to bring that public good about? As evinced by writers such as Amitai Etzioni, individual freedoms have to be balanced by the responsibility to help others. When we have shared values, then we have mutual understanding.[4] However, this understanding cannot simply arise; it has to be instilled in children by the family and other social structures. Character building is an active process in which all members of the community have a role. The positive result of this is that shared values lead to shared projects and consensus building. Ideally, communities develop metalogues – conversations about problematic subjects – in which common ground is found between formerly disparate groups.

Fast forward two decades, and notions of communitarianism live on, if in different forms. In Britain recently, the Conservative Party's rhetorical flourishes around notions of a 'Big Society', and in the USA, President Obama's healthcare reforms are merely the latest iterations of the communitarian ethic. Since the early 1980s, the communitarian ethic, which has been endorsed by political leaders and expressed in a range of speeches and policies, has become part of populist discourse. In a sense, communitarianism has formed part of the 'structure of feeling', the climate in which reality television has developed.

With this context in mind, the chapter's next task is to explore four kinds of communities – geographic, relational, utilitarian and commercial – that have been sought, constructed and re-worked by reality television, and to consider how the genre has played a role in the life of these communities.

Reality Television's Four Communities

Geographic Communities

Some of the earliest versions of reality television made it their specific brief to address communities in certain locations. For example, 1980s programmes featured car thefts captured by closed-circuit television cameras in King's Lynn in the UK. By skilfully blending CCTV footage provided by local police forces with stern messages about proper conduct, shows such as *Police, Camera, Action* became popular principally by highlighting the irresponsibility of bad drivers. Factual police programming has always been designed to engineer connections from the audience, but new reality TV formats made the claim both more explicit and insistent: you solve the crime by calling in. Also in the 1980s, *Crimewatch UK* and *America's Most Wanted* began to be followed by local versions working on the explicit premise of helping the community. Reality TV in these formats was used to create a community of responsible citizens mobilized around threatened families 'just like us'.

Watching the programme and calling in was performing a kind of public duty, a relatively easy social good. Individual testimony was integrated in the programmes and served to validate the genre. It should be mentioned that *Crimewatch UK* and *America's Most Wanted* remain amongst the longest-running factual formats in the world, so responses are being activated. However, logically speaking, the chance of viewers recognizing a crime re-enacted for a national programme but committed in a small town many months prior are remote indeed.

Perhaps more plausible are the claims of local producers: statistically speaking, there may a greater likelihood of a crime being detected, but then one might object to a focus on sensational crime potentially frightening the elderly or other members of the community. As Gray Cavender noted, police programming informed by reality TV creates anxieties in the community by underscoring 'us versus them' frameworks.[5] The crude characterizations of criminals work to make them into signs of difference, not people. Thus, whilst the community is promoted as the inspiration for such programming, what it ends up doing may be actually damaging the community. According to Cavender: 'Nothing is ever certain (or safe) for the members of the community on AMW [*America's Most Wanted*]... Pivoting on a surveil-lance culture, as so many RTV formats do, the only assurance is a kind of voyeurism: we are watching them.'[6]

In the reality TV world, it's not only crooks and criminals who threaten the community. The biggest menace can come from right next door. In *Neighbours From Hell* – released in the UK in 1996 and later franchised to the USA – specifically targeted areas were revealed to show what happens when the forces of law and order are absent. The show painted a picture of the community in dramatic language, which suggested that social collapse was only minutes away. Camcorder footage shot by the public and CCTV material were integrated into alarming stories that were made even worse by brooding, unsettling music.

In the same year *Neighbours from Hell* became a ratings success, Robert A. White published his 'Communitarian Code of Professional Ethics'.[7] The code illustrated the challenges facing media practitioners who wish to commit themselves to a communitarian ethos. A practitioner might wish to 'develop a language in the public media which makes it possible not simply to present a great quality of information but rather to present moral issues and the moral claims of different major actors so that these can be discussed'.[8] However, the increasingly aggressive marketplace made such an approach difficult. In a similar vein, the desire to 'move groups towards dialogue', as outlined in White's code, is a lot less exciting than seeing these groups engage in hand-to-hand combat in a parking lot. Thus, whilst versions of the communitarian ethos may lie behind some programming, in the case of *Neighbours from Hell*, television's market-driven needs shaped a programme that would strike fear into the community and lead to calls for extra policing, rather than more dialogue. For all the rhetoric about community that comes from a show like *Neighbours from Hell*, the authoritarian solutions it implies (more law and order) are things communitarianism largely rejects.

Anxiety and fear amongst communities are only fostered further by programmes such as *To Catch a Predator*, which claims to help alert the community to paedophiles in their midst. Again, whilst there may be some justification for the programme's tactics in some town at some time, a competing claim is that those who are caught are not typical and have been set up in ways that may make viewers doubt the producers' intentions. What is clear, however, is the effort put into the ethical claims of the programme makers, as if making the claim in and of itself did some of the work. As Jon Dovey argued: 'Individual stories are structured within an overarching public service narrative address in which we are given to understand that our viewing pleasures are safely contained by an explicit appeal to a communitarian logic of security.'[9] Programmes such as *UK Border Force* extend the logic of security further: In a climate in which national borders can be threatened at any time, we all need to pull together to control crime. The post-9/11 climate has sensitized us all to the dangers 'out there'. We are, therefore, encouraged to take our own surveillance measures. According to Sarah Manwaring-Wright: 'The use of video surveillance and the advance in television technology has not only transformed police methods but extended the role of policing further into the community.'[10]

What we find in geographically motivated reality TV is an old-fashioned claim to be working in the public interest wrapped up in the exciting and dynamic language of the form. Community is explicitly evoked as the inspiration for such strands, and results are stressed to confirm the claims and to perpetuate more of the same (programming and responses). Our behaviour in public space is a theme much seized upon, a theme that can be illustrated by the copious amounts of footage available to producers from various authorities. But it can be seen that these claims are compromised by a focus on what is ratings-worthy rather than what is useful. The need to draw an audience has to be negotiated together with the question of public service and value. Whilst it is always useful to know that the public can help solve crimes, it is difficult to avoid the conclusion that communities are being built through fear in most cases rather than through developing open and trusting relationships.

Relational Communities

A large number of reality television programmes focus on family and other groupings and ask us to consider our relationship to them. The most often evoked group remains the nuclear family, a core subject for reality TV as well as the principal target of advertisers. One can envisage the rhetoric of communitarianism shadowing the development of reality TV as the latter makes its haphazard investigations of the family only to find conflicts rather than the tools for consensus. This contrast in changing intentions was noticed by film-makers such as Paul Watson, who was responsible in the 1970s for *The Family*, a show that introduced what many have called the first reality TV family. Watson claimed that his series represented 'a genuine insight into the human condition' but that now docu-soaps and other modern reality TV formats have 'trivialised documentary'.[11]

Reality television's various approaches to the family could only have arisen with the rise of identity politics. Talk shows from the late 1970s and 1980s such as *Donahue* and *Oprah* gave space to people with non-mainstream sexual orientations, thus paving the way for a new understanding of what families might be. A new climate of emotional literacy helped usher forth new explorations of family intimacy. Paul Watson's *Sylvania Waters* and *The Family* considered the intimate matrix of communications that make up the family. Other explorations of the family via forms such as video diaries were revealing because of the conflicts and contradictions they exposed. But as the technology became more lightweight in the last decade of the twentieth and first decade of the twenty-first centuries, more extreme forms of analysis have come to the fore.

For example, *Honey We're Killing the Kids* (in the UK and the USA) and *It's Me or the Dog* (in the UK) focus on nuclear families gone awry. Here the communitarian ethos is implicit, as we are asked to consider not only what we might do in similar situations, but what families are supposed to do. Reality TV's intimate technology does open up family space, but the emphasis is on the extreme rather than the pedestrian; again, the need to sensationalize often takes priority, and as John Corner suggested, the preference for the freaky and strange now takes precedence over an interest in debate.[12]

Formats such as *The Biggest Loser* work in a slightly different way as they focus on individual family members and only include the family as an important background motivation for members to lose weight. Similarly, *Extreme Makeover* focuses on individual family members but stresses that the transformations are done to reward the individual for the sacrifices he or she has made for the family. Perhaps the success of these shows can be explained by the connection they make with audiences who can relate to this sacrifice. Here, we may see a benefit if a show helps develop any given family's mutual understanding.

In the late 1990s, as television faced increasing competition from online entertainment – particularly for younger audiences – reality TV formats became a crucial weapon in showing what television as an apparatus can do. A recent example of this is *Extreme Makeover: Home Edition* where we see actual communities being pulled together by television presenting itself as an active agent in repair work. At the beginning of each episode, viewers see camcorder material shot by the family in question. In these moments, reality TV goes back to its roots by revealing the raw, untutored footage that signifies the genuine suffering necessary to justify the expensive modifications that will occur. In the rest of the show, the reality TV element works to underscore the huge labour being undertaken by the crew.

It is important to stress the role that the onscreen community plays in this process. That community may be invoked by programme host Ty Pennington, but it is more importantly seen as the essential but usually invisible background against which families live. Again a communitarian ethic is raised: striving for the common good, involving the sacrifice of all. The fact that this marshalling of labour is taking place under a commercial banner (the sponsors are mentioned frequently, as is ABC) does to some extent obviate the altruistic motive, but it may also inspire, and ABC has promoted the good effects of its work in this way. Stories of altruism in the towns and cities where the programme has been momentarily based only underscore the potential value of the experience to different communities.

The community created in and by the international format *Big Brother* began as a form of social experiment. Here was an extended family or new relational community whose behaviour we could monitor. As the show/experiment gradually became the subject of popular debate, writers claimed specious forms of benefit in terms of learning the significance of certain intimacies from the programme and the attendant academics such as Professor Geoffrey Beattie, a body language expert who provided commentary. Perhaps viewers did become more sensitized to the subtleties of their own and others' body language as the show progressed. The gradual introduction of individuals with non-typical sexual orientation also helped generate debate, and this may have had positive effects as well. For example, when the UK version featured the trans-sexual Nadia who ultimately won the competition, some read this as a sign that the UK was now a more open and accepting society.

But equally one might argue that Nadia was included precisely to add a dimension of intrigue – the viewers knew what the contestants didn't – and that it was this revelation in the 'aftermath' show that was more important. In another year, the relentless gaze of in-house cameras in *Celebrity Big Brother* exposed the racism of its famous British participants to devastating effect. Again one might argue that the popular debate this sparked was a useful way of bringing questions of difference into the public domain. But the beneficial ratings effects for the broadcaster cannot be overlooked in such an equation.

Reality television now plays a very important role in providing access to communities at the fringes of popular culture. *Jersey Shore* (USA) and *Club Reps* (UK) feature behaviour that one feels is inspired by the need to shock rather than inform. These shows can, therefore, perform the work of reinforcing family values by suggesting that the alternatives will be unpalatable for most people.

The strength and significance of relational groupings is tested by reality TV in other ways as well. As previously noted, early talk shows were important for giving visibility to minority groups who had been marginalized by television. Increasing access to the airwaves for such groups was said to be empowering. But more recently, reality television formats have adopted a style that underlines freak value at the expense of discussion. This is seen particularly with regard to sexual orientation. Whilst it is possible that others may feel inspired to 'come out' after seeing reality programming, others may be left thinking how outlandish the people on TV are.

For example, trans-gendered people are still seen as exploitable targets. As they are framed in ways that highlight difference rather than commonality, the odds are stacked against them. One benefit, of course, is that at least the topic is entering the living room and getting discussed with a little more seriousness. But what we know of the audience would not suggest a new empathy but rather a new cynicism. As Annette Hill's research indicates, one of reality TV's unintended consequences may be the creation of communities of cynicism.[13]

However, our views have to be tempered by those less sensational reality TV formats, which illustrate the virtues of community and cooperation. *Ice Road Truckers* (USA) and *Airline* (UK) both show the extraordinary demands placed upon workers and the strength and resilience they show in overcoming these challenges. Such shows harken back to the earliest explorations of documentary that celebrated unsung heroes in the workplace and asked us to appreciate their sacrifices for the greater good – again a very communitarian ethic. Of course, in a commercial environment, the needs of producers to make profitable forms of television may entail following stories and professions that are perhaps untypical, but the lesson on cooperation and sacrifice remains a valuable one.

Utilitarian Communities

One way of considering the value of reality television would be to look at how certain communities are either taught or practically empowered by its formats. A direct line might be traced from *This Old House* in the 1980s right through to formats such as *Changing Rooms* in the 1990s or *60 Second Makeover* today. The myriad cooking shows – often on their own channels – have an even longer history that also offers learning opportunities for millions of viewers. Here the value lies in what the viewers can gain from seeing how things can change for the good (usually) on limited budgets. The commercial value of this large sector was such that the Home and Garden Television Network (HGTV), which was introduced in the USA in the 1990s, soon became one of the most profitable operations in US television. Discovery, TLC and Lifetime all dedicate space to enriching their viewing communities in this way. The value of such programming is impossible to calculate, but it would be difficult to deny that the information presented to viewers has enriched and even helped bond new communities.

Investigations of these communities will have to wait as this is one of the least researched areas of television studies, but what we do know from ratings alone is that this represents a commercially significant sector with obvious links to products and offers. Reality TV has played a very significant role in contributing to these developments and, in particular, to the rise of programming under the banner of lifestyle. Due to their low production costs and the changing nature of the industry, lifestyle programming of a utilitarian nature is now far more common than it used to be. Camcorder footage shot by subjects of such programming is often used to illustrate the 'before' of the show, which provides a striking contrast with the glamorous 'after'. Nonetheless, the ability of people to learn new skills and discover hidden abilities may be inspiring for many.

New to this sub-genre are the ways in which real people are woven into the self-improvement scripts of international lifestyle formats such as *Ten Years Younger* and *What Not To Wear*. These programmes are utilitarian in that they offer a range of skills for the user to develop. It is the aggressive style of such programming that has occasioned much comment and that raises, once more, the question of value. For example, whilst we might learn some makeup or grooming tips from *Ten Years Younger*, I am not sure we gain a great deal from seeing someone undergoing a stream of public insults or learning the details of his dental surgery. Similarly, *What Not To Wear* offers some sensible advice in terms of dressing for one's body shape, but how valuable is it to catch someone, who has dressed for comfort rather than for performance, on secret CCTV footage? Who but the subject (eventually) gains from being seen in the 360-degree mirror? Indeed, it is this aspect of *What Not To Wear* that gives it a faintly sinister air and makes possible connections with hidden surveillance in the First World. Again, the objective to offer sound, valuable advice has to be balanced against the exploitative angles.

The proof of value offered by the programmes in this category is the benefit and possibility of change; after all that the individual has been through, her situation is always presented as overwhelmingly better than before. One might argue that the meta-message here is that a dedicated approach to personal effort is worthwhile and that the trappings (the attention, the money, the advice) are merely television's ways of drawing us into the potential for all individuals represented by the format. But these programmes recommend an approach that objectifies the self, and it might be argued that the work and money required to make such changes narrow our focus and make the community less significant or determining. Indeed, the objective that informs the narrative drive is to leave the community behind. This begs the question: what communities can we speak of in respect to these programmes?

Programming such as *This Old House*, which operates under the utilitarian banner, actually addresses the decline in the skills base in the UK and USA. In this sense, shows like *This Old House* offer an oblique critique of the decline in the West's manufacturing base, and they may inspire discussions of the phenomenon. Perhaps, however, potential DIY-ers may be frightened off by their inability to match the classic hegemonic masculine ideals shown in the programme. In a similar vein, programmes such as *Ladette to Lady* – which suggests mothers adopt classic feminine behaviour by becoming better cooks and dressing to impress – may be implausible and even cruel at a time when working women are under greater financial stress that they have been for generations. As Brenda Weber pointed out, it may well be that mothers 'may no longer be on their own list of priorities', but is a makeover the ideal answer?[14] Does this build anything but communities of mutual concern?

One answer to this question may be found online: coterminous with the development of lifestyle shows that represent this utilitarian approach to the self has been the rise of online spaces to discuss programming. Here we can gain direct evidence of how advice is worked over by viewers in unpredictable ways. Consider this excerpt from the 'Althouse' blog on *What Not to Wear*:

The show ends with everyone celebrating the amazing changes in the woman's appearance. You have scenes where everyone claps and cheers and the makeover target twirls around in her new clothes – which look ugly to me – and professes to be transformed. We're assured – typical woman's TV pap – that the young woman was always a wonderful person and now her exterior matches her wonderful interior. Blah! I'd rather see a show where philosophers descend on a woman with a perfect exterior and rip into her for her intellectual and spiritual failings, put her on some kind of internally transformative regime, and turn her into a human being of substance. Can we get that?[15]

In some sense, these online communities actually constitute a form of resistance; this has value in itself and represents a public good that could not have been anticipated. On the other hand, television companies are also interested in investing in this online debate. An example of this is seen in the 'Biggest Loser Club', which further colonizes the space with commercialism and, therefore, automatically controls the debate. But in both cases, online communities constitute only a small percentage of the viewership. For the most part, the utilitarian approach – whether the improvement is directed to the home or the self – keys into the profit motive and connects to the earliest days of commercial television. Here the communities become simply discriminating consumers: reality TV aids television in its historical project to deliver audiences to advertisers. (Contrast this interpretation with this book's Chapter 9, which suggests online communities created by reality TV programmes may serve a positive role in fostering citizenship.)

Commercial Communities

One of the distinctive features of more recent innovations in reality television has been its ability to link viewer interest to income generation. Whilst we have noted this in the recommendation of particular consumer goods in certain shows and aggressive store sponsorship in others, the programmes that lie within the category of commercial communities are explicit in their aim to elicit viewer contributions. *The X-Factor*, *American Idol*, and *America's Got Talent* are the most prominent of shows whose aim is to call on the community to sponsor participants' transformation into stars. Of course, the community only plays a supporting role. As Graeme Turner pointed out, reality TV can often involve producers 'growing their own' stars,[16] and there are certainly ethical questions to consider here.

The scheduling of these programmes is very much focused around the family, and the category of commercial communities is the most lucrative of the four suggested in this chapter. As this represents a category dealt with in this book's Chapter 7, I will not go into it in much detail. However, I will point out that commercial communities are financially significant. For example, in the USA, the 2006 season of *American Idol* was claimed by the host to have generated 64 million votes for the season's winner, representing more votes than US president George Bush received in either 2004 or 2000.[17]

Reality TV has a very important function in such talent shows in that it provides evidence of the ordinary backgrounds from which the contestants emerge. According to Guy Redden, such programming keys into the 'discourse of opportunity' and the 'democratizing power that affects social mobility'.[18] In these formats, reality TV is used as a guarantor of intimacy; if the footage is shaky and in black-and-white, then all the better as this underlines the humble beginnings of the shows' proto-stars. The sign value of the real works against the huge power of glamour evoked by the noise of such formats. Reality TV legitimates the outsiders' lack of polish but also presents them as eager supplicants to those in charge. In this drama, the community is comprised of the viewer-villagers in the fairy tale whose role it is to act as a chorus, sharing the ambitions of the glamorous star-maker-gatekeepers to the kingdom beyond. All the community members need do to pledge their allegiance is pay (text or call).

What is stressed here, and what reality television helps underscore, is how valuable, warm and nurturing, the community is. Thus, whilst we may be moved by family celebrations and commiserations as the winners and losers are sorted by the industrial music-machine, we might also ask what the community was formed for: to engineer escape and, therefore, ultimately denigrate that community?

Conclusion: Reality TV, Communities and Communitarianism

This chapter has demonstrated the conflict between what a communitarian ethic might produce in terms of reality television texts and what many of those texts have become. This might be partly explained by considering the determining role of changing production contexts. A documentary culture rooted in a public service ethic and paid for by the public via forms of taxation such as a license fees or subscriptions might have a chance to make the sort of programming based on respect, tolerance and fair treatment for all that underscores communitarianism. But in a climate where the market predominates, the inclination has been to paint pictures of communities that are divisive whilst parading a 'tolerant' ethic. It is as if the noble rhetoric tries to do the work the programming cannot.

The chapter has also considered the various ways in which reality TV reaches out to call on, construct and inform different types of communities.

But we have seen that the question of its value to those communities is rather complex. As several authors have pointed out, reality TV may proffer materials, but the audience chooses what it wants to do with them. The question of value then is partly rooted in the audience. What reality TV can do is offer points of recognition; in this sense, it can always be an inspiration to debate.

In offering home camcorder footage, CCTV materials, and other recordings derived by the public, reality TV works as a guarantor of authenticity. What unites footage ranging from *America's Most Wanted* to the *X-Factor* is the promise of transformation rooted in the response of given communities. Thus, the black-and-white surveillance footage of *What Not to Wear* contestants opens the show (in the UK version), but by the end, they have been transformed and are happy to be made real in glamorous colour.

For all the evidence it provides of the real, what is often missing from reality TV is any discussion of the material context in which such realities are grounded. The consequences of living in difficult and restricting economic circumstances only play at the edges of the narrative – the better to justify the need to transform and leave communities behind. Allied to this is the treatment of class. Weber's analysis of lifestyle programmes suggests that 'though class messages are seldom overtly uttered, the significance of class is insistent in makeovers'.[19] In crime programming, it is overwhelmingly the case that the lower classes commit the crimes we are asked to solve. Those reaching for stardom in talent shows are often seen to be arising from blue-collar backgrounds – the better to stage the dramatic transformation. Thus, whilst class is clearly important, it cannot 'speak its name' for in doing so, it may reveal its connection to economic realities shared by many (rooted in economics) rather than being merely another hardship for the heroic individual to overcome.

One of reality television's roots was in the access imperative that began in the 1970s. Early forms of access allowed 'marginal groups in society' to 'present moral issues and the moral claims so that they may be discussed' (from White's code). Although such programming – in the USA on PBS and in the UK on C4 and occasionally BBC2 – appeared on the fringes, it did represent a commitment to what television could do under a communitarian ethos. Such initiatives live on today (albeit in restricted programming). The point is that communities can gain access to the airwaves but in ways they had not anticipated before the arrival of the Internet. The BBC's *Video Nation* now hosts more than 800 mini-documentaries of one to two minutes in length, each of which is a diverse contribution to the rich fabric of the nation. In this way, the challenge of community is represented in all its complexity around no single theme. This might be contrasted to the ways in which traditional television has engineered definitions of community to enliven programming. Is *Video Nation* closer to the communitarian ideal? As Iris Young has suggested, by replacing the village ideal (traditional reality TV) with one based on the city (*Video Nation*), we 'privilege heterogeneity over unity and social differentiation not exclusion'.[20]

When we consider the wide variety of programming that comes under various reality TV banners, what we find is an overwhelming reliance on the dramatic structuring of material and the need to elevate the freaky over the mundane. For the most part, reality TV adopts what Stella Bruzzi calls a mini-crisis structure in which a drama is imposed upon the material even though one may not exist.[21] As some older critics have suggested, what this does, at best, is divert rather than instruct. But perhaps it is time to accept that the views of the old guard belong to a time when television worked in a different way in the hands of a small elite. Audiences are increasingly aware of what is going on in television. This is not mere scepticism but the result of the rise of media education and a willingness on the part of the press to help explain the machinations of the form.

Reality television's relationship to its various audiences is, of course, complex. Whilst TV companies have their eye on the bottom line, myriad users have their own motivations for forming communities of interest. These communities do not develop their understanding in any logical fashion but in unpredictable ways, which may be incremental. As a final example, consider the ways in which the gay community has responded to reality TV. Some writers have suggested that reality TV has welcomed aspects of gay culture into the living room in ways that may advance understanding because of increased visibility.[22] Formats such *as Queer Eye for the Straight Guy*, *The Real World* and *Big Brother* have all featured gay characters and have made them seem ordinary – to a degree. But whilst this does represent an advance, some might suggest that defining characters by their sexual orientation remains a potentially retrograde step. Perhaps it will only be through intro-ducing a character who just *happens to be gay* (rather than being defined by this difference) that acceptance may be achieved.

Reality television will always have a complicated relationship with the communities it is seeking both to represent and to invite into its discourse. What I have attempted to do here is locate the motivations of reality TV producers and the responses of their communities under certain categories. It is difficult to predict the ways in which the situation may develop, but what we can say with a degree of certainty is that with the rise of new media, communities of all types will be heard. It will no longer be feasible for the next generation of producers to claim to speak on behalf of people when the people themselves can hear each other.

Notes

1 Annette Hill, *Restyling Factual TV* (London: Routledge, 2007) and Bill Nichols, *Blurred Boundaries* (Bloomington, IN: Indiana University Press, 1994).

2 David Reisman, *The Lonely Crowd* (New Haven, CT: Yale University Press, 1950).

3 Robert Putnam, *Bowling Alone: The Collapse and Revival of American Community* (New York: Simon and Schuster, 2000).

4 Amitai Etzioni, *The Spirit of Community: Rights, Responsibilities and the Communitarian Agenda* (New York: Crown, 1993).

5 Gray Cavender, 'In Search of Community on Reality TV', in *Understanding Reality* Television, Su Holmes and Deborah Jermyn (eds) (London: Routledge, 2004) 160.

6 Ibid., 167

7 Robert A. White, 'Communitarian Ethic of Communication in a Postmodern Age', *Ethical Perspectives*, no. 3–4 (December 1996): 207–18.

8 Ibid.

9 Jon Dovey, *Freakshow: First Person Media and Factual Television* (London: Pluto, 2000) 81.

10 Sarah Manwaring-Wright, *The Policing Revolution* (London: Harvester Press, 1983).

11 Paul Watson quoted in Stella Bruzzi, *New Documentary: A Critical Introduction* (London: Routledge, 2000) 78.

12 John Corner, *The Art of Record* (Manchester: Manchester University Press, 1996).

13 Hill, *Restyling Factual TV.*

14 Brenda Weber, *Makeover TV* (Durham and London: Duke University Press, 2009) 107.

15 Ann Althouse, "What Not To Wear' Is Not the Kind of Reality Show I Would Normally Watch', 27 April 2008. http://althouse.blogspot.com.

16 Graeme Turner, *Ordinary People and the Media: The Demotic Turn* (London: Sage, 2010).

17 Laurie Oulette and James Hay, *Better Living Through Reality TV* (Oxford: (Blackwell, 2008) 213.

18 Guy Redden, 'Making Over the Talent Show', in *Exposing Lifestyle Television: The Big Reveal*, Gareth Palmer ed. (Manchester: Manchester University Press, 2008) 136.

19 Weber, *Makeover TV*, 42.

20 Iris Young, *Justice and the Politics of Difference* (Princeton, NJ: Princeton University Press, 1990) 12–13.

21 Bruzzi, *New Documentary.*

22 Christopher Pullen, 'The Household, The Basement and the Real World', in *Understanding Reality Television*, Su Holmes and Deborah Jermyn (eds) (London: Routledge, 2004).

6

Inspiration and Motivation: If Reality TV Stars Can Do It, So Can I

Janie Harden Fritz

Reality television often is taken to task for a multitude of media sins, receiving scathing criticism from academics and the general viewing public alike[1] – and with good reason. Despite theoretical disputes and varying interpretations of findings, mass media researchers have established that what we watch shapes our beliefs, attitudes and impressions of the social world.[2] In short, our conceptual television diet affects our existential health, and reality TV fare sometimes is the worst kind of junk food, as some chapters in this collection attest.

However, not all reality programmes are marked by a dearth of philosophical nourishment. Among the hundreds on offer, some reality shows may actually provide opportunities for viewers to experience something more than the frisson of *schadenfreude*, the guilty pleasure we feel when something bad happens to someone else,[3] or the voyeuristic thrill of being a "fly on the wall" observing others' uncontrollable emotional outbursts.[4] Some reality shows have the potential to move us to greater flourishing as human beings – to seek personal growth and to be more generous, tolerant, understanding and discerning as citizens and neighbours, as some media scholars have pointed out.[5] Reality shows can provide an ethical lens for viewing the world, inspiring and motivating us to live what virtue ethicists consider a truly good human life. Reality TV can "tutor our imagination"[6] by helping us to see new possibilities for our own lives, the lives of others, and our common life together.

Reality shows have the potential to work on our imagination to inspire us, motivate us and expand our horizons because they take the form of stories. Philosopher Richard Kearney echoes what scholars since Aristotle have noted and what rings true in our own lives – stories matter; stories are what make us most truly human.[7] Because of its narrative nature, just as the best literary fiction does,[8] reality TV at its most constructive can provide motivational impetus to our best impulses rather than our worst. Reality shows that portray narratives of people exhibiting perseverance under challenging circumstances, striving for a better life against difficult odds, and showing generosity toward others display values that, despite our differences, define ethical common ground, a location where we can stand together to find inspiration and motivation for worthy personal goals and laudable collective aspirations.

This type of virtue-laden narrative functions much like Aristotle's ceremonial or "epideictic" rhetoric, celebrating agreed-upon values that bind communities together. This joining of epideictic rhetorical form with the narrative action of "ordinary" participants in reality shows has the potential to enrich what philosopher Charles Taylor calls the "social imaginary," those taken-for-granted expectations of social life that help us make sense of our surroundings.[9] Reality shows can enlarge the scope of the social imaginary by showing us elements of human life and sides of human experience that we may know little about – for example, the lives of the marginalized and suffering.[10] As Deni Elliott's Chapter 9 in this book shows, reality television can give us new ways of understanding others' experiences, yielding more charitable insights into the behaviour of those we might otherwise find inexplicable or strange and helping us to be more accepting of human difference. Reality programming reminds us of both the frailty and resilience of the human condition and of our responsibility for one another.

In the remainder of this chapter, I discuss the potential for reality TV to inspire and motivate viewers towards richer, fuller lives through an expanded vision of self and others. While not all reality TV shows lend themselves to such positive influence, a growing number promise that possibility, holding out hope for a constructive role for reality TV in our increasingly fragmented social world. First, I address how the narrative format of reality TV shapes the moral imagination. Next, I address how reality TV takes the form of epideictic rhetoric, highlighting common values to bring communities of difference together. Finally, I discuss how reality shows as "epideictic narrative" reflect and make visible larger narratives or worldviews as a background for inspiration and motivation to virtuous action and expanded horizons to foster generosity of spirit toward others.

Reality TV, Narrative and the Moral Imagination

Human beings have been drawn to stories since the beginning of recorded history, from Homer's relating of Odysseus's adventures to J. K. Rowling's seven-year saga of Harry Potter and his struggle against Lord Voldemort. Narrative is fundamental to human experience; we engage life in story format. A narrative understanding of human life and action frames our lives as stories lived out in interaction with others who are also living out their stories.[11] Communication theorist Walter Fisher considers human beings story-telling creatures, suggesting that good stories are persuasive in a different way than logical arguments.[12] George Gerbner, who proposed the cultivation hypothesis a half-century ago, was convinced that much of what we know about the world comes to us from the stories we hear and tell.[13] Stories give us insights into who we are and reflect a moral vision of the world, presenting particular understandings of right and wrong, and helping us reflect on and evaluate our own behaviour.[14] From a narrative perspective, the way we act, communicate and carry out our daily activities is inherently ethical as we protect and promote particular goods that give meaning to our lives.[15]

Much of the content of television today consists of narratives of one kind or another. From made-for-television movies and soap operas to serial sitcoms, contemporary programming offers a wide range of options that take the form of stories. The History Channel recognizes the power of an exciting tale, and some of the most interesting television commercials contain story-like elements.[16] Even news stories are framed as narratives to appeal to viewers who enjoy following the action of an unfolding drama.[17] Perhaps that is one of the reasons we are drawn to reality television shows – they tell us part of the story of others' lives, and that is immensely attractive.[18] In fact, Lisa Godlewski and Elizabeth Perse offer an operational definition of reality TV that reflects this key to its appeal: "unscripted programs that record real people as they live out events in their lives, as these events occur."[19]

Reality TV is not new or unique in offering a glimpse into the storied lives of others. Depictions of "everyday" people in their authentic lived experience have emerged in many modalities and genres over the centuries. In print form, autobiographical accounts and daily journals have brought the personal past of historical and contemporary figures to present audiences, and early television programming featured several offerings that presaged the beginning of reality TV; for example, *Candid Camera* was a prototype of today's reality show. The documentary format was designed to bring issues that had hitherto been neglected into the public eye, serving a civic function understood as necessary for a democratic society to flourish.[20] Contemporary shows that focus on issues with implications for the public sphere continue the documentary tradition. For example, *16 and Pregnant* and its spin-off *Teen Mom* provide glimpses of the lives of young women who face challenges of teenage pregnancy, and *Extreme Makeover: Home Edition* makes us aware of hardships that many families face.

Several popular print counterparts to the reality show today draw audiences through stories. *People* magazine offers glimpses into the lives of public figures, from film stars to politicians. *Reader's Digest* has long been popular for its stories, particularly the "Drama in Real Life" feature, which typically features ordinary people. *Guideposts* magazine, founded by legendary icon of positive thinking Norman Vincent Peale, features stories of people coping with life events – illness, catastrophes, career changes, recovery from addition, relational distress and forgiveness. The story-tellers are people from all walks of life and include regular screen, television, athletic or recording stars. In the form of retrospective descriptions of events, these narratives provide a realistic glimpse of people in situations evoking a range of responses grounded in or leading to a new or enlarged sense of self, others and the world in general. *Guideposts* bills itself as containing true stories of hope and inspiration; these narratives draw their strength from the actual experiences of ordinary people – one of the reasons some viewers offer for the appeal of reality TV shows.[21] Reality TV rests within this genre of story-telling: common people reacting to a range of events with realistic, authentic responses. The reality shows that have the most potential to inspire, motivate, and expand viewers' horizons are akin to these types of stories.

Walter Fisher suggests that a narrative understanding of the world stands in contrast to what he identifies as the "rational world" paradigm.[22] The contrast between the rational world paradigm and the narrative paradigm is nowhere seen more clearly than in philosophers' discussions of the paradox of fiction[23] – we experience pity, fear, joy and other emotions when reading novels or watching fictional portrayals on the movie or television screen. Logically, we should not experience such emotions because the events portrayed and the characters involved in them are not "real." Yet we do experience them, because, through imagination invited by the narrative structure of the events, we enter into the experience of the characters. Empathy and fiction are closely connected,[24] and this connection emerges when we encounter print and visual fictional forms – novels, plays, movies and television shows. Such portrayals help us reflect on how we should live and what we should do as participants within a larger understanding of the shared goods that define our common public space. These narratives shape what philosopher Martha Nussbaum calls the "moral imagination."[25]

Imagination, as I am using it here, refers to envisioning what is possible but not yet visible in our lives or in the lives of others.[26] For example, you may see your friend Natasha's potential for leadership as you interact with her on a daily basis, although she may not yet hold an elected office in any club or organization nor see herself as a leader. "Moral imagination" refers to our sense of how this "possible" fits within a larger framework or vision of what is good to be or to do and how our actions or the actions of others may bring us or them closer to or farther away from this ideal.

In Aristotelian terms, this ideal is known as a "telos" or aim for a virtuous human life.[27] In reality TV, imagination tied to the morally possible meets the contingency of opportunity under conditions of uncertainty. We don't know how the participants in *The Amazing Race* will do next; indeed, even with so much of the action contrived and reconstructed through editing, no one can predict the outcome as the action unfolds. The responses of the characters are "actual," if not completely unplanned,[28] and capture the sense of choices emerging spontaneously as the participants encounter the unexpected. That is part of the appeal of reality TV, a feature that connects to the fundamental concern of communication ethics: making decisions in everyday life according to our sense of the "good."[29] Although reality TV is not traditional fiction, it takes the narrative form that gives fiction its effect – and it offers more.

As viewers observe the characters' actions within a reality TV episode, the anticipation of what the participants will do next rests within a horizon of ethical expectations, expectations that we may only become aware of when they are violated. In this sense, even the worst reality shows remind us of a community's limits. As a respondent in one study noted, some shows go "too far"[30] in subjecting participants to humiliation and ridicule. We believe that people should not be deliberately degraded, so we find this type of exploitation problematic.[31] The boundaries of community morality become clear when we have the chance to contrast behaviours beyond the pale of expectations with those that rest within the horizon of ethical acceptability.

Reality TV, because of its display of ordinary participants of culture in narrative form, works in a liminal space between the "is" of real life and the "ought" of a moral framework to cultivate our moral imagination. This perspective resonates with Nussbaum's description of how fiction works to translate general or abstract principles into the particular and concrete reality of lived experience: Principles remain abstract and static until they meet the messiness of human lives.[32] As participants in reality shows respond to events, their actions become part of contexts requiring application of ethical principles that viewers can evaluate and reflect upon. These actions contribute to viewers' understanding, defining those principles through exposure to their appearance in everyday life. We learn how to be generous – and understand generosity better – when we see an action that illustrates generosity. Furthermore, the horizons of our understanding of the virtue of generosity expand when we see what we have come to recognize as generosity moved into action in new situations represented before us.

Many of the participants in reality TV shows provide a powerful ethical option for action through their behavioural choices because they are similar to the general viewer. The people we see on reality shows are ordinary people making those choices, for good or ill. Because we perceive participants to be similar to us, their actions become messages that support our efficacy beliefs. As learning theorist Albert Bandura might note,[33] when audience members identify with participants[34] and see them performing a given action, they see that action as something they can do, too, whether it be sticking with an exercise program (e.g. *The Biggest Loser*) or helping a disadvantaged family renovate a dilapidated home (e.g. *Extreme Makeover: Home Edition*). Not only are participants similar to viewers in their "ordinariness," the choices are actual decisions made in real time, as well. These shows, therefore, offer the moral imagination added traction. Reality shows offer a narrative of lived experience that is unfolding at the moment of viewing. Witnessing a story apparently in the making is a different experience than reading a story whose ending is already known – viewers witness participants in the midst of multiple possibilities, moving toward a future that has not yet arrived. Each human life has a beginning, middle and end,[35] and reality shows typically show people in the middle part of the story – in the midst of the action that follows from a past and moves toward a gradually revealed future or destiny.[36] Participants on *The Biggest Loser* shape new futures for themselves as they learn to make different choices related to diet and exercise; their actions create visible changes in these developing life stories.

Even when reality shows feature people who are no longer "ordinary" because of unexpected celebrity from their repeated participation in such shows (e.g. Bethenny Frankel), expectations associated with the genre may bring attributes of these now-well-known participants closer to the category of the typical viewer. Such participants' lives may be viewed as examples of what might happen to any viewer. After all, this person got a start through reality TV while still part of the ranks of the "ordinary" person. Current "pseudo-celebrity" status may be brought closer to the horizon of expectations of viewers – Andy Warhol's famous "fifteen minutes of fame" expected for everyone has simply, in this case, expanded to a longer temporal moment. In an era of You Tube, where ordinary people apparently bursting with potential talent populate cyberspace, the celebrity of reality show participants may actually be quite ordinary. Such fame becomes part of the action of an ordinary person's life.

This portrayal of the life of the participants in the unfolding action of a personal story is the common thread across reality shows. The story is typically one of becoming, of a life in process – just as most of our lives are. This "becoming" feature is a vital element for the moral imagination, because it is the choices and decisions made in daily encounters during the course of a life that shape possibilities for future action and define participants' actions as worthy of praise or blame, as ethically significant. At the same time, reality shows focus our attention on human experience and reactions in a very immediate way; there is little phenomenological – felt or experienced – distance between oneself and the characters. The video-like format of the program contributes to this sense of extreme immediacy for the viewer.[37] The closeness of the characters enhances the focus on the present that James Chesebro[38] and Neil Postman[39] describe as characteristic of television and reflects the "narrative middle" of participants' lives for the viewer. Reality TV as a medium for inspiration, motivation and expanded horizons gathers part of its power from the immediacy of display of these salient elements: characters' lives in story format, the presentation of moral choices requiring ethical decision making, and similarity of characters to viewers. However, the larger virtue structure or moral framework within which the action occurs may be the key factor shaping the potential for reality TV to work in these ways. When the stories of reality TV represent prominent values within a moral universe that falls within a viewer's horizon of meaning, they promise great potential for inspiration, motivation and expanded viewer horizons.

Virtue, Traditions and Epideictic Rhetoric: Community Goods and Reality TV

Particular human stories, including those portrayed on reality TV, gather meaning from larger narrative frameworks within which they are situated – political, religious or philosophical perspectives on the world that define right and wrong, better and worse ways of being, or worldviews. A religious perspective is an example of a larger narrative or worldview, as are secular philosophies and political ideologies.[40] Virtue ethics philosopher Alasdair MacIntyre uses the term "tradition" to refer to a way of life handed down within a community over time that includes distinct ways of living life and engaging the world. A tradition includes prescriptions for right and wrong behavior, which define virtues that shape persons' actions toward a particular understanding of the good life.[41] These community virtues define valued characteristics of human action and are expressed in images and artifacts of a given culture or society and serve as touchstones of "the good" for those who subscribe to those values. Mediated messages both reflect and shape a community's values, providing insight into what matters for a society or culture and reinforcing those values – they interact with people's under-standings of everyday life, or the "social imaginary."

Philosopher Charles Taylor describes the social imaginary as the ways ordinary people imagine their social existence and surroundings – their relationships with others, the expectations that guide social interaction, and normative images and understandings that underlie such expectations.[42] The social imaginary is carried in images, stories, legends and is shared by large groups of people or even an entire society. The social imaginary makes collective, shared practices possible and gives social life a sense of legitimacy. It gives us a sense of how things normally go and what behaviors (either enacted or failed to be enacted) would violate those practices. In fact, it is through violations of the shared common sense of the social world that we bring to the surface those implicit practices that are taken for granted. In this sense, our expectation of what "is" fuels our moral sense of what "ought" to be the case.

Fiction, or story-telling, and its associated generic cousins of biography and autobiography, in which the details of a narrated story are understood to be grounded in actual events, are one important element of human discursive activity, an element mirrored in important ways by reality TV shows. Another modality of human discursive activity is rhetoric, communicative action designed to persuade under conditions of uncertainty, often contrasted with philosophy, or speculative cognitive activity designed to discover truth. Rhetoric and fiction have been connected theoretically, most notably in the twentieth century by literary critic Wayne Booth in The Rhetoric of Fiction.[43] One element of rhetoric with connection to fiction is epideictic or ceremonial rhetoric, which focuses on community virtues or values and often takes a particular ritualized form such as a eulogy at a funeral, an address during a crisis such as war (for example, Lincoln's Gettysburg address), or a speech during an awards ceremony. Rhetorical scholar Robert McKenzie argues that television talk shows function as epideictic.[44] Likewise, television advertise-ments can function rhetorically as narrative examples displaying community values;[45] in this case, they function as a type of epideictic narrative. Many reality programs appear to work this way, as well, as either positive or negative examples of shared community values.[46]

Epideictic rhetoric, like stories and other symbolic formations, reflects the virtue structure of a community. Epideictic rhetoric takes the form of communicative events that highlight characteristics of importance to a community – noteworthy acts of service, bravery, courage and perseverance.[47] There are multiple moral communities among us with various degrees of overlap; we don't always agree on what is praiseworthy or blameworthy, and our own standpoint on the good encounters those of others. In terms of reality TV, imagine Johanna, an avid reality TV fan, enjoying *The Swan*. She finds it wonderful that an average looking woman can become "beautiful" through a personal makeover; the courage of this participant to make a change inspires her. Melinda, another regular reality TV viewer, may find the idea of conformity to societal standards of attractiveness oppressive and hegemonic and find the show not only uninspiring, but morally problematic.[48] Such diversity of standpoint suggests that it may be difficult to predict which reality shows may inspire, motivate or broaden the horizons of particular audiences in a given instance. However, despite differences in standpoints on the good, it may be possible to identify some minimal shared virtues among many moral communities in a particular society.[49]

Amid the many traditions, communities and competing understandings of "the good" in today's diverse world, some minimal patches of common ground[50] exist on which a large proportion of citizens can stand together. For example, philanthropy and the ability to transform one's life are two long-standing touchstones of agreement within US culture.[51] So, referring back to our hypothetical viewers of the makeover beauty show, although they disagree about the values portrayed in *The Swan*, perhaps both would agree that the recipients of care and generosity in *Extreme Makeover: Home Edition* deserved a break, and on this point they stand on common ground. This reality show brings viewers together on one square of the "patchwork quilt" of common sense that says: "That was the right thing to do!"[52]

Reality TV: Inspiration, Motivation and Expanded Horizons

Reality TV at its best works at the intersection of (televized) fiction and epideictic rhetoric, engaging the imagination to move viewers toward virtuous engagements of self and others in the world. Reality TV's work on the imagination operates for viewers through responses to particular persons in a show presented through the immediacy of the visual image and through resonance with a worldview implicit in the portrayal. The work is done at the personal or individual level by means of empathy evoked by viewing persons similar to the self (as opposed to larger-than-life celebrities) and at the level of the worldview by portrayal of a particular understanding of a "good" human life – a portrayal that taps often implicit elements of narrative virtue structures that guide our lives – by shaping the social imaginary.

Epideictic rhetoric is "concerned with training the habitual virtues of character through praise and blame."[53] Many reality shows work as epideictic rhetorical narrative displays to celebrate agreed-upon virtues, for example, generosity or helping others.[54] These shows cultivate a particular view of the world, prime viewers to recall particular virtue-connected possibilities for action in similar situations, and provide models for action for viewers through the behavior of similar others.[55] Tonny Krijnen and Ed Tan refer to reality game shows as an "emotional-moral laboratory."[56] When viewers of reality shows praise characters' behavior or larger "project"[57] as good, worthy or laudable, or deride it as bad, unworthy or detestable, reality shows function as a type of epideictic performance highlighting values or virtues that exemplify or violate a common view of the world – a view of the world that has the potential to connect communities of difference around a common good despite other differences. From a rhetorical perspective, the praise and blame of epideictic rhetoric in its many cultural forms reinforces or shapes virtuous practice.

Because reality TV appears to gain much of its symbolic life through communities of discourse[58] that help to shape the social imaginary, the extent to which these shows motivate and inspire viewers and expand their horizon of possibilities for understanding others may depend on the conversational texture of what could be considered our moral viewing communities – those persons with whom we discuss what we see in terms of the ethical and moral implications of the action. Reality shows, by giving viewers the opportunity to respond to and discuss participants' actions, may serve to shape our moral imagination through celebration of community values – or consensual censure or blame – in response to the narrative portrayed in the show. Such discussions broaden our horizons of self and others, making space for new ideas and shaping our understandings of what is possible, desirable and good. When the ethical implications of reality shows become "conversational currency,"[59] engaged in a reflective way through talk with others, then we may be primed to respond in ways displayed by characters in reality TV shows when confronted with situations that offer the opportunity to respond similarly because of the availability of these responses in memory.[60] However, such a response must be within our capacity to enact. In such case, our likelihood of response is reinforced, or contextual opportunities to enact particular responses become salient. If we are thinking about these issues, reality shows may prepare us to be alert for opportunities to act in these ways.

Media scholar Laurie Ouellette sees hope for reality TV. She notes that shows like *The Biggest Loser* and *The Apprentice* may help viewers navigate and negotiate life as citizens in a changing information world by learning appropriate forms of "civic conduct and problem solving."[61] She points to many of the "helping" shows, such as *American Idol Gives Back* and *Oprah's Big Give*, as "do good" programs that can redeem reality TV's tarnished reputation. She notes that on *Extreme Makeover: Home Edition*:

> TV viewers are 'activated' to practice compassionate citizenship by volunteering for non-profit partners such as Habitat for Humanity and Home Aid. The ABC website provides direct links, publicity on sponsors and partners, advice on getting involved, and tips from volunteer agencies, thus further stitching the production and active consumption of reality TV into privatized networks of assistance and self-care.[62]

The show *Exiled* sent debutantes to impoverished places in the world. Helping shows are becoming an element of network brands highlighting corporate social responsibility (CSR) and "citizen branding," so they are responding with what the historical moment is calling for. ABC brands itself as "a better community," for instance.[63] VH1's *Charm School* participants are learning what it means to be good citizens by volunteering and providing community service.[64] *Secret Millionaire* works similarly; viewers vicariously experience the lives of impoverished others and the generosity of a millionaire who goes into deprived areas and gives away money.[65]

These examples suggest that reality TV can cultivate expanded horizons – yielding generosity of spirit toward others – through expanding the possibilities for understanding others with whom viewers have limited or no contact in their daily lives. Writing in the 1980s, media theorist Joshua Meyrowitz foreshadowed theoretically and practically how reality TV may work in this way. In *No Sense of Place*,[66] Meyrowitz argued that television portrays images of backstage behavior, or private behavior, of social groups or roles of those whose private behavior we seldom see. Although Madeleine Esch points out in Chapter 3 of this book that putting backstage behavior in front of a camera can raise privacy concerns, images of backstage behavior on TV can also create potential benefits. From the perspective of a child, for example, parents' conversation about daily troubles that takes place behind closed doors is a type of backstage behavior seldom encountered. But when children witness a backstage conversation between parents on a television programme, they as viewers become privy to the private discourse of persons like their parents, and this new image opens possibilities for them. "My parents may discuss these issues, too" may be the message a child takes away from these images.

Reality TV provides a vast panorama of backstage behavior for people and groups about whom we would otherwise know very little or nothing, permitting us to see the lived experience of others. When we observe persons struggling to make ends meet, trying to lose weight, or encountering discrimination, our horizons expand. We can come to understand others and develop attributional generosity when generating explanations for behavior as we learn about what others face in their daily lives. *Hoarders* teaches us that our neighbor's cluttered house may not be the result of laziness; he may be afflicted with a mental illness. Members of a socioeconomic class we had perceived as uninterested in work appear before us in a different light as we see their efforts to seek employment met with refusal after refusal on *Trading Spouses*.

Some reality shows are premised on the value of the experience of a different other's life to provide a new perspective on their own and of those others – *Wife Swap* is one such show. Viewers experience these encounters vicariously and may come to expand their horizons to encompass new understandings of others. The assumed "actuality" of the experience of the persons on the show and the experience of viewing a set of different others through the medium of the show both may create new possibilities in the mind of viewers.

Conclusion

Aristotelian virtue ethics assumes that there is an end or "telos" for human life and human beings, what human beings characteristically are, or are meant to be and do as human beings. Virtues dispose us to behave in ways that move us toward that goal of the good. Aristotle noted that dispositions to moral action are embodied – they are not primarily cognitive, and they are "caught" rather than "taught" through participation in culture.[67] In order for us to recognize virtue when we see it, we must have a background that defines the "telos" for human life, a background that tells us what is virtuous. That background could be considered a moral story, narrative or worldview – a tradition – often religious, or from a philosophical framework that offers a picture of human beings and their place in the world. In MacIntyre's virtue ethics framework, a tradition defines an understanding of the good for human life that gives rise to virtuous practices. These practices can be engaged reflectively as part of a meaningful human life. Recognition of a virtue as part of a tradition provides the ability to reflect on action as constituting a particular virtue and as being worthy of praise or blame.

If a reality show is to inspire and motivate us to practice virtue and expand our horizons for understanding others, it must portray for us a narrative or a vision of the good for human life. The show must demonstrate how particular behaviors enact or instantiate some good for human life. For an action to become habituated as a character trait, the behavior enacted must be conceived as existing within a larger narrative framework – within a story that depicts a particular understanding of a good human life. The social imaginary may be shaped through the work of reality shows depicting particularly economies of virtue, providing a meaningful background narrative against which a given character's action may be evaluated as praiseworthy or blameworthy, or the narrative itself as a whole understood as a type of epideictic narrative displaying or demonstrating a virtue representing a valued symbol for a community.

Reality shows like *The Biggest Loser*, *The Amazing Race*, *Secret Millionaire* and *Hoarders* provide opportunities for viewers to envision alternatives for engaging in a life marked by civic participation, personal enrichment and deeper appreciation of the lives of others. However, many reality shows do not offer such benign portrayals. The bulk of scholarship on reality TV focuses on the potential for programing to perpetuate unhelpful stereotypes and stimulate increased demand for humiliation and degradation of partici-pants.[68] If constructive reality shows work the way I've described them here, problematic ones hold such potential, as well. The difference rests, perhaps, with the attitude of viewers and the moral discourse communities within which they are situated – and the extent to which networks responsive to communities with concerns see positively-themed shows as opportunities to brand themselves as good corporate citizens. The fact that some viewers of reality TV are reluctant to identify themselves as viewers and articulate concerns about shows that they believe are problematic[69] suggests that viewers may be more reflective than not about the shows they watch.

As further research continues on this growing genre and as media criticism related to the ethics of reality TV works its way into classrooms and the public sphere, we may find opportunity to highlight the positive elements of reality TV shows that represent a world we hope to see. Just as audience demand is often sufficient to call forth markets for fiction books catering to particular markets, we may witness the growth of positive reality shows in response to calls for programs that portray the best we can be instead of the worst. For that, at least, we can hope.

Notes

1 Wendy Wyatt, "Humiliation TV: A Philosophical Account of Exploitation in Reality Television." Presentation, Annual Convention of the Association for Education in Journalism and Mass Communication, Denver, CO, 4–7 August 2010.

2 Jennings Bryant and Dolf Zillmann, "A Retrospective and Prospective Look at Media Effects," in *The Sage Handbook of Media Processes and Effects*, Robin L. Nabi and Mary Beth Oliver (eds) (Thousand Oaks, CA, 2009), 9–17.

3 Alice Hall, "Viewers' Perceptions of Reality Programs," *Communication Quarterly* 54, no. 2 (2006): 204.

4 Clay Calvert, *Voyeur Nation: Media, Privacy, and Peering in Modern Culture* (Colorado: Westview Press, 2004); Rachel E. Dubrofsky, "Fallen Women in Reality TV: A Pornography of Emotion," *Feminist Media Studies* 9, no. 3 (2009): 353–68.

5 Heather Havrilesky, "Three cheers for reality TV," *Salon*, 13 September 2004. http:// dir.salon.com/story/ent/feature/2004/0-2/13/reality/index.html (accessed 8 May 2011); Sara B. Miller and Amanda Paulson, "The Latest Buzz in TV Programming – Generosity," *Christian Science Monitor*, 16 September 2004, 1; Laurie Ouellette, "Reality TV Gives Back: On the Civic Functions of Reality Entertainment," *Journal of Popular Film and Television* 68, no. 2 (2010): 66–71; James Poniewozik, "Why reality TV is good for us," *Time* (17 February 2003), 65–7; Wyatt, "Humiliation TV."

6 Caroline Simon, *The Disciplined Heart: Love, Destiny, and Imagination* (Grand Rapids, MI: Eerdmans, 1997) 5.

7 Richard Kearney, *On Stories: Thinking in Action* (New York: Routledge, 2002).

8 Simon, *The Disciplined Heart*; Martha C. Nussbaum, *Love's Knowledge: Essays on Philosophy and Literature* (New York: Oxford University Press, 1990).

9 Charles Taylor, *A Secular Age* (Cambridge, MA: Belknap, 2007), 171–4.

10 Ouellette, "Reality TV Gives Back."

11 Simon, *The Disciplined Heart*.

12 Walter R. Fisher, "Narration as a Human Communication Paradigm: The Case of Public Moral Argument." *Communication Monographs* 51, no. 1 (1984): 1–22.

13 Michael Morgan, "Cultivation analysis and media effects," in *The Sage Handbook of Media Processes and Effects*, Robin L. Nabi and Mary Beth Oliver (eds) (Thousand Oaks, CA, 2009) 69–82.

14 Simon, *The Disciplined Heart*.

15 Ronald C. Arnett, Janie M. Harden Fritz and Leeanne M. Bell, *Communication Ethics Literacy: Dialogue and Difference* (Thousand Oaks, CA: Sage, 2009).

16 Janie Marie Harden, "Rhetorical Example as Narrative: A Case Study of Selected Television Commercials" (master's thesis, University of Georgia, 1984).

17 Gaye Tuchman, *Making News: A Study in the Construction of Reality* (New York: Free Press, 1978).

18 Robin L. Nabi, Erica N. Biely, Sara J. Morgan and Carmen R. Stitt, "Reality-based Television Programming and the Psychology of its Appeal," *Media Psychology* 5 (2003): 303–30.

19 Lisa R. Godlewski and Elizabeth M. Perse, "Audience Activity and Reality Television: Identification, Online Activity, and Satisfaction," *Communication Quarterly* 58, no. 2 (2010): 149.

20 Ouellette, "Reality TV Gives Back."

21 Hall, "Viewers' Perceptions," 205–6.

22 Fisher, "Narration."

23 Jerrold Levinson, "The Place of Real Emotion in Response to Fictions," *The Journal of Aesthetics and Art Criticism* 48, no. 1 (1990): 79–80.

24 Mary-Catherine Harrison, "The Paradox of Fiction and the Ethics of Empathy: Reconceiving Dickens's Realism," *Narrative* 15, no. 3 (2008): 256–79.

25 Martha Nussbaum, "'Finely Aware and Richly Responsible': Moral Attention and the Moral Task of Literature." *Journal of Philosophy* 82, no. 10 (1985): 516–29; *Love's Knowledge: Essays on Philosophy and Literature*.

26 Simon, *The Disciplined Heart*. Simon uses imagination to refer exclusively to one's insight into the destiny of another, but I refer here to insights about one's own and others' potential.

27 Alasdair MacIntyre, *After Virtue* 3rd edn (Notre Dame, IN: Notre Dame University Press, 2007); Nussbaum, *Love's Knowledge*.

28 Beverly Skeggs and Helen Wood, "The Labor of Transformation and Circuits of Value 'Around' Reality Television," *Continuum: Journal of Media & Cultural Studies* 22, no. 4 (2008): 559.

29 Arnett, Fritz and Bell, *Communication Ethics Literacy*.

30 Lisa K. Lundy, Amanda M. Ruth and Travis D. Park, "Simply Irresistible: Reality TV Consumption Patterns," *Communication Quarterly* 56, no. 2 (2008): 215–16.

31 Wyatt, "Humiliation TV."

32 Nussbaum, "Finely Aware."

33 Albert Bandura, "Social Cognitive Theory of Mass Communication," in *Media Effects: Advances in Theory and Research*, Jennings Bryant and Dolf Zillman (eds) (Mahwah, NJ: Lawrence Erlbaum, 2002) 43–67.

34 Godlewski and Perse, "Audience Activity."

35 Kearney, *On Stories*.

36 Simon, *The Disciplined Heart*.

37 Skeggs and Wood, "The Labor of Transformation," 559.

38 James Chesebro, "The Media reality: Epistemological Functions of Media in Cultural Systems," *Critical Studies in Mass Communication* 1 (June 1984: 111–30.

39 Neil Postman, *Amusing Ourselves to Death: Public Discourse in the Age of Show Business* (New York: Penguin, 1985).

40 Ninian Smart, *Worldviews: Cross-cultural Explorations of Human Beliefs*, 3rd edn (Upper Saddle River, NJ: Prentice-Hall, 2000).

41 MacIntyre, *After Virtue*.

42 Taylor, *A Secular Age*, 172.

43 WayneC. Booth,*The Rhetoric of Fiction* (Chicago: University of Chicago Press, 1961).

44 Robert McKenzie, "Audience Involvement in the Epideictic Discourse of Television Talk Shows," *Communication Quarterly* 48, no. 2 (2000): 190–203.

45 Harden, "Rhetorical Example as Narrative: A Case Study of Selected Television Commercials."

46 Tonny Krijnen and Ed Tan, "Reality TV as a Moral Laboratory: A Dramaturgical Analysis of *The Golden Cage*," *Communications* 34 (2009): 449–72.

47 McKenzie, "Audience Involvement."

48 Lundy, Ruth and Park, "Simply Irresistible," 216.

49 Sissela Bok, *Common Values* (Columbia: University of Missouri Press, 1995).

50 Arnett, Fritz and Bell, *Communication Ethics Literacy*; Charles Taylor, *Sources of the Self: The Making of the Modern Identity* (Cambridge, MA: Harvard University Press, 1989).

51 Miller and Paulson, "The Latest Buzz."

52 Arnett, Fritz and Bell, *Communication Ethics Literacy*, 66–7.

53 Jim Garrison, "Prophetic Epideictic Rhetoric: Poetic Education Beyond Good and Evil," *Educational Theory* 53, no. 2 (2003): 224.

54 Ouellette, "Reality TV Gives Back."

55 Bandura, "Social Cognitive Theory."

56 Krijnen and Tan, "Reality TV as a Moral Laboratory," 454.

57 Ibid.

58 Alice Hall, "Perceptions of the Authenticity of Reality Programs and Their Relationships to Audience Involvement, Enjoyment, and Perceived Learning," *Journal of Broadcasting & Electronic Media* 53, no. 4 (2009): 515–31.

59 Ibid., 527.

60 AmosTversky and Daniel Kahneman, "Availability: A Heuristic for Judging Frequency and Probability," *Cognitive Psychology* 5, no. 2 (1973): 207–32.

61 Ouellette, "Reality TV Gives Back," 68.

62 Ibid.,69.

63 Ibid.

64 Ibid.

65 Ibid., 70.

66 Joshua Meyrowitz, *No Sense of Place: The Impact of Electronic Media on Social Behavior* (New York: Oxford University Press, 1985).

67 Garrison, "Prophetic Epideictic Rhetoric."

68 Wyatt, "Humiliation TV."

69 Lundy, Ruth and Park, "Simply Irresistible."

7

Commercialization: The Intersection of Economics and Ethics in Reality TV

Bastiaan Vanacker

Reality TV as Big Business

While examples of what we would now label reality TV can be found throughout television history, it wasn't until the late 1980s that reality TV developed as a distinct genre. Labor conflict and financial hardship marked the television world in the USA during that time, and this forced networks to look for cheaper, unscripted content. This led to the development of shows such as *FBI: Untold Stories, America's Most Wanted,* and *Top Cops.*[1] Ten years later, a second wave of reality programing hit the screens when shows such as *Survivor* and *Big Brother* made their way to the USA from Europe.[2]

Initially, the potential of this new crop of reality TV shows went unrecognized, and they were considered best suited as filler during the quiet summer months. By the middle of the decade, however, reality TV was heralded as the savior of broadcast network television for its success in stopping, or at least stemming, the exodus of audiences to cable.[3] In the years since, despite occasional reports of its death, reality TV has carved out its niche in the broadcast and cable lineups. One journalist counted no fewer than 560 reality shows in 2010.[4]

Clearly audiences are watching reality TV, but that's only part of the story. Equally important in explaining the success of reality TV is the economics behind it. Reality shows are relatively cheap to produce. An hour of lower-budget reality TV can cost as little as $300,000, while even the bigger network productions such as *The Biggest Loser* still cost less than $1 million per hour. The hourly rate to produce a scripted drama, on the other hand, is between $2 million and $3 million.[5] What's more, most reality TV programs don't have to pay the people who appear in them. By comparison, for the last season of *Friends*, the six main cast members earned $1 million each per episode. Exceptions exist in reality TV, of course. As shows such as *The Real Housewives*, *The Hills*, *Jon & Kate Plus 8*, or *Jersey Shore* become popular, their reality "stars" begin to demand bigger payouts. But even these salaries are modest in comparison: at the peak of their success, the Gosselins of *Jon & Kate Plus 8* fame earned $22,500 per episode.[6]

In addition to relatively low production costs, reality TV has provided advertisers with an ideal vehicle for product placement. During the first three months of 2008, Nielsen Media Research counted almost 118,000 instances of product placement on US television. Eight of the ten shows featuring the most product placement were reality shows, with *The Biggest Loser* leading the way.[7] While product placement revenue is still only a fraction of that of traditional advertising, its importance will only grow as more people circumvent traditional ads by using digital recorders such as Tivo.[8]

All of this doesn't mean there are no financial drawbacks to reality television. It tends to perform poorly in off-network syndication, as the timeliness and topic matter of reality shows don't always lend themselves well to syndication. In other words, audiences may be more willing to watch reruns of *Seinfeld* than *Survivor*. In addition, the unpredictability and tawdry nature of some reality programs can chase advertisers away or make them leery, forcing networks to sell advertising for these shows at lower rates.[9] Reality TV is a global phenomenon in which successful concepts, such as *Big Brother*, are sold to foreign networks to be produced locally. Some of the most successful exporters of reality TV formats are Dutch Endemol (*Big Brother*, *Fear Factor* and *Deal or No Deal*) and British Fremantle Media (*Idol*). However, exporting television formats still requires that the format be made into an actual program in a local market, and this is less profitable than exporting finished television products.[10]

Even with these challenges, reality TV is big business. Many people make a living from it, and it provides a source of revenue for networks and producers.

While the tendency may be to equate big business with ethical shortfalls, we have to resist the urge to label cultural products as unethical merely because they are made with an eye toward profit. The drive for profit only becomes an ethical issue if it comes at the expense of other, more important, values.

The goal of this chapter, then, is to investigate the business of reality TV from an ethical perspective and determine whether ethical values are being trumped by economic values. The chapter begins with an introduction to deontology and outlines how that philosophy can be applied to reality TV. Next, it considers the ethical implications of content used to attract audiences and promotional techniques used to attract advertisers. Finally, it examines whether reality TV is turning audiences into mere consumers and participants into mere commodities.

Deontology and Reality TV

Deontology is an ethical framework based on duty. This is a relatively straightforward approach to understand when analyzing professions, such as journalism, that have specific and widely understood duties. But how can we apply duties to something like reality TV? After all, it's *just entertainment*. It falls outside the ethical realm.

The reply to this claim is two-fold. First, all reality TV is made by people, and, from a deontological perspective, all people, just by virtue of being human, have certain universal duties they must live up to. Second, reality TV isn't just entertainment. It – along with all other forms of pop culture – informs and educates, it socializes and provides societal bonds, and it helps create our identities and our views of the world.[11] With this kind of power comes ethical responsibilities.

Immanuel Kant, deontology's most famous adherent, argued that duties to respect human dignity, to refrain from treating others merely as a means to an end, and to universalize one's actions are central to living an ethical life. In Kantian ethics, certain actions – lying, for example – are inherently wrong. A Kantian duty-based ethic is often touted as one that has no regard for consequences. It is more accurate, however, to view it as one that adheres to certain principles and values, even if the immediate consequences of not doing so might seem preferable. Those principles are not random; they are those around which a society can be organized because they can serve as universally valid standards of behavior. In this sense, a duty-based ethic does concern itself with consequences.

We have already pointed out that one duty of reality TV producers comes from the economic realm: making a profit. What we turn to next is an exploration of whether actions that stem from this duty can be reconciled with duties that fall in the ethical realm.

Scandal, Controversy and the Quest for Audiences

All reality shows compete for viewers. Without them, a show has little hope of succeeding. In its quest for audiences, one show may require its participants to eat cockroaches, another may expect them to expose private and embarrassing moments, and a third may encourage them to lie. After all, outrageousness, disclosure of private facts, and conflict created by deception help a reality show stand out, and the tactics seem to attract viewers. Even if the people participating in reality shows somehow are wronged, is this really an ethical issue? If participants voluntarily agree to have their struggles with hording, obesity or teenage pregnancy broadcast to the world, or if they welcome the opportunity to sit in a bucket filled with camel snot to win a trip to Jamaica, why should we be concerned? After all, the participants aren't doing anything against their will.

A Kantian-inspired deontological ethicist would disagree. It simply doesn't suffice that everyone agrees and no one is harmed; these actions could still be considered unethical. While this perspective may seem strange, particularly in Western libertarian societies where self-determination is considered a crucially important value, it is actually a rationale supported by many policies of those societies. They wouldn't, for example, allow someone to sell his kidney to the highest bidder, nor would most of them allow prostitution, even if all parties agree. According to this perspective, certain actions are simply wrong, even if no one involved objects. From a deontological perspective, a similar rationale can be applied to reality TV. Some reality shows might be considered wrong because they violate fundamental human values, even if all participants agree and no one seems to be harmed.

Let's now turn back to the question of whether the commercial nature of reality TV is a factor that pushes the genre toward the theoretical ethical brim, toward violating fundamental human values. One argument supporting this claim is that many shows seek scandal and controversy and use them as a selling point. In fact, Daniel Bilteryest, borrowing from French sociologist Dominique Mehl, has argued that reality TV is surrounded by the "perfume of scandal."[12] This scandal results from shows that explore controversial moral, psychological and social issues, and from the criticism and moral panic that often accompany their launch. In these cases, the controversy, rather than the show itself, becomes the attraction. France's regulatory body, for example, forced the *Big Brother*-like program *Loft Story* to undergo changes before it could move forward. These included allowing participants at least two hours of real intimacy per day and limiting the use of cigarettes and alcohol. Other European countries saw similar reactions to the launch of *Big Brother*. In an ironic twist, these reactions – many of which came from intellectual and political elites – were smartly used when promoting the programs.[13]

Reality shows that combine pushing the envelope and outraging the intellectual elite have become a pattern. In 2005, for example, the Belgian commercial channel VTM sent three Belgian families to "primitive tribes" in Africa and Asia for the reality show *Toast Kannibaal*. Criticism soon followed. Cultural anthropologist Rik Pinxten sharply denounced the show, arguing that it presented the rest of the world as a playground for rich Westerners to use at will and that it portrayed members of the tribes as less valuable than Westerners.[14] Media ethicist Johan Taels argued that the program fell short of its goal to provide a realistic view of a clash of cultures: "The producers continue to search for media-friendly confrontations. What do we consider to be unusual, dirty, laughable or ridiculous?"[15] When the format was sold to the Netherlands, Dutch producers went one step further – despite requests by the Belgian producers not to do so – and invited tribe members to the Netherlands to record the ensuing culture clash,[16] adding yet another layer of controversy to the show and another presumed "hook" for audiences.

Toast Kannibaal isn't the only example from the Netherlands where a quest for audiences has pushed the boundaries of reality TV ethics. In 2006, Dutch commercial station Talpa aired *De Gouden Kooi* (*The Golden Cage*). In the show, ten people paid a €10,000 entrance fee to a luxurious villa where all their needs were met. The person who remained the longest in the villa won €1,000,000 and the villa, while the other players lost their money. Contestants were eliminated either by being voted out unanimously or by exiting voluntarily because they could no longer stand it. Unlike *Big Brother*, where people only stayed in the house for three months, *De Gouden Kooi* did not have a time limit and lasted as long as contestants remained. The show, therefore, ended up airing from October 2006 until May 2008. Even though the program was heavily criticized because it encouraged the use of bullying and psychological pressure to force people out, audiences stuck with it through its entire run.

Do these examples confirm the fear that commercial pressures on reality TV drive the genre to the ethical abyss? Not necessarily. In many instances, the controversy dies once the programs start airing and the things that caused the ethical fears do not become reality. While controversy and scandal might provide an initial selling point for reality TV, they are not always good long-term strategies. In fact, controversial and ethically questionable hoax shows have faded from most channels' line-ups altogether. For instance, American shows such as *My Big Fat Obnoxious Fiancé, The Assistant*, and *The Joe Schmo Show* – all involving elaborate schemes designed to make people believe they were on a different kind of reality show than they actually were – lasted only one or two seasons. In the UK, *Space Cadets*, which aired on Channel 4, led contestants to believe they were training to be the first space tourists. What they thought was a Russian cosmonaut camp was, in fact, a disused airbase near Ipswich, and what they thought was a blast-off into space was actually a cabin being rocked by hydraulic lifts.[17] The show was expensive ($7 million) to produce, and because of the need to keep the project under wraps, producers could not secure sponsorship before the show started airing.[18] This indicates the marketplace does not favor hoax-type shows whose premise has to remain hidden.

Economic drawbacks of hoax shows include their difficulties in attracting audiences and advertisers. They also can't be turned into a franchise. Reality contestants can only be fooled once. It is, therefore, not surprising that in recent years, we have witnessed a decline in this type of reality television. Controversy, it turns out, is more a gimmick than a recipe for lasting success. At the end of the day, reality TV has to have audience appeal, so the envelope can only be pushed so far. Still, what constitutes "too far" might be relative. ABC considered buying the format for *The Golden Cage*, which resulted in a wave of indignation flooding the blogosphere and news sites.[19] Citing cost concerns, ABC ultimately did not go forward with the project.[20] Whether it was cost or fear of a backlash, this example does indicate that the market-place can also act as a brake on perceived unethical practices in reality TV. In the Netherlands as well, the heyday of controversial reality TV seems to be over, and more wholesome reality TV programming has become more popular than the contrived "reality soaps."[21] The successor to *De Gouden Kooi*, for example, struggled in the ratings and only survived due to its online following. All in all, as the genre has matured, what were once crucial ingre-dients have become occasional byproducts, and the trend seems to be that the market doesn't, in fact, reward ethically questionable programs that thrive on scandal and controversy.

Product Placement and the Quest for Advertisers

Most reality TV shows rely on advertising to foot the bill, and one appeal of reality TV is that it offers ample opportunity for integrated advertising or product placement. Of course, product placement is not unique to reality TV;

shows like *Sex and The City* and *Dawson's Creek* and movies like *Cast Away* and *ET* have prominently featured product placement. It is also not exclusive to the USA. Although product placement has traditionally been regulated more strictly in other countries,[22] change is underway. In the European Union, for example, bans on product placement have been (or are about to be) lifted. A 2007 European Union directive ordered member states to allow product placement under certain conditions.[23] When the ban was lifted in the UK in early 2011, critics voiced concerns that it would become as rife there as it is in the USA.[24]

While producers of scripted shows usually have to find ways to integrate products seamlessly into the storyline (e.g. the Absolut Vodka storyline in *Sex and the City*), reality TV doesn't have this challenge, so opportunities for product placement seem endless. But do these opportunities simultaneously create ethical problems, and are these ethical problems somehow more prominent in reality TV than in other types of programming? Ed Wasserman presents three potential problems with product placement: (i) it is deceptive; (ii) it jeopardizes the artistic integrity of writers and producers; and (iii) it violates and destroys the trust of the audience.[25] Because the second objection applies primarily to scripted entertainment, we will only concern ourselves with the first and third objections.

Product placement is deceptive, according to Wasserman, because it catches us with our guard down, without the filters we usually erect "when dealing with content that we know is deliberatively manipulative."[26] One could, of course, argue that as audience members, we are not really harmed by the practice. Who cares if someone on our TV screens drinks a bottle of water with the label prominently featured? This no-harm-done argument is a convenient one for so-called stealth advertisers,[27] but that is unlikely to impress a Kantian deontologist. As Patrick Plaisance argues, the notions of transparency, humanity and respect are all closely connected in Kantian ethics. By being transparent in our communications with others, we acknowledge and respect their ability to make free choices as rational human beings. It is our duty to do so: "We must interact with others in ways that maximize their ability to exercise free will, or reason. To fail to do so is to fail to recognize our existence as rational beings who, by the presence of our will to reason, are obliged to act morally toward others."[28] By trying to sneak up on audiences, product placement does not acknowledge and respect their decision-making abilities.

Wasserman does point out, however, that we no longer live in an environment where every ad is clearly delineated:

> After all, traditional TV ads aren't labeled as such. We've been trained to recognize the pause, the changes in voice, visual cues and the like, and

we say, oh, this is a commercial. Time to go to the bathroom. If we are retrained to understand fictional forms as some mongrel form of integrated marketing and creative expression, we'd no longer have a basis to object to product placement – not, that is, on grounds of deceptiveness.[29]

We are exposed to thousands of advertisements every day, and very few of them announce themselves explicitly as advertising. But in most situations, we understand that we are being advertised to. When we see a billboard along the road suggesting that we give the Big Mac a try, we understand that McDonalds paid for the space to communicate its advertising message. What, then, do we understand when we're watching a reality TV show? When the candidates of *Top Chef* shop for their groceries in a Whole Foods Market whose logo is shown repeatedly, should we be told that the grocery chain paid for this exposure, or do we already know this? Do we have a moral right to be told, or do we owe it to ourselves to be media-savvy viewers? Is it really *our duty* – rather than the duty of advertisers or producers of reality shows – to educate ourselves about the ubiquity of advertising in our societies?

The latter argument should be used with caution, as this "buyer-beware" defence can be applied to any kind of advertising practice. If we make audiences responsible for being aware of all advertising techniques, we hand the ethical equivalent of a get-out-of-jail-free card over to advertisers. On the other hand, advertisers work within a society in which audiences have certain expectations of and hold certain beliefs about advertising. Because different types of reality television create different types of expectations, these expectations should be taken into consideration when evaluating the deceptiveness of product placement in the context of reality television.

Research has shown that audiences' resistance to product placement is relatively small.[30] In reality shows where producers set the stage for real people to compete against each other, product placement seems to be acceptable as part of that stage, much the same way we expect to encounter advertising on the sidelines of a sports arena. Viewers are adept at distinguishing between the real and the fake, which is, in fact, one of the reasons people enjoy watching reality TV.[31]

If viewers are proficient at spotting the real and the fake, the obviousness of much product placement in reality TV should alert them to the fact that they are watching covert advertising. When a tribe winning a challenge on *Survivor* is rewarded with some chilled Mountain Dew, the product placement is obvious. While the really blatant examples of product placement might be off-putting, they are arguably the least deceptive, exactly because they are so apparent. The more an expectation of product placement is present, the less deceptive it is. By contrast, if one is watching content in which no product placement is expected, it would be more deceptive. (Consider, for example, the product placement that occurs when content-starved news programs make use of corporate video news releases.) While product placement is a practice that requires continuous ethical scrutiny, this analysis suggests that obvious instances of product placement in staged reality shows are not more deceptive than product placement in other television programs or in other instances of advertising we encounter in our daily lives.

The analysis changes for reality shows that fit within the documentary tradition. Shows such as *Little People, Big World* make a greater claim to reality than staged shows such as *Survivor* or *Big Brother*. TLC describes *Little People, Big World* as "in-depth television documentation" of the lives of little people in which "viewers look into the lives of the Roloffs as they face the pressure of being little in an average-sized world and the financial burdens of operating Roloff Farms."[32] When such claims of authenticity are made, it is the duty of the producers to live up to the expectations that these claims generate. In this instance, product placement becomes more troublesome because viewers do not expect staged elements such as product placement in a documentary. Not only is product placement in this context less expected and, therefore, potentially more deceptive, it erodes people's trust in the genre, which is another of Wasserman's concerns. To illustrate this concern, consider a specific example from *Little People, Big World*.

Episode 40 of season 3 shows the Roloffs as they struggle to finance the remodeling of their home. The episode documents what happens when an ambitious husband's plans clashes with concerns of a fiscally prudent wife. The struggles and conflicts provide the drama that draws in viewers. While what happens on the screen is authentic, there is also something fake about it. As husband Matt researches chandeliers for the new addition online, he says to his wife: "There is an internet special on Home Depot, Mom." Multiple times throughout their exchange, the camera zooms in on his computer screen where The Home Depot logo and slogans are prominently displayed. The scene ends with a cutaway shot of the farmhouse and Matt Roloff's voiceover: "And free shipping ...."

The next scene shows the whole family shopping for a new farm vehicle. Matt claims the family outing is supposed to lift everyone's spirits after the tension brought on by the ongoing construction. The footage shows family members drooling over various Polaris Wrangler vehicles, while Mom stands off to the side with a skeptical look on her face. The farm vehicles are shot from various angles, most of them in ways that prominently display their logos. After the boys are heard singing the praises of the vehicle, the salesman tops it off by pointing out some of the vehicle's stand-out features: "This vehicle can hold 1,000 pounds in the bed, and it can also tow one ton.

You got some dual accessory power right there, so if you want to charge your cell phone …" Not able to resist this much quality in one vehicle, the family – who in the previous scene was struggling to make ends meet – drives off with the biggest farm vehicle on the lot.

Even though Matt's voiceover declares that the purchase of the vehicle really makes economic sense, a critical viewer is left wondering whether the Roloffs got it for free or at a discount in exchange for the exposure. What exactly did they get out of The Home Depot exposure and what did TLC get out the deal? If Matt had decided to do some comparison shopping and had gone to a competitor's web site, would that have made it into the episode? Or if he thought that The Home Depot's customer service was poor, would that have been allowed to air? The details of product placement agreements usually remain under wraps, so we can't definitively answer these questions, but such instances do illustrate the erosion of trust that can be bred by such blatant forms of product placement.

Once product placement dictates storylines and creates the reality in which the subjects operate, a project with documentary ambitions is turned into a staged one. This is a violation of trust. To the extent that *Little People, Big World* is advertised as "television documentation," its integrity is jeopardized in a much more fundamental way than when a winner of a challenge on *Survivor* receives a bag of Doritos. While one can again ask, "what's the harm?" a deontologist would argue that this practice is based on a principle that, if used by everyone, would erode the whole genre of documentary-based reality television, which is anchored in the premise that what we see might be edited, but not staged. In this instance, sacrificing authenticity to make revenue through product placement cannot be defended because it represents a maxim that cannot be universally applied within the documentary context. For the same reason, we cannot argue that people should expect or wise up to the fact that these shows use product placement. The duty one assumes by producing television content that makes claims of authenticity cannot be discarded so easily.

Consumer Culture and the Commodification of Life

The previous two sections analysed specific instances in which the commercial nature of reality TV and the quest for both audiences and advertisers can lead to potentially unethical behavior. In this section, we will turn our attention to a more abstract argument and address ethical concerns about reality TV that are rooted in a general criticism of consumer culture as a whole. This objection fits within a larger tradition of cultural criticism that has decried the effects of the capitalist system on culture. Based on Marxist theory, which criticized capitalism for reducing every resource into something that can be traded and sold in the marketplace, scholars from the Frankfurt School, such as Theodor Adorno and Max Horkheimer, argued that under the pressures of the market, culture is reduced to just another commodity. The goal of these cultural products, they argued, is not to inform or enlighten, but to perpetuate the dominant capitalist ideology by addressing audiences as consumers rather than as autonomous human beings. For some, the nature of our postmodern world makes this criticism sound outdated. After all, research has dismissed the notion of a passive audience uncritically absorbing everything it is presented, and the distinction between high and low culture upon which this criticism is based seems elitist. However, reality TV's tendency to glorify consumer culture and reduce human life and human experiences to sellable commodities presents issues that call for ethical analysis.

In shows such as *Joe Millionaire* or *Temptation Island*, participants reside in luxurious surroundings, and lodgings in MTV's *The Real World* usually resemble a luxurious frat house complete with pool table and high-end amenities. As Jennifer Pozner points out, shows such as *Meet My Folks* and *Marry My Dad* relocate families into houses that are significantly more upscale than the ones in which the families actually reside. These McMansions provide advertisers with better branding opportunities than the participants' real, middle-class dwellings.[33]

Beyond the settings for reality shows, affluence rears its head in other ways. Many reality TV shows portray people doing just about anything to win prizes or money. Those who attribute a high degree of power to the media might deem this unethical and agree with Jennifer Pozner when she writes about the glorification of material wealth in reality TV: "The magnification of affluence in reality TV plays a dangerous game with our expectations, our desires, our spending patterns – and our country's economic stability."[34] According to critics like Pozner, reality television shows reduce their audiences to mere consumers and produce shows that not only reflect but reinforce materialistic beliefs. (See also this book's Chapter 4, which discusses the conflation of spiritual and material values in reality marriage shows.)

Of course, not all reality shows are steeped in this kind of materialism, and even some challenge us to question the materialism on display. It's possible that reality TV can actually be seen as a cautionary tale of what people will do for fame and money. As June Deery points out:

Reality TV represents, among other things, the triumph of the market, the notion that everyone as well as everything has its price and that people will do pretty much anything for money. But it also relies on the fact that its capitulation still has the power to shock. Its trivial dramas transfix audiences in part, I believe, because they tap into deep cultural anxieties about the profit motive taking priority over everything, especially over moral judgments concerning truth, deception, betrayal, and trust.[35]

At a time when today's young people are labelled as narcissistic,[36] some reality shows can be seen as a cultural exponent of the obsession with self, celebrity and materialism but at the same time as an invitation to question that obsession. Some have expressed fear that rewarding and glorifying behavior could "contribute to lowering thresholds in regular viewers for reprehensible, transgressive conduct."[37] However, while many shows glorify consumption and encourage the notion that people will do anything for money, audiences can and do interpret these messages in critical ways. For example, Jaap Amesz, the winner of the previously mentioned Dutch reality show De Gouden Kooi ended up with fame, money and a new villa, through engaging in tactics that earned him the nickname "Terror Jaap." However, it is possible that audiences enjoyed watching him not because they consider his actions to be morally defensible, but because they enjoyed the performance and the element of play involved. Audiences are able to recognize there is an element of gamesmanship to these types of shows, and they recognize actions need to be evaluated within the context of the shows. As such, the shows act like moral laboratories where experiments are being conducted that might stimulate reflection rather than copycat behavior.[38]

When we argue about effects of reality TV's glorification of consumer culture, we are engaging in an outcomes-based ethical analysis. However, a Kantian perspective would ask us not to look so much at the outcomes but at the actions themselves. From this ethical viewpoint, we can question whether the whole premise behind some reality shows – turning genuine human struggles into for-profit entertainment – is ethically questionable. Consider this example.

In 2007, the Dutch network BNN aired De Grote Donor Show (The Big Donor Show). On the show, a terminally ill patient who allegedly had only six months to live would consider three candidates in need of a kidney transplant and then decide to whom she would donate her own kidney. Viewers could weigh in by sending text messages supporting their candidate of choice. The show attracted worldwide attention and criticism but in the end turned out to be a hoax purportedly designed to raise awareness of the scarcity of kidney donors in the Netherlands. The dying patient was an actress; the candidates were real patients in need of a kidney, but they were in on the hoax. As a result of the show, the number of potential kidney donors in the Netherlands skyrocketed. This is certainly a positive outcome, but sidestepping the argument about whether the elaborate deception was justified in this case,[39] let's focus on why so many people thought the show crossed ethical boundaries, even before it was revealed as a hoax. Although the show could bring about some greater good, critics rejected it because – among other things – it made a spectacle and entertainment of disease and human suffering. Surely, no one objected to bringing the issue of organ donor shortages to the forefront (an outcomes-based concern), but many thought this forum, a reality TV show with conventions derived from competitive pressures, was not the right one.

From this critical perspective, not only the most egregious examples are troublesome. Many shows raise concerns that human life and emotions are being reduced to commercial products and in the process dehumanized, deprived of authenticity and ultimately destroyed, even if, as in the case of *De Grote Donor Show*, the goal was ultimately a laudable one. A Kantian might also wonder about programs such as *Jon & Kate Plus 8*, where familial struggles associated with raising eight children become the central plotline of a ratings hit. An outcomes-based ethical argument might point out that the couple divorced and, therefore, claim the show was unethical. A Kantian analysis, however, would stay away from this kind of Monday-morning quarterbacking and instead analyze the ways in which the Gosselin family became a mere commodity. On the same basis, shows like *Celebrity Rehab, 16 and Pregnant* or *Intervention* would also likely receive a thumbs-down from a deontologist because of their tendencies to use human crises as commodities. A Kantian would argue that once these true human experiences become commodified as cultural products that are employed to compete with other shows, the people featured in them become merely a means to an end. This fundamental criticism reinforces the notion that certain areas of human life should not become the plotline for reality shows that have to compete for viewers. Instead, these issues should become the purview of media that are not as explicitly profit-driven (and have better developed ethical codes and standards) such as documentary film-making or journalism. While this position may seem to adopt an elitist bias against popular culture, it is fundamentally situated in a justified concern for the value of common humanity and the respect that humanity demands.

Conclusion

In this chapter, we used a Kantian deontological analysis to investigate the ethical implications of the commercial nature of reality TV. While there are some indicators that a quest for audiences could lead reality TV producers to push ethical boundaries, these fears seem to be mitigated by the fact that most controversial reality TV shows have been weeded out as a result of poor audience response. In fact, commercial pressures might actually have led some reality TV producers away from boundary-pushing formats. Next, we considered reality TV's quest for advertisers and explored product placement. While audiences have come to expect product placement in reality TV shows that contain staged elements, the practice cannot be defended in the context of shows that follow the documentary tradition because product placement erodes trust in the genre. Finally, we addressed the more abstract criticism that reality TV treats people as a means to an end. While audiences can actively and critically engage with reality TV, viewers are frequently seen as mere consumers, while participants – and their often highly personal life issues – are reduced to mere commodities.

In the end, the story of commercialization on reality TV is not a simple one. Examples are answered by counter-examples, and questionable tactics must face up to audiences who are becoming increasingly sophisticated and critical. Like any commercial enterprise, reality TV must seek to live up to its duty of being economically viable while simultaneously committing itself to an ethic that offers authentic respect for all involved.

Notes

1 Chad Raphael, "The Political Economic Origins of Realiy TV," in *Reality TV: Remaking Television Culture*, 2nd edn, Susan Murray and Laurie Ouellette (eds) (New York: New York University Press, 2009) 128.

2 Ibid., 130.

3 Claire Atkinson and Jon Fine, "New Reality Dawns for TV Economics," *Advertising Age*, 27 September 2004, 75.

4 Aaron Barnhart, "Reality TV Shows Find Success With Small Budgets, Strong Personalities," *Kansas City Star*, 5 December 2010. http://www.kansascity.com/2010/12/05/2499791/biggest-loser-other-reality-shows.html.

5 Ibid.

6 Brian Stelter, "As Unknown Faces Become Stars, Reality Shows Fight Pay Escalation," *New York Times*, 27 July 2010, B1.

7 Nielsen Research, "Product Placements Rose 6% in First Quarter, Nielsen Reports," 5 May 2008. http://www.nielsen.com/us/en/insights/press-room/2008/product_placements1.html.

8 Ted Magder, "Television 2.0: The Business of American Television in Transition," in *Reality TV, Remaking Television Culture*, Susan Murray and

Laurie Ouellette (eds) (New York and London: New York University Press, 2009) 155.

9 Raphael, "The Political Economic Origins of Reality TV," 137–8.

10 Magder, "Television 2.0," 149–50.

11 See Leah R. Vande Berg, Lawrence A.Wenner and Bruce E. Gronbeck, *Critical Approaches to Television*, 2nd edn (Boston: Houghton Mifflin, 2004); F. Miguel Valenti, Les Brown and Laurie Trotta, *More Than a Movie: Ethics in Entertainment* (Boulder, CO: Westview Press, 2000); Jeffery L. Bineham, "The Construction of Ethical Codes in the Discourse and Criticism of Popular Culture." In *Communication Ethics, Media and Popular Culture*, Phyllis M. Japp, Mark Meister and Debra K. Japp (eds) (New York: Peter Lang, 2007) 13–39.

12 Daniel Biltereyst, "Media Audiences and the Game of Controversy: On Reality TV, Moral Panic and Controversial Media Stories," *European Culture and the Media*, Ib Bondebjerg and Peter Golding (eds) (Bristol, UK: Intellect Books, 2004) 117.

13 Ibid., 123–4.

14 Jan Debackere, "EenFout en GevaarlijkProgramma," *De Standaard*, 12 March 2005. http://www.standaard.be/artikel/detail.aspx?artikelid=GQFD8DAT.

15 Ibid.

16 Jan Debackere, "Op Zoeknaar de Cultuurclash," *De Standaard*, 4 September 2006. http://www.standaard.be/artikel/detail.aspx?artikelid=G84113ET7.

17 Denise Robertson, "Bad Taste Reality TV? There's Worse to Come," *Western Mail*, 13 December 2005, 20.

18 Emma Hall and Laurel Wentz, "'Space Cadets' Takes off Without a Sponsor," *Advertising Age*, 12 December 2005, 14.

19 Tonny Krijnen and Ed Tan, "Reality TV as a Moral Laboratory: A Dramaturgical Analysis of the Golden Cage," *Communications* 34 (2009): 449–50.

20 Andy Dehnart, "ABC Rejects Golden Cage Because of Costs," *Reality Blurred*, 8 May, 2008.http://www.realityblurred.com/realitytv/archives/future_shows/2008_May_09_abc_rejects_golden_cage.

21 Stijn Bronzwaer, "Lachen! Je Bent Op TV!" *NRC.Next*, 17 March 2011, 1.

22 Amit M. Schejter, "Art Thou for Us, or for Our Adversaries? Communicative Action and the Regulation of Product Placement: A Comparative Study and a Tool for Analysis," *Akron Law Review* 39 (2006): 207–42.

23 Mark Sweney, "EU to Allow Product Placement on TV," *The Guardian*, 23 November 2007. http://www.guardian.co.uk/media/2007/nov/30/advertising.television.

24 Tom Leonard, "Thirsty Simon, or Are You Trying to Sell Us Something? How Product Placement Is about to Transform British TV," *Mail Online*, 24 January 2011. http://www.dailymail.co.uk/news/article-1349936/Simon-Cowells-American-Idol-Coca-Cola-product-placement-transform-UK-TV.html.

25 Ed Wasserman, "The Ethics of Product Placement." Presentation at the annual convention of the Association for Education in Mass Communication

and Journalism, San Francisco, CA, 3 August 2006. http://ewasserman.com/2006/08/03/the-ethics-of-product-placement/.

26 Ibid.

27 Stealth advertising generally means advertising that tries to hide the fact that it is advertising. It can, for example, refer to hiring actors to talk to strangers and praise a product or service.

28 Patrick Plaisance, *Media Ethics: Key Principles for Responsible Practice* (Thousand Oaks, CA: Sage, 2009) 54.

29 Wasserman, "The Ethics of Product Placement."

30 Jay Newell, Jeffrey Layne Blevins and Michael Bugeja, "Tragedies of the Broadcast Commons: Consumer Perspectives on the Ethics of Product Placement and Video News Releases," *Journal of Mass Media Ethics* 24, no. 4 (October 2009): 212.

31 Annette Hill, "Big Brother, the Real Audience," *Television and New Media* 3, no. 3 (August 2002): 337.

32 "Little People, Big World," *TLC Family Guide: Monday Night Schedule*. http://tlc.discovery.com/guides/family/tlc-family-night/schedule.html.

33 Jennifer Pozner, *Reality Bites Back: The Troubling Truth About Guilty Pleasure TV* (New York: Seal Press, 2010) 133–4.

34 Ibid., 135.

35 June Deery, "Reality TV as Advertainment," *Popular Communication* 2, no. 1 (2004): 2.

36 Jean Twenge, *Generation Me: Why Today's Young Americans Are More Confident, Assertive, Entitled and More Miserable Than Ever Before* (New York: Free Press, 2006).

37 Krijnen and Tan, "Reality TV as a Moral Laboratory," 469.

38 Ibid.

39 While it might have brought about the greatest good for the greatest number of people, from a deontological perspective, the use of deception to reach this goal would likely not pass ethical muster.

8

Deception: Reality TV Playing Us False

Edward H. Spence

Introduction: Epistemological Deception

Is reality TV deceptive, and if it is, does it matter? Before we proceed to answer that question, let us begin by making a fair assumption: reality television viewers are not stupid. People who watch reality TV do so mainly for its entertainment value rather than its veracity. They know these shows undergo a lot of editing, scripting and staging, so they aren't easily fooled into thinking what they are watching is the entire, raw truth. Come on – who believes that! We can reasonably expect a certain degree of suspension of disbelief on the part of viewers. So, that's not the kind of deception this chapter will examine. Rather, it will examine whether substantial values such as loyalty, honesty, friendship and love are being misrepresented in reality TV. For if they are, that kind of deception is undoubtedly worthy of our attention and concern. To that end, this chapter uses conceptual philosophical analysis – with the help of some stories, myths and legends – to provide a theoretical framework for understanding and reflecting upon how deception can occur in reality television.

Reality TV can be considered deceptive in at least two ways. The first is epistemological and primarily concerns matters of knowledge, including information and matters of fact. The second is ethical and concerns matters of right and wrong moral behaviour. However, deception in the epistemological sense also involves deception in the ethical sense because misinformation (the unintentional dissemination of false information) as well as disinformation (the intentional dissemination of false information) can also constitute unethical conduct. This is because information as a type of knowledge must be true.[1] Knowledge is defined traditionally by philosophers as justified true belief. For any statement to count as knowledge, either written or spoken, it must meet at least three necessary conditions: (i) it has to be believed by someone; (ii) it has to be justified on the basis of sufficient demonstrable evidence in support of that belief; and (iii) it must also be true. Typically, deception – either through statements and claims or through visual images – involves some degree of falsehood. This can either be unintentional or intentional, and it is the latter that is of greater ethical concern. However, deception caused through negligence is also ethically wrong, albeit to a lesser degree, than intentional deception. This is because it amounts to misinformation.

The concern of this chapter is *not* deception in the epistemological and its related ethical sense; in other words, we are not concerned with deception concerning matters of knowledge and information. Why? First, as viewers of reality TV, we are not and cannot always be in a position to be certain if epistemological deception is taking place. We may, of course, suspect that there is some degree of deception through the staging, scripting and editing of the narrative plot of reality shows to make them more dramatically engaging and appealing to viewers. Drama, after all, relies on creating conflict between characters, and that can't just be left to chance. We can therefore expect, even if we can't be certain, that in order to capture and hold audience attention and secure ratings, reality TV has to be dramatic; its production cannot but be under the control of the producers. It follows then that reality TV cannot be as 'real' as the 'reality' it purports to depict.

Plato's 'Allegory of the Cave' very aptly describes this disparity between reality and the mere appearance of reality. In the allegory, a strange story is related to Glaucon by Socrates, Plato's protagonist in *The Republic*:

> And now, I [Socrates] said, let me show in a figure how far our nature is enlightened or unenlightened: – Behold! Human beings living in an underground den, which has a mouth open towards the light and reaching all along the den; here they have been from their childhood, and have their legs and necks chained so that they cannot move, and can only see before them, being prevented by the chains from turning round their heads. Above and behind them a fire is blazing at a distance, and between the fire and the prisoners there is a raised way; and you will see, if you look, a low wall built along the way, like the screen which marionette players have in front of them, over which they show the puppets.

And do you see, I said, men passing along the wall carrying all sorts of vessels, and statues and figures of animals made of wood and stone and various materials, which appear over the wall? Some of them are talking, others silent.

You have shown me a strange image [Glaucon], and they are strange prisoners. Like ourselves, I replied; and they see only their own shadows, or the shadows of one another, which the fire throws on the opposite wall of the cave?

True, he said; how could they see anything but the shadows if they were never allowed to move their heads?

And of the objects which are being carried in like manner they would only see the shadows?

Yes, he said. And if they were able to converse with one another, would they not suppose that they were naming what was actually before them?

Very true. And suppose further that the prison had an echo which came from the other side, would they not be sure to fancy when one of the passers-by spoke that the voice which they heard came from the passing shadow?

No question, he replied. To them, I said, the truth would be literally nothing but the shadows of the images.[2]

Like the prisoners in Plato's 'Allegory of the Cave', we may have no option as viewers of reality shows but to simply accept at face value the shadows created by the unseen puppeteers – or simply leave the cave. This brings us to the second reason why our concern in this chapter will not be primarily about epistemological deception and its related ethical wrongness. That reason involves suspension of disbelief and its related absence of epistemic care about whether our favourite reality show is as 'real' as it pretends to be. If the show is sufficiently entertaining and dramatic, do we really care (or should we care) about the degree of reality in an otherwise enjoyable show? At best, reality TV is an interesting, engaging and entertaining dramatic hybrid of fiction (the scripting, staging and editing of the narrative plot) and reality (the real characters/wannabe actors in the show). Would we as viewers, for example, wish that Russell or Boston Rob on *Survivor* be more real in their cunning, double-crossing tactics for supremacy than they appear to be?

Would it make any difference to viewers in terms of their pleasure in watching the two rat-cunning and unconscionable antagonists go head-to-head for the one million dollar prize while their opponents fall apart and are eliminated one by one? Would viewers care to know if the 'apparent' reality they are seeing is less than the 'real' reality behind the scenes? If reality TV could be *more* entertaining if it were *less* real, wouldn't we probably wish that to be the case? After all, reality TV has to be entertaining and engaging, and if it can't be that and fully real at the same time, then the reason for watching reality shows becomes redundant.

Like Plato's cave prisoners, we are prepared to accept a bit less reality for a bit more fun. If nothing else, we do know that things outside the cave can be rather grim and inhospitable to good times and having fun. Let's face it, the caves of our living rooms are rather cosy. Why not shut out the world for a while and immerse ourselves in the images we see and hear in our favourite reality show? At least shadows seem less threatening and dangerous than reality – real wars, real poverty, economic downturns, natural disasters and all the other 'slings and arrows of outrageous fortune'[3] and the vicissitudes of the cut and thrust of real life. For a while at least, shadows that entertain are comforting, and strictly speaking, there's not much ethically wrong with that. So the epistemological deception is not what may be ethically problematic about reality TV. The problem lies elsewhere and has to do with the things our societies seemingly value and care for, at least a great deal of the time. If there is something ethically problematic with deception in reality TV, that is where we may find it.

Deception and the Corrosion of Values

Let us now explore the question of whether some types of reality TV may be conducive to the corrosion of values through some kind of deception. What kind of deception other than epistemological deception might that be? If epistemological deception primarily concerns deception with regard to knowledge, can there be a type of deception that concerns not facts but values? To explore whether reality TV involves deception about values, I will first provide a general account of such deception on the basis of another illuminating passage from Plato's *Republic*. It concerns Plato's legendary quarrel with the poets. I will then apply that analysis more specifically to the question of deception and the corrosion of values in reality shows.

Plato's Quarrel with the Poets

What was Plato's quarrel with the poets, and why should it concern us now? Before we explore the contemporary relevance of Plato's complaint against the poets and more specifically its relevance to reality TV, let us first ascertain what Plato's complaint was. Plato addresses his complaint against the poets through his protagonist Socrates, who is having a dialectical duel with Adeimantus about the appropriate education for the Guardians of the State. To Adeimantus' astonishment, Socrates finds fault with two of the greatest poets of the time, Homer and Hesiod. The thrust of his complaint is that these and other poets 'who have ever been the great story-tellers of mankind'[4] lie through their teeth. In short, they lie about the true nature of the gods and that of the heroes.

According to Socrates, the poets misrepresent the gods by depicting them as cunning, dissembling, profligate, quarrelsome, lascivious, hot-tempered, self-serving and vain individuals who are morally no better, and sometimes worse, than ordinary men and women. That's a pretty big complaint! To back up his argument, Socrates gives several examples of ways in which Homer has depicted gods behaving badly. One, in particular, is Homer's allusion to the various transformations of Zeus, leader of the gods, who changes into bulls, swans and other disguises so he can seduce and have his carnal ways with earthly women. According to Socrates: 'It is impossible that God should ever be willing to change; being, as is supposed, the fairest and the best that is conceivable, every God remains absolutely and for ever in his own form.' Socrates goes onto say that 'God is perfectly simple and true both in word and deed; he changes not; he deceives not, either by sign or word, by dream or waking vision'. He concludes that 'the gods are not magicians who transform themselves, neither do they deceive mankind in any way'.[5] Socrates' argument about the true nature of God is based on a conceptual analysis that ascribes to God, as the supreme and best of all beings in the whole of existence, the quality of perfection. Being perfect, God would not want to change to something less perfect, especially as a self-seeking means for deceiving humans for his or her own selfish ends.

According to Socrates, the poets misrepresent not only the gods but also the true nature of heroes by depicting them as grabbing, selfish, arrogant, greedy and callous egotists. Achilles, for example, is depicted by Homer in the *Iliad* as a thug. Not only does Achilles kill Hector, he desecrates Hector's body by tying it up to his chariot and dragging it around the walls of Troy. In contravention of divine and human laws, Achilles then refuses to surrender Hector's body for burial. Socrates asks: Is such a depiction of Achilles, the greatest of all the heroes, a true representation of what a hero is or at least ought to be? And what of the harmful effect that such a depiction might have on the impressionable minds of children? As Socrates argues, 'the young man should not be told that in committing the worst of crimes, he is far from doing anything outrageous'. Socrates continues, 'a young person cannot judge what is allegorical and what is literal; anything that he receives into his mind at that age is likely to become indelible and unalterable; and therefore it is most important that the tales which the young first hear should be models of virtuous thoughts'.[6]

We can now see that Plato's complaint against the poets is a fundamental and deep concern for moral education and how false depictions of gods and heroes in the poetry of his time can have a detrimental effect on the character of impressionable young persons who are not yet capable of the critical and reflective thinking that, through knowledge and experience, would allow them to discern truth from falsehood. Socrates' arguments against the false depictions of gods and heroes in Homer's poetry are of two kinds.

The first kind is a deontological argument, which seeks to demonstrate that the depictions of gods and heroes by poets are inherently inconsistent because those depictions are contradictory and in direct negation of the essential attributes that characterize or should characterize gods and heroes alike. With respect to ethics, a deontological argument is a rational argument that purports to show that something is morally wrong if it involves an inherent logical contradiction. Therefore, according to Plato's deontological argument, gods and heroes cannot behave badly and immorally in any way that denies their inherent excellence of character and divine perfection respectively. Vices and immoral conduct are inconsistent with excellence of character and divine perfection.

Given that heroes by conceptual definition possess or should possess excellence of character instantiated by virtues and the absence of vices, and gods possess perfect natures, which cannot of necessity admit the imperfection of vices, depictions of gods and heroes that are inconsistent with heroes' and gods' essential characteristics amount to lies. So, for example, Achilles as a hero par excellence cannot, by definition, be ill-tempered, arrogant, petulant, greedy, malicious, cruel, sulking and unjust in the way described by Homer. Those are vices and in direct negation and contradiction to the cardinal virtues such as courage, moderation, prudence and justice that a hero must of necessity possess. Note also that according to Plato and later the Stoics, virtues come in a bundle, so if one is virtuous, one must be in possession of all the cardinal virtues such as courage, prudence, moderation and justice and not just some of them; it's either all or nothing. Even if we grant that Achilles as depicted by Homer was brave, the absence of moderation, prudence and justice in his character and conduct would render him vicious, not virtuous. After all, history has shown us that a lot of bad people can act bravely even when they do so unjustly. To be just, one must sometimes moderate one's anger, and that takes more courage than giving vent to it.

As Aristotle would say, such conduct is characteristic of the foolhardy person, not of the truly courageous individual whose courage is guided by reason and prudence.[7] To be prudent, one must also be reverential to the gods. Achilles wasn't reverential when he desecrated Hector's body and refused to give it back to the Trojans for burial. To be just, one must sometimes constrain one's self-interest with regard to the legitimate interests of others. Achilles, by contrast, allowed his self-interest and sulking pride to jeopardize the interests of his fellow Greeks by withdrawing from a battle that almost cost the Greeks the war. Based on this discussion, Achilles – as depicted by Homer – was either not a hero, or he was a hero but was falsely depicted by Homer as being vicious rather than virtuous. Either way, Homer lied. In one case, he lied about the true nature of heroes; in the other, he lied about the true character of Achilles. In the end, Homer's depiction of heroes generally, and his depiction of Achilles' character specifically, was a misrepresentation and thus a lie.

The second argument Socrates uses against false poetic depictions of gods and heroes is a consequentialist argument. This argument demonstrates that young people can be adversely influenced by false depictions. As they are encouraged by those depictions, young people may learn to act viciously and immorally, mimicking the behaviours of their false models of gods and heroes. This is an overall detriment to the good of the state. A consequentialist argument is a rational argument that purports to show an action is morally wrong if it results in overall bad consequences and morally good if it results in good consequences for the greatest number of people affected by that action.

By combining the deontological and consequentialist arguments, Socrates can rationally conclude that the false representations of gods and heroes in poetry must be censored for the good of society. Furthermore, he argues that the young must be educated to be sceptical and critical of poetry; in other words, they must be equipped to recognize the many ways in which poets such as Homer distort the truth of many things, including the truth about gods and heroes.

The Contemporary Relevance of Plato's Quarrel with the Poets

If we grant that Plato's complaint against the poets is of historical interest, and may even be of philosophical interest, what possible relevance is it to us today, particularly given the lack of any significant influence of poets in contemporary society? If we understand poetry in the traditional sense, then the answer would have to be that Plato's quarrel with the poets has no practical relevance or application. However, if we extend the meaning of poetry to include the most influential creators and communicators of information and persuasion in the mass media today, then Plato's quarrel with the poets becomes immensely significant and relevant.

Who in contemporary life is equivalent to the influential poets of Plato's time? Who is today's Homer or Hesiod? I suggest that the most influential poets today (in terms of popularity) are the various creators and producers of popular culture: the film-makers, musicians, radio and TV celebrities, media moguls, computer game designers, magazine writers, public relations spin doctors, advertisers and, of course, the creators and producers of reality TV shows.

Insofar as these pop culture 'poets' bend or manipulate the truth to various degrees, then Socrates' arguments apply to them as well, and insofar as the moral training of young people is adversely undermined and thwarted by the false messages of these 'poets', should we not at least consider whether their messages should be censored for the good of society? In addition, should we not also consider whether young people should be educated, in particular in media ethics, to recognize and be sceptical and critical of those false messages – messages that may undermine the moral fibre of society?

It is beyond the scope of this chapter to span the whole spectrum of mass media to locate examples of the many ways in which pop culture's contemporary poets lie to us or mislead us about what is morally and aesthetically valuable and worthy. Based on our own collective cultural experiences, however, what we can say with some justification is that what pop culture's poets are generally promoting, at least some of the time, is an amoral hedonism. Reality shows such as *The Bachelor* and *Temptation Island* promote pleasure-seeking egoism where lust is confused for love; *Big Brother* and *Master Chef* promote shallow popularity as true friendship; *The Apprentice* promotes corporate and material success as well-being and happiness; *Survivor* promotes the view that winning at all costs amounts to success; and most reality shows, if not all, promote the view that temporary fame in front of a TV camera – for the sake of TV producers and advertisers – amounts to self-fulfilment.

Reality TV and Axiological Deception

Does reality TV constitute axiological deception – deception concerning values? Before we proceed to answer that question, it would be useful to have a philosophical definition of 'deception' by which to orientate our discussion. I will use, as a working definition, the following definition by James Edwin Mahon:

> Deceiving must be intentional; deceiving requires that another acquires or retains a false belief, and not merely loses or fails to gain a true belief; deceiving must involve the agency of the deceived; and the deceiver must know or truly believe that what the deceived believes to be true is false.[8]

This definition will be useful in determining whether some of the phenomena in reality shows constitute deception and what sort of deception it is.

The intentional condition for deception is problematic with regard to reality TV because it is not always clear if and when the deception caused is intentional. To be sure, some epistemic deception in reality TV caused by scripting, staging and editing may be intentional and would qualify as deception according to the above working definition. That is, it is intended to deceive, and it actually succeeds in deceiving by making viewers of reality shows believe what is, in fact, false. As was said in the introduction, we can reasonably assume that quite a few people who watch reality shows do so for the shows' entertainment value rather than for their veracity. Therefore, they would know that these shows are not as 'real' as they appear to be, and so viewers wouldn't be easily fooled into believing that what they are watching is, in fact, the whole truth. We can also expect a certain degree of suspension of disbelief on the part of viewers. So, to reiterate, even if epistemic deception does take place, it is not the primary ethical issue in reality TV deception.

Therefore, the substantial ethical problem with reality TV deception concerns not epistemic but axiological deception. Derived from the Greek word 'axia' meaning value, axiological deception can be understood generally as deception that concerns not facts but values. Such deception is conducive to the corrosion or corruption of those values. It is the corrosion of values that renders axiological deception an ethically significant phenomenon, and it is the primary ethical issue on which my final analysis will focus.

Do the creators and producers of reality shows intentionally produce axiological deception in their audiences by intentionally causing them to have false beliefs about values, which creators and the producers of reality shows know to be false? If that were the case, it would certainly constitute deception, according to our working definition. But things are not that simple. It is not at all clear if the creators and producers of reality shows go out of their way to intentionally deceive their audiences in this way. Perhaps they themselves are either deceived or even ignorant about the truth of the values their shows promote and encourage. On the other hand, they may simply not consider the falsehood of those values to be a matter of any moral significance. So what's the problem?

Let's go back and reconsider Plato's quarrel with the poets and see whether it may help us advance the case for axiological deception in reality TV. According to Plato's arguments against the poets (the deontological and consequentialist arguments), both Homer and Hesiod were engaged in axiological deception conducive to the corrosion of values. But did Homer intentionally deceive his audience by misrepresenting the gods and the heroes, knowing the misrepresentation to be false and intending his audience to believe it to be true? Or is that misrepresentation something other than strict epistemic deception? Could it be some other kind of deception – a deception that does not need to meet the epistemic criterion of intention – that may help us understand how reality TV is conducive to axiological deception? For even if reality TV deception is not intentional in the relevant epistemic sense, is it – at least according to Plato's deontological and consequentialist arguments – morally harmful nonetheless just because it is conducive to the corrosion of societal values? The answer that seems to suggest itself is that reality TV is misrepresenting false values as true (axiological deception) whether intentionally or not. That is, something false is presented as true whether or not there's an intention to do so. If that misrepresentation is potentially conducive to the corrosion of values by causing at least some viewers to be misled, deceived or confused about those values, then that would constitute axiological deception.

Sissela Bok calls an untruth that unintentionally deceives others 'confabulation'. According to Bok:

> There is a large category of statements where deceit is not intended but where truthful communication is far from being achieved. In considering this category, it is important to take into account all that can help to distort communication quite apart from an intention to deceive. When people convey false information in the belief that it is true, they may be tired, mistaken, uniformed, inarticulate, intoxicated, or duped by others; but so long as they do not intend to mislead anyone, they are not acting in a manner that is in any way deceitful. Their statements may be false, but they have not knowingly uttered falsehoods.[9]

However, immediately before this passage, Bok does say: Such cases show that the moral dimensions of choices concerning truthfulness and deceit *are not exhausted by referring to the intentions of those who make statements* [emphasis added].[10] Bok's explanation of deception through confabulation helps explain how deception can occur by effect if not by intention; others may be led to believe an untruth or falsehood even if that is not the intention of those who cause the deception.

'Sweet lord, you play me false:' A Closer Look at Axiological Deception

To further explore the notion of axiological deception in reality TV, consider a scene from Shakespeare's *Tempest* in which Miranda and Ferdinand are playing a game of chess:

> Miranda: *Sweet lord, you play me false.*
> Ferdinand: *No, my dear'st love, I would not for the world.*
> Miranda: *Yes, for a score of kingdoms you should wrangle, and I would call it, fair play.*[11]

Just as Miranda claimed that 'Ferdinand played her false', can we claim that reality TV shows 'play their audiences false?' Perhaps. Through staging, scripting and editing, participants in reality shows fake values and sentiments, and make what is essentially phony and false, at least some of the time, appear real and true. This seems to point to an important and interesting difference between reality shows and fictional shows such as dramas: in reality TV, participants *play their real selves false* through axiological deception (by feigning their values and sentiments for dramatic effect); in 'fictional' dramas, actors endeavour to *play their fictional characters true* for realistic effect. I will refer to this difference as the inversion of reality phenomenon – a phenomenon in which the 'real' in reality shows appears false and the 'fictional' in movies appears true. The irony of this inversion of reality is quite startling when one considers how, for example, the character Marshall Rooster Cogburn played by John Wayne in the original film *True Grit* comes across as vividly true, authentic and believable, in contrast to the so-called friendships, loyalties, disloyalties, betrayals, frustrations and multiple other values and sentiments expressed by reality TV participants. These come across as fake, false and anything but authentic. Yet, the former is meant to be fictional, the latter real.

It is this inversion of reality, by which fictional movies or novels play us true and reality shows play us false, that may help explain what can be fundamentally deceptive about reality TV and why that deception matters axiologically, even it does not matter (that much) epistemologically. It matters axiologically – and by extension ethically – because reality shows pretend to be something they are not; they can be considered deceptive because they pretend to be real and truthful when they are not.

In this way, reality TV shows are like advertorials (advertising messages masquerading as news commentary). The 'reality' in both advertorials and reality shows is pure camouflage to make us believe that which is fake and phony is true and real. In the case of reality shows such as *Survivor* and *Big Brother*, for example, the camouflage is created by having the 'characters' in those shows depicted by real people who play themselves and – if the above analysis is correct – play themselves false (at least some of the time). In the case of advertorials, it is the facts or opinions that are fake (they are not facts or opinions but paid advertisements), and in the case of reality shows, it is the values and sentiments that participants display, or are manipulated into displaying by the shows' producers. The reason for the deception, quite simply, is that the label of 'real' gives both advertorials and reality shows alike more credibility with audiences. Credibility is a good ploy to use when you are selling something, which is what all reality shows are really doing, whether that means selling an audience to advertisers or selling a product that appears on a reality show to viewers.

Does Reality TV Corrode Values through Axiological Deception?

Even if we accept on the basis of the aforementioned analysis that some reality shows exhibit features of axiological deception, does it matter? To answer that question, we now need to apply the above theoretical framework to examine if and how axiological deception can corrode societal values – values such as honesty, trust, truthfulness, integrity, loyalty and love, which we as a society consider important and worth preserving and promoting. If we find that some reality shows have the tendency to corrode – or even potentially corrode – values though axiological deception, then this is a matter of ethical concern.

Applying Plato's deontological and consequentialist arguments to our analysis of axiological deception, we can make the following evaluative assessments with regard to the axiological deception in reality TV and its propensity to contribute to the corrosion of societal values.

Deontologically

To the extent that shows such as *Survivor* and *Big Brother* play their audiences false, that practice can be understood as axiological deception. For there seems to be an inherent inconsistency in displaying values and sentiments by real people in reality shows as 'real' when they are designed to be false – when those sentiments are faked or manipulated through staging, scripting, editing and other tactics. Although comprised of real people, these reality shows play their audiences false by simply pretending to be real. Like Homer's presentation of Achilles as a 'hero' who displays behaviour uncharacteristic and conceptually inconsistent with that of a real hero, the deontological inconsistency in reality TV is the use of reality to create something unreal and then label it 'real'. The inconsistency lies in presenting falsehood as truth.

Consequentially

The effect of falsely presenting values and sentiments by real people in reality shows as 'real' may have the unwelcome consequence of influencing the belief that people in similar circumstances in real-life settings would behave in a similar manner and, perhaps, ought to behave in that manner. In the case of *Survivor*, for example, it may influence the belief that the 'winner takes all' and that rules of 'winning by whatever it takes' are ethically justified principles to guide conduct. That may lead to the corrosion of ethics itself through encouraging viewers to believe that ethics is about using the most effective means to achieve one's self-regarding goals, whatever those happen to be. Of course, ethics is concerned and ought to be concerned not just with the goodness of the means but also with the goodness of the ends, so fostering this kind of belief is ethically problematic.

By contrast, some reality shows that promote good social ends and values may, in fact, turn out to be consequentially good and, as such, ethically praiseworthy. This is illustrated by the recent Australian reality show *Go Back To Where You Came From*.[12] The show follows six Australians on a sea voyage to places from which asylum seekers have fled. It compares the 'before-and-after' attitudes of the six contestants, the majority of whom are initially hostile to asylum seekers who have 'jumped the migration queue' and come to Australia uninvited. At the conclusion of the four-part reality show, we see a dramatic change in the attitudes of the six participants. They seem more compassionate and understanding as a result of having experienced what the asylum seekers went through to get to Australia in their leaky boats. Even if we are sceptical about the veracity of the show and how real the participants' change of heart is, the consequence of getting viewers to see the problem from the asylum seekers' standpoint can be considered a worthy and commendable ethical result because it may promulgate in the general public values of compassion and understanding. If it is based on a lie, it is what Plato might describe as a 'noble lie' – a lie whose consequence is to promote good ends. (For other examinations of how reality TV can help viewers to see problems from others' perspectives, see also this book's Chapter 2 on stereotyping and Chapter 9 on democracy and discourse.)

Conclusion

Back to the Cave: The World's a Stage

All the world's a stage,
And all the men and women merely players;
They have their exits and their entrances,
And one man in his time plays many parts,
His acts being seven ages.[13]

In response to the claim that reality TV is deceptive for all the reasons adduced above, one might object that if reality TV is deceptive, that's because reality itself is deceptive. As Plato demonstrated through his 'Allegory of the Cave' we can't always be certain of what's real and what merely appears to be real.

We are all in the cave. If we rely on our perceptions to apprehend reality and can't always tell the difference between appearance and reality – there being no conclusive distinguishing marks between the two – then what's so different between real 'reality' and the apparent 'reality' of reality TV? As Renee Descartes pointed out so poignantly in his *Meditations*, reality or what we perceive reality to be, could be a dream or a grand illusion caused by the mere logical possibility of a 'deceitful demon' who lies to us about the very existence of an external world.[14] The contemporary equivalent of Descartes' argument of the 'deceitful demon' is the 'brains in vats' scenario. For all we know, the argument posits, we could be brains immersed in vats on Alpha Centaury and connected to a super-computer that manipulates us to make us believe falsely that we are at home watching our favourite reality show or reading this chapter. Our clever objector may proceed to add that if it is all a deception and a grand illusion, and we can't be certain of any reality let alone that of reality TV, we may as well sit back, relax and enjoy it. Not bad advice if you enjoy watching reality shows or are anxious of flying.

To Thine Own Self Be True

Even if we accept this radical sceptical stance about the certainty of reality, there is the significant and all-important matter of integrity, honesty and truthful sentiments and values. For even in a totally illusory and unreal world, our consciousness of who we are, irrespective of what we are and where we are, must be real in order to experience this total deception and mull over it. That lived consciousness that makes us who we are must still be true to itself. For as the bard reminds us:

> *This above all: to thine own self be true,*
> *And it must follow, as the night the day,*
> *Thou canst not then be false to any man.*[15]

Reality TV is no exception to that fundamental human principle. Being true to oneself is the bottom line of ethics and the human condition. It is called integrity. If we don't know or can't know the ultimate truth of reality or can't be certain of the values reality shows promote, we can at least be truthful to ourselves and by so being, be true to others.

Notes

1 Edward H. Spence, 'A Universal Model for the Normative Evaluation of Internet Information', *Ethics and Information Technology* 11, no. 4 (2009): 243–53; and Edward H. Spence and Aaron Quinn, 'Information Ethics as a Guide for New Media', *Journal of Mass Media Ethics* 23, no. 4 (2008): 264–79.

2 Plato, *The Republic*, Book VII, The Internet Classics Archive. http://classics. mit.edu/Plato/republic.8.vii.html.

3 William Shakespeare, *Hamlet,* Act 3, Scene, 1, William Shakespeare Literature. http://www.shakespeare-literature.com/Hamlet/8.html.

4 Plato, *The Republic*, Book II, The Internet Classics Archive. http://classics.mit. edu/Plato/republic.3.ii.html.

5 Ibid.

6 Ibid.

7 Aristotle, *The Nicomachean Ethics*, 5th edn, trans. F. H. Peters (London: Kegan Paul, Trench, Truebner & Co., 1893).

8 James Edwin Mahon, 'A Definition of Deceiving', *International Journal of Applied Philosophy* 21, no. 2 (2007): 192.

9 Sissela Bok, *Lying: Moral Choice in Public and Private Life* (New York: Vintage Books, 1999) xxi.

10 Ibid.

11 William Shakespeare, *The Tempest*, Act, Scene 1. The Complete Works of William Shakespeare. http://shakespeare.mit.edu/tempest/tempest.5.1.html.

12 SBS Television, *Go Back to Where You Came From*, 2011. http://www.sbs.com.au/shows/goback.

13 William Shakespeare, *As You Like It*, Act 2, scene, 7, lines 139–43. http://www.enotes.com/shakespeare-quotes/all-world-s-stage.

14 René Descartes, *Meditations on First Philosophy*, ed. John Cottingham (Cambridge: Cambridge University Press, 1996).

15 William Shakespeare, *Hamlet*, Act, 1, scene 3. http://www.enotes.com/shakespeare-quotes/thine-own-self-true.

9

Democracy and Discourse: How Reality TV Fosters Citizenship

Deni Elliott

Through reality TV, we are introduced to the families of *Teen Mom*: "A year after the adoption, Catelynn and Tyler have an emotional reunion with their daughter Carly. Amber & Gary try to work out custody of Leah now that they are broken up and dating other people."[1]

... And those of *Little People, Big World*: This is a "reality series about life in a family of little people, also sometimes called midgets or dwarves. Standing only four feet tall, Matt and Amy Roloff are struggling to raise their four children, who are mixed in stature, on their 34-acre farm."[2]

... And *Sister Wives*: "Meet husband Kody – along with his four wives: Meri, Janelle, Christine and Robyn and their combined 16 children – and see how they attempt to navigate life as a 'normal' family in a society that shuns their lifestyle. From their unconventional family structure and living arrangements to financial challenges, each episode exposes the inner workings of a polygamist household, revealing the unexpectedly tight-knit and loving relationships between Kody's wives." [3]

These shows are intriguing, but what do they have to do with democracy, the subject of this chapter? It's easy to think that the values portrayed by reality TV and those that support democracy are at opposite ends of a spectrum. According to this view, reality TV is all about exploitation of private individuals who sacrifice dignity and integrity to achieve fame and fortune. Reality TV promotes deception as contestants in direct competition first befriend and then betray each other in their climb to the top. Dating and performance shows seem to delight in denigrating and rejecting untalented participants or those who don't conform to mainstream society values. The programs themselves are deceptive in that producers snip and attach material to create a patchwork-quilt storyline of their own invention. The dramatic narratives are comprised of living, breathing quotes and segments that have momentary truth but that lack contextual accuracy. They are exploitative, fictional and intentionally hurtful, according to the accounts of many of the wounded characters.

At the other end of the spectrum, we have democracy, a governing and societal ideology that promotes the values of individual freedom and community good. It is relational and trusting of the outcomes of both liberty and civic process in that it asks each to speak his or her truth, drawing citizens together for civic (and civil) discussion while simultaneously allowing maximum freedom for individuals.

Of course, neither of these extremes addresses the variety of experiences that occur on reality TV or in the practice of democracy. Reality TV can certainly be argued to cause unjustified harms, and those arguments can be found elsewhere in this volume. While democracy preaches acceptance and equality, a long string of minority groups including women, people of non-European descent, people who identify as gay, lesbian, bi-sexual or trans-gendered, people who aren't Christian, and people with disabilities have historically been denied a place in the polis by law and by convention.

It is precisely because of the limitations of how democracy is practised – and because of the limitations that individuals create for themselves by gravitating toward sources and resources that simply reinforce their own prejudices – that reality TV can be instrumental in promoting a more vibrant and accepting civic life. This chapter reviews communication essentials for the ideal practice of democracy and illustrates how the presentation and viewing of alternative lifestyles through reality TV can be instrumental in supporting those communication essentials.

Reality TV helps promote democracy in the following ways: First, viewers have a safe opportunity to see how people who are different from them think and live. Yes, editing can skew the "reality" of reality TV, but when comparing participants in reality TV with actors in situation comedies or made-for-television dramas, viewers believe that reality TV participants are presenting real lifestyles and beliefs. Second, reality shows help viewers better understand what they think, believe and value. Viewers imagine themselves in reality TV situations and try on how they might respond in those situations. The vicarious experience provides an opportunity for viewers to think more deeply about themselves. Finally, through reality shows, viewers have an opportunity to experience democratic action. Some shows demonstrate community involvement and philanthropy, others promote the common good through encouraging individuals to develop a democratic sensibility, and still other shows lead to discussions that are governed by the rules of civil discourse, where individuals can practice having conversations that contribute to a truly deliberative democracy.

Each of these ways in which reality TV can promote democracy will be explored later in the chapter. Before that, however, the chapter will set some foundations by, first, introducing the fundamentals of a deliberative democracy, which can be applied to reality TV, and, second, considering reality TV's origins and how those have contributed to its development as a genre that can promote democratic practice.

The Dream of Democracy

Democracy at its best is self-governance that grows out of citizens engaging in civic discourse about controversies and choices facing their communities. At its core, democracy requires that, first, citizens know what they believe about public controversies and, second, that they express those beliefs through actions they think enact or reinforce those beliefs. Or, if citizens choose not to actively participate, it follows logically (although not necessarily emotionally) that they should be content to let other citizens make public policy decisions on their behalf. Democracy that is deliberative, however, demands much more than expressing an opinion.

Deliberative democracy is based on collective engagement rather than individual expression of belief. This sophisticated view of group decision-making starts with the assumption that citizens cannot understand their world or even their own views without actively engaging the ideas of others. Long before reality TV and an interactive internet, British philosopher John Stuart Mill argued that it is essential for citizens to seek out opinions different from their own because they have a duty to "form the truest opinions they can."[4]

Mill noticed that few people looked beyond their own beliefs. We can see this today when people listen only to those who reinforce their own viewpoints or consume only those media sources that reflect their particular worldviews. What communication scholars today call "selective exposure" Mill argued was a sign that people didn't have justification for whatever they might believe. He said that most people "have never thrown themselves into the mental position of those who think differently from them, and consider what such persons may have to say; and consequently they do not, in any proper sense of the word, know the doctrine which they themselves profess."[5]

Mill offered four reasons citizens need to seek opinions different from their own: (i) the contrasting opinion might be true or partly true; (ii) even if the contrasting view is completely false, there is good reason to seek it out because looking at our own point of view against one that is completely false helps us remember why we believe what we do. Our true opinion is better understood when tested against alternative points of view; (iii) it is likely that an opposing view has some elements of truth that we might have previously ignored; and (iv) the constant testing of beliefs is good for society. An opinion shared by a group, a nation, even a world of people may lose its meaning or context – that is, become "dead dogma" in Mill's words – if it goes unquestioned.[6]

The process citizens use to form the truest opinions possible so they can best participate in self-governance is the process of civic discourse. Citizens hear different points of view, check out the facts, and really work to understand how other people think and why they think it. Mill describes a person who engages in this process as someone "who has the calmness to see and honesty to state what his [or her] opponents and their opinions really are, exaggerating nothing to their discredit, keeping nothing back which tells, or can be supposed to tell, in their favour." Mill adds that, "this is the real morality of public discussion."[7]

Mill argued that as citizens become educated about the differences and needs of their fellow citizens, they begin to understand that each person's self-interest is benefited by making the community as a whole good for everyone. Rather than compete for societal goods, enlightened citizens are propelled to recognize the common humanity among people and make choices that support the good of the whole. This can be understand philosophically, in that one's own need is no more important than the basic needs of every other individual. Or it can be understood pragmatically, in that we are certainly happier if we live in communities that are safe where individuals are not driven to steal what they need.

Contemporary scholars have put the argument for engaged and thoughtful discussion in a slightly different context than Mill did. They emphasize that what's important is not just the expression of opinion, but of deliberation about which opinion is best and why. For example, according to political theorist Jane Mansbridge:

If a deliberative system works well, it filters out and discards the worst ideas available on public matters while it picks up, adopts, and applies the best ideas. If the deliberative system works badly, it distorts facts, portrays ideas in forms that their originators would disown, and encourages citizens to adopt ways of thinking and acting that are good neither for them nor for the larger polity. A deliberative system, at its best, like all systems of democratic participation, helps its participants understand themselves and their environment better.[8]

The Familiar Frame of Reality TV

With the proliferation of reality TV programs that focus on narrow, segmented and specialized portions of the audience, such as bargain shoppers (*Extreme Couponing*) or people with problem dogs (*The Animal Whisperer*), it's easy to forget that television has a history of encouraging viewer inter-activity from the mass audience and giving viewers a peek at lives different from their own.

Television has long served as a medium that allows selected private individuals to exchange exposure for fame and fortune. Historically, quiz shows did not ask contestants to risk bodily injury or eat live bugs, but they selected and reinforced individuals who demonstrated exaggerated responses or otherwise played best to the medium. For examples, the producers of shows like *The Dating Game* (which first aired on ABC from 1965 to 1973) and *The Newlywed Game* (which ran on ABC from 1966 to 1984) edited their shows to serve up half-hour programs rich with conflict and sexual references that kept audiences coming back for more.

Queen for a Day, which ran weekly on NBC from 1956 to 1960 and then on ABC for an additional four years, provided an eerily prescient example of audiences selecting their favorite contestant and deciding who should be eliminated. *TV.com* describes this precursor to reality TV like this:

> Four women, each having a sob story to tell, told [host Jack] Bailey why they believed they should be crowned the show's "Queen For a Day." Usually, each contestant asked for a merchandise prize such as a washer and dryer. After all four sad stories were told, the audience chose the winner by applause (determined via the "applause meter"). The winner was awarded her prizes and was bedecked in a sable-trimmed red velvet robe and jeweled crown. Interspersed between the contestants' stories was fashion commentary.[9]

PBS's *An American Family* in 1973 and then MTV's *The Real World* in 1992 and CBS's *Survivor* in 2000 were "earthy anthropological experiments," according to *The New Yorker's* Kelefa Sanneh, that showed the economic worth of creating drama from encounters between "real people" instead of actors.[10] Over time, the genre has evolved to include the theme of reality TV participants bettering themselves in the process. The "transformation" narrative that Sanneh describes[11] fits neatly into the American assumption that individuals have the freedom to gain self-knowledge and become better – physically and spiritually – than they were prior to some pivotal experience (such as appearing on a reality TV show). This assumption fits nicely into the notion that citizens have a duty to grow and develop through public exposure and public discourse. The viewers' vicarious experience complemented by their ability to express their ideas and hear the ideas of others in interactive community discussions potentially allows viewers to learn as much as the participants do. In fact, Laurie Ouellette and James Hay call reality TV a contemporary source of "guidelines for living" for viewers, who see the ordinary people on reality TV as examples of what – or what not – to do to succeed as citizens.[12]

Experiencing People With Different Ideas and Lifestyles

One attraction of reality TV is that it exposes viewers to participants who are strongly perceived to be "like" them. As one *Survivor* viewer said: "I like the fact that it's real people – people I can identify with instead of superstars and Olympians." Another viewer who is part of the predominant demographic to which reality TV caters, women aged 18 to 25, wrote: "I can see myself or others I know in the actions of those on television."[13] Involving participants who are seen by the audience as "regular" people also suspends "the typical dominance of expert and official knowledge over television content."[14]

But reality TV also exposes viewers to people who are perceived to be *unlike* them. This is important for democracy. As Mill argued, citizens must try on the ideas of others to really know their own and to find the best truth possible. Reality TV can open a window for viewers into a community larger than their own circle of family, friends and neighbourhood. Andy Dehnart, who runs the reality TV website *Realityblurred.com*, said: "Television can provide an intimate entry point into the lives of people who are otherwise misunderstood or underestimated." [15] We're offered this entry through a non-threatening process that allows us to simply "take it all in," to see how others live, how others think, and what others value. We may not have any sense what it's like to be a teenager with a child, but *Teen Mom* gives us an idea. We may have never met a little person, but *Little People, Big World* gives us that chance. We may have definite perceptions about polygamy, but *Sister Wives* helps show us how accurate – or inaccurate – those perceptions are. (This book's Chapter 2 on stereotyping also makes the case that viewers have an ethical duty to try to get used to those who may differ from them.)

Exposure is the first step; interaction comes next. Viewers of many reality shows are encouraged to engage with one another in blog discussions hosted by network- or interest-based websites. The discussions, or community groups as they are sometimes called, provide further opportunity for viewers (or "posters") to be exposed to beliefs and opinions different from their own. Through discussion with others, viewers can further formulate their own ideas regarding the lifestyle or situational challenges posed by reality TV participants.

Sister Wives provides an example of this point as viewers discuss the polygamous lifestyle examined in that reality TV show. Using the familiar "argument by analogy," discussants in this Celebitchy blog[16] struggle to decide what polygamy is like:

> *Heatheradair*: My problem with the entire glamorization of their lifestyle is the message it sends their kids. These kids are being taught that it's OK not to expect your dad to be around more than a night or so a week … and this is different than kids of divorced parents who might only see their parents on the weekend.

> *Hakura*: You make some very good points … I don't think it's right for the state to pursue a prosecution for 'polygamy' when Kody is only *legally* married to one of the women. Polygamy, like gay marriage, is an example of the law applying 'traditional religious moral standards' to people's lifestyle choices … I'm torn as to how this affects children.

> *Pakka*: So what – he's not forcing me to be his wife so I don't care … I am … fascinated by it.

> *Carol*: I love this show. I wanted to hate him but I thought he came off better on the show.

> *Lisa*: Leave this family alone! They are wonderful parents and they seem to love each other very much.

Mandy: Who are WE to judge their lifestyle? ... I'm sure people thought the first women to ask for voting rights or the first black people to insist on being able to sit in the front of the bus with the whites were "disgusting" as well but thankfully our world continues to grow and evolve and accept.

These viewers use analogies and disanalogies to express their own beliefs, and the common comparisons help them to understand how other viewers think. They are all trying out the foreign lifestyle against those with which they are more familiar. "What is polygamy *like*?" might be the theme of this exchange. Is it like same-sex marriage or other civil rights issues from the past? Is the relationship of a child to a polygamous parent like that of the relationship between a child and divorced parent, or not? What viewers think polygamous marriage is like helps inform their opinions. In exchange, trying on others' analogies opens new pathways for how to think about the unfamiliar lifestyle.

In another example, a *Supernanny* discussion group member, who is wondering how to control her daughter when she becomes a toddler, starts off a thread with this question: "Are there some alternative techniques, other than those shown by the Nanny, that are equally effective?" In response, spanking is suggested, which leads to a discussion of how to discipline small children. Other posters warn readers to "steer clear of physical punishment/violence." Instead, they are encouraged to put the child to bed with kisses and cuddles after a warm bath. "Don't use your words! Just hit," says one poster, "is not a lesson I want to impart to my child."[17]

Not all conversations about reality TV, however, encourage diversity of thought. *Blind Date* is a show that uses animated pop-ups for producers to comment on participants' clothes or actions, or to superimpose what participants "really" think or mean (or what interpretation the producers think makes for good entertainment). According to one analysis, "*Blind Date* aims to reinforce stereotypically desirable characteristics for partner selection, related to gender, class and ethnic representations, by framing the divergent participants via the supertext in a manner that comically punishes deviance from hegemonic norms,"[18] Indeed,

producers go out of their way to attract and select daters from outside the mainstream who do not embody the traditionally desirable characteristics of a mate ... [Then] the show seizes the opportunity to poke fun at daters who exhibit marginal or unorthodox characteristics, going so far as to place participants in situations designed to make their deviance from social norms appear comical.[19]

In doing so, producers are implicitly telling viewers how they should respond – with derision to men who value something other than high income and with ridicule toward women who try to relate to something other than men's physical attributes.

Ultimately reality TV shows are controlled by their producers. Do producers want viewers to believe that a woman's breasts are her most important assets regardless of her graduate degree and professional career? If so, animated pop-ups in *Blind Date* point the way to that conclusion. On the other hand, producers can provide viewers the opportunity to compare their own ideas with others but without the inclusion of canned judgments that lead viewers to the "right" conclusion. Consider, for example, the parenting styles of families portrayed on *Supernanny*. It is assumed that the families chosen to appear on that show and other similar help-oriented programs have a problem to solve. But the locus of the problem and the nanny's treatment are transparent enough that viewers can feel engaged and provoked by the *process* as well as by the outcome.

Developing Self-Knowledge

After being exposed to the ideas of others, the next step essential for democracy is to apply that new knowledge to better understand what we ourselves think, believe and value – in other words, to further develop our sense of self. Mill argued that one can come to know the truth only by testing one's views against the views of others. Hearing others" ideas is not simply an exercise in tolerance but rather an instrumental part of developing a coherent view of one's own. Mill warned that the ability to change or clarify one's values and beliefs is fragile. "Capacity for the nobler feelings is in most natures a very tender plant," he says. "Easily killed, not only by hostile influences, but by mere want of sustenance."[20] Viewing reality TV can provide that sustenance needed for developing those "nobler feelings," as can participating in community discussion groups about reality TV.

Viewers confronting their own biases or assumptions can recognize alternative perspectives offered by reality TV participants. In one example, Zach Anner, a comedian with cerebral palsy, received hundreds of phone calls after co-winning *Your OWN Show: Oprah's Search for the Next TV Star*, on which he proposed a wheelchair-based travel program. One of those calls came from a man whose son had just been in an accident. "He was crying because my idea gave him inspiration that he and his son could travel someday."[21] The reality TV participant inspired this viewer to think of new possibilities for himself. Sarah Reinertsen, an amputee who finished seventh on *The Amazing Race 10*, taught a viewer a similar lesson. While taking a walk in a short skirt that exposed her metal prosthetic leg, Reinertsen was stopped by a stranger who recognized her from the show. This man's friend had recently lost his leg in Iraq. According to Reinertsen, the friend had been "totally depressed, but watching me on the show had totally renewed his hope... That's when I realized just how powerful the show really was and that it could help change perceptions and lives."[22] This power of reality television illustrates what Ouellette and Hay mean when they call television a "cultural technology" that can shape individuals and democracy.[23]

Online discussions about reality TV can also prove powerful as we develop coherent views about ourselves and about the world around us. A 21-year-old *Teen Mom* viewer and poster who said she was a mother of four, started an online discussion thread on the MTV website by saying that she "got pregnant at 15 and [has] had it very hard and complicated ever since ... I'm sick to death of these teenagers coming on these shows and putting on a show that life is so hard for them, when they have no idea."[24] The clear statement provoked others into stating their own truths:

Maybe you need to stop having kids and get a job.

I'm very sorry for it all, but it will turn out to be ok.

Everyone's situation is different. The girls on the show lucked out by getting a nice paycheck for having their lives taped. But there are thousands of others who have it just like you or worse.

You have it hard because you have made it hard for yourself.

We all have our own hard knock story as teen moms ... we need to prevent future girls from following the same road ... use your story to help with prevention and education.[25]

Through this online discussion, the mom who started the thread is given the chance to consider (or reconsider) her own views about herself in light of those offered by other posters.

While growth and change is a laudable goal for those watching reality TV and participating in discussions about it, the result can also be simple reinforcement of viewers' beliefs. For Mill, this reinforcement is one reason for listening to false opinion: we remember why we hold the true ideas that we do. For at least one *Supernannny* poster, this is exactly what participating in the online discussion accomplished. "I have to say, watching this show makes me think I'm a pretty darn good mom, and my kids' behavior is fantastic (relatively speaking)."[26]

Experiencing Community Involvement, Democratic Action and Civil Discourse

Community Involvement

Mill recognized that happiness is found, in part, through realizing that society has shortcomings and that individuals can be actively involved in making the world a better place. While Mill acknowledged that relieving human suffering is "grievously slow," those who engage in helping others "will draw a noble enjoyment" from the act itself. [27] Shows like *Extreme Makeover: Home Edition* and *Secret Millionaire* provide examples of individuals and corporations joining forces to help those in need. Philanthropic action requires that those who can help must first recognize the need, then think creatively about how they might best help, and finally have the motivation to carry through with helpful action. Philanthropic reality shows demonstrate all three of these requirements. The formula results in both individuals who are better off by the end of the show and satisfied participants who contributed to the good action. Mill would find the formula an effective illustration of what he considers true individual happiness.

Ouellette and Hay suggest that philanthropic reality shows fill a public and social service role that government in an era of deregulation and privatization has failed to fill and that the shows may introduce needy people to active roles as functioning citizens.[28] However, these shows are not without their detractors. Media critic Christian Blauvelt says of *Secret Millionaire*: "While it's admirable that ABC is giving deserving non-profit organizations much needed publicity that they wouldn't receive otherwise, the narrative impulse of the series – based largely around rich folks encountering the less fortunate – reveals much about how lacking our national dialogue on poverty remains."[29] But Blauvelt's comments did not go unchecked. In true illustration of the interactivity of realty TV discussion groups, many of the viewer-commentators critiqued Blauvelt's criticism. They said the good works should be celebrated, not "bashed."

Democratic Action

Reality TV history is littered with the tarnished crowns of program heroes whose avarice has led to tragic ends. But among the "teen moms" charged with drunk and disorderly conduct and "survivors" who are arrested for domestic violence or assault, we also see participants turn the popularity of their shows into political power. In July 2011, *Sister Wives* provided a good example of how reality TV can lead directly to democratic action when Kody Brown and his four wives filed a federal lawsuit, asking that Utah's bigamy statute be declared unconstitutional.[30]Jonathan Turley, the attorney representing the family, said: "What they are asking for is the right to structure their own lives, their own family, according to their faith and their beliefs."[31] Turley added that "the focus of the lawsuit is really privacy – not polygamy," and the suit follows the principles of other lawsuits that have held "private intimate relationships between consenting adults' are constitutionally protected.[32]

The same month, ABC announced that first lady Michelle Obama would appear on an upcoming episode of *Extreme Makeover: Home Edition*. Obama was to help expand a centre for homeless female veterans located near Fort Bragg in Fayetteville, North Carolina, another of her efforts intended to assist those in the armed services.[33] Real life public officials stepping into reality TV reinforces the truth of the experience, as do reality TV participants stepping from the front of the television camera into the courtroom.

Another example of combining reality TV with a view toward the democratic goal of promoting the community good is the network, OWN, The Oprah Winfrey Network. OWN calls itself "the first network about living your best life."[34] According to a 2009 news release announcing the network, its goal "is to create an innovative experience for that broad audience of people who are living their lives with a purpose."[35] Audiences are rewarded for viewing by being identified as "living their lives with a purpose," and shows are classified as "Best Life All Stars," "Best Life Experiences" and "Best Life Inspiration." The network airs documentaries, magazine shows and fictional programs but also reality shows. Viewers are recruited to participate in some of these reality shows through a "Casting Call" page on the website, which also invites community discussion of the shows.

Civil Discourse

For deliberative democracy to truly be promoted, deliberations must be productive. Oprah.com "House Rules" provide specific guidance for those who wish to participate in online conversations about the network's reality shows, OWN as a whole, and *O* magazine.[36] In doing so, Oprah.com also helps shape *civic* discourse by insisting on *civil* discourse. "[W]e require respect and good manners from everyone participating in our online communities, commenting forums, twitter feeds, message boards, blogs, O Groups, chat rooms, user review forums or other interactive communities."[37] Oprah.com explicitly states hallmarks of deliberative democracy in providing the boundaries of participation:

> Our community is a place where people can strive to live their best lives, achieve personal growth and generate positive, thoughtful dialogue. Members can come to one another for support, comfort and shared experiences. While we invite healthy debate, Oprah.com is not intended as a forum for personal attacks and destructive postings.[38]

Consuelo Arroyo, President of NETIZEN Media Solutions, who manages the OWN communities, said that no messages are trimmed or edited for content. A message is either judged as appropriate within the guidelines or is not posted to the site. The writer is then notified of the reason the message was denied.[39]

Reality TV World, a website devoted to all things reality TV, is more explicit in its warning to posters and more aggressive in its moderation of discussions. The following warning appears at the top of the discussion forum page:

> The Reality TV World Message Boards are filled with desperate attention-seekers pretending to be one big happy PG/PG13-rated family. Don't be fooled. Trying to get everyone to agree with you is like herding cats, but intolerance for other viewpoints is NOT welcome and respect for other posters IS required at all times. Jump in and play, and you'll soon find out how easy it is to fit in, but save your drama for your mama. All members are encouraged to read the complete guidelines. As entertainment critic Roger Ebert once said: 'If you disagree with something I write, tell me so, argue with me, correct me – but don't tell me to shut up. That's not the American way.'[40]

In contrast to OWN with its "use it or lose it" approach to viewer messages, Reality TV World posts a "flag" button next to each post, inviting readers to alert the forum moderator to violation of rules or standards. On a variety of discussion groups, posters have indicated that parts of their messages have been edited, although they contend those messages did not violate the site's guidelines.[41] As this example demonstrates, the tension between free speech and regulation aimed at keeping civic discourse non-offensive is no different online than it is in the physical world.

Reality TV as Stimulus but Not Solution

Passive consumption of reality TV, or even the more active involvement in web-based discussions of the programs, will not alone make viewers better citizens. Freedom of expression, in reception and in production, is of instrumental worth only. The emotional involvement provoked through reality TV and interactive community groups does not fulfil citizens' responsibility to act; it is just a start. Education is needed to help citizens recognize both their power to act directly in the public arena and the methods they can use to take direct action. Nonetheless, reality TV can provide an easy avenue for citizens to be exposed to lifestyles different from their own, to develop self-knowledge, and to experience a variety of forms of democratic action.

Notes

1 MTV, "Season 2, Episode 212 Summary," *Teen Mom*, 2011. http://www.mtv. com/shows/teen_mom/season_2/episode.jhtml?episodeID=170102#mor einfo.

2 TV.com, *Little People Big World*, 2011. http://www.tv.com/little-people-big-world/show/61776/summary.html?tag=page_nav;main.

3 TLC, "About the Show," *Sister Wives*, 2011. http://tlc.howstuffworks.com/tv/ sister-wives/about-sister-wives.htm.

4 John Stuart Mill, "On Liberty," in *John Stuart Mill: On Liberty and Other Essays*, John Gray ed. (New York: Oxford University Press, 1859/1991) 59.

5 Ibid., 42–3.

6 Ibid., 59.

7 Ibid., 61.

8 Jane Mansbridge, "Everyday Talk in the Deliberative System," in *Deliberative Politics: Essays on Democracy and Disagreement*, Steven Macedo ed. (New York: Oxford University Press, 1999) 211.

9 TV.com, "Show Overview," *Queen for a Day*, 2011. http://www.tv.com/queen-for-a-day/show/20880/summary.html.

10 Kelefa Sanneh, "The Reality Principle: The Rise and Rise of a Television Genre," *The New Yorker*, 9 May 2011, 72.

11 Ibid., 75.

12 Laurie Ouellette and James Hay, *Better Living Through Reality TV: Television and Post-Welfare Citizenship* (Malden, MA: Blackwell, 2008).

13 Mark Andrejevic, *Reality TV: The Work of Being Watched* (Lanham: Rowman & Littlefield, 2004) 9.

14 Justin DeRose, ElfriedeFürsich and Ekaterina Haskins, "Pop (Up) Goes the 'Blind Date': Supertextual Constraints on 'Reality' Television."' *Journal of Communication Inquiry* 27 (2003): 173.

15 Neal Justin, "Reality TV Gets More Real," Star Tribune, 17 April 2011, 1E.

16 These excerpts have been edited for space and emphasis. Deleted sections are indicated by ellipsis marks. See Celebitchy.com, "Sister Wives Husand Kody Admits He Gets his Wives' Names Mixed Up," 10 March 2011. http://www.celebitchy.com/145013/

17 Ibid.

18 DeRose, Fursich and Haskins, "Pop (Up) Goes the Blind Date," 172.

19 Ibid., 176–7.

20 Mill, *On Liberty*, 141.

21 Justin, "Reality TV gets more real," 1E.

22 Ibid.

23 Ouellette and Hay, *Better Living Through Reality TV*, 2–3.

24 MTV, "Message Board," *Teen Mom – Your Story*, 2011. http://community.mtv.com/Content/Discussions/DiscussionResults.aspx?tcid=39738.

25 Ibid.

26 Reality TV World, "Message Board Forum," *Super Nanny*, February 2005. http://community.realitytvworld.com/boards//DCForumID17/1171.shtml.

27 Mill, *On Liberty*, 146.

28 Ouellette and Hay, *Better Living Through Reality TV*, 14–33.

29 Christian Blauvelt, "ABC's 'Secret Millionaire': Why it Sends the Wrong Message," Entertainment Weekly.com, 6 March 2011. http://popwatch.ew.com/2011/03/06/secret-millionaire.

30 Associated Press, "'Sister Wives' Stars Challenge Utah Bigamy Law," 14 July 2011. Available at First Amendment Center. http://www.firstamendmentcenter.org/sister-wives-stars-challenge-utah-bigamy-law.

31 Ibid.

32 Ibid.

33 Peter Gicas, "Michelle Obama to Guest Star on Extreme Makeover: Home Edition," Eonline, 20 July 2011. http://www.eonline.com/news/michelle_obama.

34 Discovery Communications, "OWN: The Oprah Winfrey Network Gives Sneak Peek of New Network Dedicated to Living Your Best Life," 2 April 2009. http://corporate.discovery.com/discovery-news/own-the-oprah-winfrey-network-gives-sneak-peek-of-/.

35 Ibid.

36 See Oprah.com, "House Rules," 22 June 2011. http://www.oprah.com/oprahdotcom/House-Rules.

37 Ibid.

38 Ibid.

39 Consuelo Arroyo (president of NETIZEN Media Solutions), in discussion with the author, July 2011, personal communication.

40 Reality TV World, "Guidelines," *Message Board Forums*, 2011. http://community.realitytvworld.com/cgi-sys/cgiwrap/rtvw2/community/dcboard.cgi?

41 Ibid.

10

Exploitation: When Reality TV Becomes Degradation TV

Wendy N. Wyatt

Perhaps more than any other, one criticism is routinely leveled against the reality television genre: exploitation.

For instance, in a January 2009 piece in *The Boston Globe*, TV critic Joan Anderman said that by watching reality television, we've "finally cultivated a taste for pure humiliation, hostile confrontation and all-purpose exploitation."[1] Anderman's British counterpart, Fiona McIntosh of the Sunday *Mirror,* agreed: "Reality TV has been around long enough for every man and his dog to know it's exploitation by any other name. It brings out the worst in anyone."[2]

Many allegations of exploitation relate to reality shows involving children. In Canada's *National Post*, Kathryn Blaze Carlson wrote a story headlined "Rise of kidsploitation: They're in the spotlight like never before, but are the children all right?." [3]The article considered the treatment of children appearing in such reality shows as *Kid Nation*, *Jon and Kate Plus 8* and *Baby Borrowers*. David Aaronovitch offered a similar critique in his *Times* of London story. His headline read: "We must hate kids to put them through this; People moan about invasion of privacy but are happy to see children exploited for their own sneering entertainment."[4]

Some members of the press have accused not only reality shows of being exploiters but also the media that cover those shows so incessantly. In her article, "Squirming, but watching a dying reality star," Sara Lyall, London correspondent for *The New York Times*, reflected on the life and impending death of Jade Goody, the UK's most famous resident of the *Big Brother* house and a reality TV celebrity. When Goody was diagnosed with terminal cervical cancer, a handful of media outlets bought the rights to her end-of-life story. Many of those same outlets were, in Lyall's words, "intermittently nasty about Ms Goody, holding her up as a sorry symbol of vulgarian, instant-gratification Britain." But with her death, media were "squirming with unease at their collusion in the endless building up, knocking down and exploitation of a woman they always counted on to increase their own sales." [5]

The charge of exploitation has been leveled so often against reality television – a July 2011 Google search for "reality TV" and "exploitation" yielded 3.24 million hits – that a number of critics have changed its name to humiliation TV. Some, such as American Studies professor Nicolaus Mills, have gone as far as to say that today's reality TV has created a *culture* of humiliation where no one – participants nor producers nor audience members – comes away with his or her dignity intact.[6] As *Time* magazine television critic James Poniewozik, the author of this book's Foreword, once noted, reality TV is the one mass-entertainment category that thrives because of its audience's contempt for it.[7] Although some of this contempt is for reasons such as aesthetics, the case against exploitation by reality TV is largely a moral one.

This chapter is a philosophical analysis of the charge that reality TV exploits. It uses Ruth Sample's account of exploitation from her book *Exploitation: What It Is and Why It's Wrong*[8] to determine, from a theoretically grounded position, whether and in what cases the charge is justifiable. The impetus behind the analysis is a concern that if reality television truly is exploitative, then we as audiences – as stakeholders with a good deal of power to determine a show's future – should feel morally obligated to do something about it.

The Assumption

A thread that connects many moral critiques of reality television is an assumption that the meaning of exploitation is both clear and shared.[9] A critic who charges reality TV with being exploitative may give specific examples from different shows, but rarely does that critic explore fully *how* the example satisfies the conditions of exploitation. In fact, many pieces of scholarship on reality TV explicitly recognize the exploitative nature of the shows,[10] but they stop short of grappling with what exploitation means. Of course, media critics are not necessarily philosophers, and those critics shouldn't be prohibited from using a word like exploitation in the ordinary, pedestrian sense. But if we truly want to understand whether reality TV is exploitative – a forceful charge that, as noted earlier, may obligate people to act against it – a more sophisticated application of the word is required.

While no one has fully explored the nature of exploitation in reality television, a few scholars have hinted at what, particularly, makes the programs exploitative. Annette Hill, for instance, noted that viewers are more likely to levy exploitation charges against reality shows that mistreat animals and children because they are "perceived as 'vulnerable' and, therefore, cause for concern."[11] Hill, then, connects exploitation with vulnerability. Clifford Christians and his colleagues argued that "reality television as a genre must face up to Kant's claims that each person should be valued, no one should be treated as fodder for another's exploitation. To violate this principle is more than 'dissing' an eighteenth-century philosopher. It is, rather, to put human relationships in jeopardy."[12] This approach considers exploitation a violation against Kant's categorical imperative that requires treating people not as mere means to an end, but as ends in themselves. Also adopting a Kantian approach are Angela Cooke-Jackson and Elizabeth Hansen, who considered the ethical implications of depicting stereotypes of subcultures, specifically Appalachia, in CBS's proposed reality show *The Real Beverly Hillbillies*.[13] Comparing the proposed show with works of fiction such as *The Beverly Hillbillies*, the authors argued that the proposed show was not ethically justifiable: "Stereotypes used by the producers of fiction may harm the members of the subculture as a whole but do not target individuals as directly as a reality television show that exploits an Appalachian family."[14] Finally, in her analysis of weight loss/makeover reality shows, Berrin Beasley also implied a Kantian-based prohibition of participants' exploitation based on their negative body images.[15]

The Theoretical Framework

The specifics of Sample's approach to exploitation are outlined in the sections below, which apply her theory to reality television, but a few key ideas are important to point out first. The work both builds on and critiques two of the leading philosophical accounts of the wrongness of exploitation: Alan Wertheimer's "unfairness" approach[16] and Robert Goodin's "vulnerability" approach.[17] While Sample agrees with Wertheimer that exploitation can be voluntary and mutually beneficial, she critiques his theory "for failing to be able to account for exploitative interpersonal relationships."[18] She also disagrees with Wertheimer's market-based claim that exploitation cannot occur if workers are paid a competitive wage. Likewise, Sample sees virtues in Goodin's account but ultimately rejects its consequentialist nature as "too implausible" and "also at odds with our basic understanding of exploitation."[19] What Sample arrives at, then, is a largely Kantian account of exploitation (although she notes it is compatible with a wide range of moral theories). Her account defines exploitation as interactions with another that seek advantage and that fail to recognize the value inherent in that being. The account is both descriptive in that it aims "to capture what we seem to mean when we complain of exploitation" as well as normative in that it describes what we *ought* to mean.[20]

Sample's theory does have its critics.[21] But Yusuf Has argued that her book is "systematic and open-minded" and "capable of forcing anyone who reads it to rethink his established notions about what exploitation involves and what makes it wrong."[22] Jon Mandle called Sample's work "a powerful and original account of exploitation that distinguishes exploitation from other moral faults and explains precisely why it is morally objectionable."[23] Even Alan Wertheimer, whom Sample critiques, noted that the book "raises many important questions and should be read by anyone interested in the concept of exploitation." [24]

Exploitation as Degradation

Although Sample doesn't consider reality television in her book, she does introduce several cases outside the reality TV realm, apply her own account to those cases, and test them for exploitation.[25] This chapter extends Sample's examples and seeks to identify whether exploitation occurs on reality TV. Because it is producers of reality TV who most routinely are charged with being exploiters, the chapter will focus on their potential blameworthiness.[26] But one question is worth posing, if only rhetorically, here: Can any of the other stakeholders who contribute to the success and perpetuation of the genre be implicated as exploiters? In other words, even though this chapter doesn't explore the full range of stakeholders, I believe it is worth considering the role played by reality TV participants, by the media that cover and comment on reality TV, and even by reality TV viewers.

My analysis draws primarily from the third chapter of Sample's book where she outlines her specific account of exploitation. Along with considering whether reality television participants are exploited, I will also consider two other sub-issues that she addresses: whether the (possible) exploitation is unintentional and whether it is systemic.

According to Sample, exploitation involves interacting with another being for the sake of advantage in a way that degrades or fails to respect the inherent value of that being. In other words, there is no commitment to the dignity of the other. Exploitation is, therefore, degradation; it is a feature of interactions – of transactions or of relationships – where there is a lack of respect. That lack of respect falls generally into three broad divisions: (i) that which results from neglecting what is necessary for a person's well-being or flourishing; (ii) that which results from taking advantage of an injustice done to a person; and (iii) that which results from commodifying, or treating as a fungible object of market exchange, an aspect of that person's being that ought not be commodified.[27]

Consider Sample's definition of exploitation in the context of reality television participants. Do the producers of reality TV lack respect for those who take part in their shows? Do they fail to place value in the participants and fail to make a commitment to their dignity? Perhaps each of the three broad divisions that encompass lack of respect is applicable to the analysis.

Neglecting a Person's Well-Being

It's easy to think of instances where reality TV participants' well-being or flourishing is neglected on a reality show. Most obviously, consider *Survivor* and its contestants who are denied basics like food and shelter. Or *Big Brother* participants who are kept confined inside the four walls of a house and denied most outside contact for the duration of their participation. Or *Kid Nation* participants – all ages 8 to15 – who are denied adult guidance or supervision. In each of these shows, the neglect is purposeful. In fact, it is part of the shows' very design and a feature around which the central plots are built. When Sample speaks of neglect as exploitation, she is not referring to the kind of neglect that occurs from a simple lack of interaction, from *ignoring* the needs of others. Rather, exploitative neglect involves *denying* the needs of those with whom one is interacting. Although the *consequences* of simply ignoring someone's needs may be worse (imagine a prospective reality TV participant who desperately needs the money she would receive by appearing on the show but is ignored by the casting director), Sample argues that the exploitation that results from denying the needs of those to whom one is connected is actually worse than the simple neglect that occurs when one fails to interact with another.[28] "When we interact with intrinsically valuable others, we come face to face with their value."[29] In the context of reality TV, this interaction has been initiated, and by neglecting the well-being or flourishing of those to whom reality TV producers are connected, those producers fail to recognize the value of the participants. Under Sample's first division, then, at least some reality shows can be charged with exploitation.

Taking Advantage of an Injustice

Sample's second category of "lack of respect" is taking advantage of an injustice done to a person. Is this evident on reality television? In several cases, it appears that shows not only take advantage of an injustice but facilitate or even create that injustice. Consider, for example, the frequent deception that occurs on reality TV – so frequent, in fact, that it has become part of the very fabric of the genre. While some shows contain only deceptive elements, others are built entirely on deception. Whatever the extent, deception surely involves injustice. As one example, consider *My Big Fat Obnoxious Fiancé*. During this reality show, participant Randi Coy was told that she and another participant would win a large sum of money if they married. But her "fiancé" turned out to be an actor hired by the producers to make Coy's life a living hell. The show used this deception, this injustice, as the basis for weeks of amusing or (depending on your perspective) heart-wrenching episodes in which Coy endured the consequences of being completely and unknowingly duped. The same logic applied in *Joe Schmo*, a reality show parody that led "average Joes" to believe they were contestants on a competition reality show when, in fact, they were victims of an elaborate hoax designed to amuse viewers. Even the "feel-good" show *What Not to Wear* routinely begins episodes with deception, persuading would-be participants to talk about their personal style by telling them they're being interviewed for a documentary film.

Reality TV has capitalized on other kinds of injustice as well. Consider the wildly popular *Jon and Kate Plus 8*, which became simply *Kate Plus 8*. From the series' inception, critics raised questions about the wisdom of exposing Jon and Kate Gosselin's eight children to the constant glare of the public through their reality show, but criticism increased significantly when the Gosselins very publicly divorced. In this case, the potential injustice of that divorce for the Gosselin children was made worse by the media spectacle it created. The injustice of divorce also became fodder for the producers of *The Real Housewives of Beverly Hills*. As the show taped, Camille Grammer's 13-year marriage to actor Kelsey Grammer unraveled and her realization of his infidelity became one of the show's key plotlines.

Turning a Person Into a Commodity

Perhaps it's the third kind of interaction that most demonstrates the lack of respect reality show producers have toward their participants. The lack of respect that results from interactions that commodify people, Sample says, is at the heart of much exploitation, and this gets to the heart of what reality television is all about. The people behind reality TV are engaged in a business enterprise wherein they produce a commodity that is consumed by audiences and one that is, relatively speaking, a bargain to produce. Among other cost-saving features, reality television does not need elaborate sets, special effects, scriptwriters or actors who require union wages. In return, reality show producers get a product the public seems to love. Millions of people have tuned in to reality shows, which makes for high ratings and, in turn, translates into networks being able to demand higher advertising rates. The bottom line makes all the sense in the world, particularly in nations such as the USA where commercial TV is facing an economic crisis. So a formula begins to emerge. After the first successful *Bachelor*, it's all that much easier to do *The Bachelor*, Season 2 and *The Bachelorette* and *The Bachelorette*, Season 2, and on and on. To boot, some participants on the shows end up rich, employed, beautiful, even married. Of course, some of them also end up rejected, kicked out, tossed aside, and some of them go on to become the stars of the shows' next incarnation. In fact, the first "bachelorette" was the second choice in *The Bachelor*. She was rejected on that show but was then given a chance to do the rejecting the next time around.

We vividly remember some reality "stars," but most of them simply fade into obscurity; the show got what it needed out of them and then sent them packing. In the context of exploitation, these cases seem the clearer ones. When the consequences are bad for someone, it's intuitively easier to think that person was exploited. But what about people who benefit from their participation on reality TV?

Mutually Beneficial Interactions

What happens when participants on reality shows end up rich, employed, beautiful or married? An important part of Sample's account of exploitation is that the consequences of interactions that involve disrespect are connected to, but do not constitute the exploitation.[30] Much exploitation, Sample argues, is mutually beneficial; just because the situations of both parties in the interaction are improved doesn't mean the transaction or relationship is free of exploitation. So even the man who wins *The Apprentice* and gets a job working for Donald Trump, or the woman who gets an engagement ring from the handsome bachelor, or "the swan," a former "ugly duckling," who gets not only a brand new body (through extensive, medically questionable plastic surgery) but a title to go with it, may be exploited.

Sample might find these cases the most interesting because so many reality show participants seem extremely competent. Particularly in the cases of participants who take part in the second, third or fourth incarnation of a particular show, they know exactly what they're getting themselves into. For competent individuals, Sample asserts that there is some kind of vulnerability or need. In many cases, it is exploiters making use of this need that makes for the exploitation.[31] Vulnerability, according to Sample, is typically, if not always, at the heart of exploitation, and a person cannot be exploited if no vulnerability is made use of.

Returning to reality television, is there a particular need that reality partici-pants have and that reality show producers take advantage of? Perhaps it relates to ego: the need to be recognized, to be noticed, to be in the spotlight. For many of the would-be actors and models who populate the reality television world, the relation to ego is clear. But they aren't alone. As Rochelle Riley of *The Detroit Free Press* noted: "It is painfully obvious, based on the general direction of American television, that the most coveted thing in America truly is that elusive 15 minutes of fame we all grow up wanting, and, as lore holds, we are due at some time."[32]

Then again, perhaps the need is for self-respect. This intuitively makes sense for shows like *Extreme Makeover* and *The Swan*, where contestants' lack of self-respect is a common storyline. Or perhaps the need is for power, opportunity or wealth; that's exactly what participants on *The Apprentice* are promised. Or perhaps the need is for something else altogether, but something that nonetheless relates to an individual's flourishing. Whatever it is, the claim remains that producers are making use of some genuine need that more vulnerable participants have. The key, according to Sample, is that the dignity of these individuals has not been respected. They have not been valued but instead treated, in Kantian terms, as merely a means to an end.

Unintentional Exploitation

One of the conundrums of exploitation has been whether unintentional interactions can be considered exploitative. In other words, if someone didn't *mean* to exploit another, can it rightfully be called exploitation? Sample says "yes" and gives three conditions under which unintentional exploitation can occur. The first is when the exploiter believes that the interactor is not deserving of respect or when the exploited person believes he or she is not deserving of respect.[33] Could this *unintentional* exploitation be the case for reality television? Yes. Does this make the exploitation any less problematic? No. In the former case, we can see where the exploiter (the reality show producer) doesn't believe the interactor (the participant) is deserving of respect; after all, if the participant is truly viewed as a commodity – a mere means to ratings and revenues – then it seems quite likely that the person isn't viewed as deserving of respect. It's as if the participant's moral agency has been stripped away. Robert Bianco of *USA Today* described "the true, sick glory" of *The Swan* like this: "We convince these women their self-worth is wrapped up in their physical appearance, alter them to meet some unspecified standard of beauty and then tell all but one, 'Sorry, you're still not worthy enough'."[34]

In terms of participants' belief that they deserve respect, to hear some of them talk, particularly those on makeover shows, it's as if they have rarely been treated respectfully by others and, therefore, have little *self*-respect. In describing participants on *The Swan*, Ian Kilroy of *The Irish Times* said: "The essential characteristic of the women chosen for Fox's treatment seems to be low self-esteem. They're putty in the hands of the team of 'experts' – plastic surgeons, a dentist, a personal trainer and a therapist – who have the task of transforming them into beauty queens."[35] Of course, it's important to remember that what we see on reality shows has been strategically chosen by the producers; a portrayal may not fully or even accurately represent a person's self-esteem. But these manufactured snapshots do give us a glimpse of participants' attitudes, and many of those glimpses paint a picture of people who quite clearly lack respect for themselves.

Beyond not believing a person is due respect, Sample also says that unintentional exploitation can occur if the exploiter is mistaken in his or her account of what respectful treatment requires, or if the exploiter is mistaken in his or her judgment of what it takes to fulfil the requirements of respect, even if that person understands generally what respect requires.[36] In the case of a program like *The Swan*, we might imagine the show's producers claiming that they do, in fact, respect their participants and that their desire to make participants' lives better is grounded in the very notion of respect. The trouble with this argument is that regardless of how producers feel about participants, their interactions with those participants falls short of respect. In other words, producers aren't living out their convictions through their actions.

As *The Swan* demonstrates, all three instances of unintentional exploitation are possible in the case of reality TV. None of them, however, justifies the treatment. Even if the exploitation is unintentional, it is still exploitation. The challenge in the case of unintentional exploitation, therefore, is dealing not only with a change in behaviour but also with a change in attitude.

Exploitative Systems

The arguments I've presented so far have covered ways in which individual reality shows may exploit participants, but I haven't addressed whether reality TV on the level of genre is exploitative. Sample argues that exploitation can be routine and that exploitative interactions can come to be systematically favoured and promoted.[37] For reality television, this charge is particularly relevant but also difficult to assess. The difficulty arises in the question: Do all reality TV shows fit together in one category, or has reality TV become too big and too complex to call it a single genre? Although not every show demonstrates clear evidence of exploitation as defined by Sample and although behaviors endorsed by some shows are not endorsed by others, I would argue that all shows are still part of a single genre that we know as reality TV, and this genre as a whole has shown itself ready to endorse exploitative tactics. Regardless of differences, for instance, between *Extreme Makeover* and *Extreme Makeover: Home Edition* – differences in intention, in content, in reception – the two shows are both considered reality TV. The genre may encompass a large range of programs, but they all share an identity, and like all identities, the one called reality TV can prove remarkably resilient.

It was the success of early reality TV shows that led to the creation and growth of the genre. The fact that many participants in early shows became bona fide celebrities led to the willingness of many others to participate and then to the opportunity for other shows to take advantage of that willingness. This eventually led to an entire system of reality TV (and its associated identity). While this chapter has focused on instances of producers exploiting participants, a thorough exploration of systemic exploitation would also consider the potential for exploitation of viewers and perhaps even exploitation of shows' creators, who have become tangled in a system that seems to foster a continual slide toward ethically problematic behavior. As Mills noted: "Whether there are boundaries these shows will not cross in the future is hard to know... Rather than looking for ways to tone down humiliation TV, the networks are looking for copycat shows to take it to the next level."[38]

My argument, then, is that while every show may not be exploitative, every show can be implicated as part of an exploitative system. Talent shows such as *American Idol*, *America's Got Talent* and *Dancing with the Stars* do not seem, at least by design, to meet any of Sample's three divisions of exploitation as degradation: (i) the well-being of participants is not neglected; (ii) an injustice is not being capitalized on; and (iii) although participants' talents are viewed as commodities – just as they are for athletes, musicians and actors – the participants themselves are not being commodified (or they are knowingly engaged in self-commodification). Still, as previously noted, even non-exploitative shows are part of a genre that endorses exploitative behaviors. Does this mean a handful of "bad apples" are spoiling the whole bunch? To some extent, yes. At this point in its development, the reality TV basket is full of bad apples. Some good ones may be mixed in, but they're fewer and further between. As Sample points out, systemic exploitation means that exploitation is routine, and exploitative transactions are favored. Systemic exploitation, therefore, relates to the norms of a system. For the reality TV system, the norm seems to be exploitation; the exception is found in shows that *don't* exploit.

The Dilemma of Reality TV

It's important to point out that other scholars and critics, some of whose work appears in this book, have argued that reality TV can be good for society. James Poniewozik has noted that the good-natured response of most participants on reality shows – even those who fail – can inspire average Americans to pursue their dreams.[39] This argument is played out in Chapter 6 by Janie Harden Fritz, who notes, along with others, that reality TV can inspire, motivate and expand horizons.[40] A number of analysts have claimed that reality TV represents a diversification of television culture and a democratization of the media.[41] According to them, reality TV is "a changing vehicle for the representation of ordinary (that is, non-elite) people and a platform for the projection of ordinary voices."[42] What's more, Deni Elliott in Chapter 9 notes that reality TV promotes all-important democratic discourse. For others, reality TV can simultaneously create goods and harms. In Chapter 5, Gareth Palmer discusses reality television's potential to build community, even if that potential most often goes unrealized or if the communities created are communities of concern,[43] and in Chapter 2, Kristie Bunton argues that reality TV can reinforce harmful stereotypes but also debunk them.[44]

So reality television is a complex phenomenon. It is clearly one that presents a dilemma of competing values and one that, therefore, begs the question: does the good outweigh the harm? Is the inspiration, the democratization, the community building worth the exploitation? My critique of some work that highlights the value of reality TV but doesn't simultaneously consider its harms is that that work stops at the descriptive and fails to make an ethical, an evaluative, claim. Taking a Kantian perspective much like Sample's, I argue that the goods achieved by reality TV – even when those goods are quite substantive – should not trump the routine degradation of its participants. Exploitation, therefore, is a harm in itself that cannot be mitigated by good consequences such as those that occur when the exploitation results in mutually beneficial consequences between producers and participants or even larger goods for society.

Confronting the Exploitation

We are left, then, with the question: What ought we do in response to the exploitative nature of reality television? Whether individual interactions on reality TV are exploitative or the exploitation occurs on a systemic level, questions about our obligations to confront this exploitation surely arise. Do we, particularly in our role as viewers, have a moral obligation to try to stop the exploitation? Interestingly, and perhaps surprisingly, Sample would say "no" – at least in most cases – because doing so would interfere with the freedom of the exploited. According to Sample, "competent individuals must be free to choose among their options when they can do so without coercion or distress."[45] For this argument, Sample turns away from Kant and toward John Stuart Mill, who argued that individuals are the best judges of their own interests. If someone finds that getting involved in an exploitative situation is his or her best course of action, we as observers aren't necessarily justified in preventing the transaction.

While I share Sample's concern about the autonomy of people – in our case, reality TV participants – I would argue that her prohibition on interfering doesn't mean we have to *support* the exploitation. The media and audiences should share a collaborative relationship in which they have mutual obligations.[46] Audiences have an obligation to respond to all kinds of media that they consume, and viewers, therefore, ought to register their distaste for the exploitative nature of reality TV.[47] The easiest way to do this is by simply refusing to watch. In a market-based media system driven by ratings, viewers (and advertisers) collectively have the power to influence programming decisions. In fact, some of the most egregious cases of exploitation on reality TV ended when viewers stopped tuning in. *The Swan* was cancelled after two seasons, and *Kid Nation* lasted just one. In far too many other cases, however, viewers – tens of millions of them – are tuning in to reality TV and tacitly endorsing the ongoing exploitation that reality TV breeds. Put simply, viewers can influence the direction of reality TV without interfering with someone's freedom.

Isn't it possible that we can have the goods of reality television – the shows that inspire, that represent ordinary people, that build connection – without the exploitation, the degradation, the humiliation? Why not? Perhaps reality TV is not a true moral dilemma; it isn't only a choice between the good and the harm. To get the inspiration, we don't need the exploitation. If reality TV producers recognize this and take strides to move away from the exploitative model, we may discover that a more ethically justifiable genre lies beneath the wreckage and if, in changing the model, we discover that viewers turn away, perhaps it is they, or we, who are really the exploiters.

Notes

1 Joan Anderman, "Critic's Corner," *The Boston Globe*, 5 January 2009, G12.

2 Fiona McIntosh, "Exploiting Kids… Just for the Sake of TV Viewing," *Sunday Mirror*, 8 February 2009, 29.

3 Kathryn Blaze Carlson, "Rise of Kidsploitation; They're in the Spotlight More Than Ever Before, but Are the Children All Right?" *National Post*, 24 October 2009, A6.

4 David Aaronovitch, "We Must Hate Kids to Put Them Through This; People Moan About Invasion of Privacy but Are Happy to See Children Exploited for Their Own Sneering Entertainment," *The Times* (London), 17 February 2009, 22.

5 Sarah Lyall, "Squirming, but Watching a Dying Reality Star," *The New York Times*, 20 February 2009, A1.

6 Nicolaus Mills, "Television and the Politics of Humiliation," *Dissent*. (Summer 2004): 79–81.

7 James Poniewozik, "Why Reality TV Is Good for Us," *Time*, 17 February 2003, 65–7.

8 Ruth Sample, *Exploitation: What It Is and Why It's Wrong* (Lanham, MD: Rowman and Littlefield, 2003).

9 It's important to note that a good deal of work done on reality TV doesn't engage with the moral questions at all. Scholars, particularly those from the cultural studies field, tend to be more interested in understanding reality TV (as a cultural form and representational practice and as a source of meaning and pleasure) than in offering an ethical critique. Support for reality TV by many of these scholars is discussed briefly towards the end of the chapter.

10 See, for example: Karen Lury, "For Crying out Loud: The Repression of the

Child's Subjectivity in 'The House of Tiny Tearaways'," *Semiotica*, 173, no. 1 (2009): 491–507; Anita Biressi and Heather Nunn, *Reality TV: Realism and Revelation* (London: Wallflower Press, 2005); and Sam Brenton and Reuben Cohen, *Shooting People: Adventures in Reality TV* (London: Verso, 2003).

11 Annette Hill, *Reality TV: Audiences and Popular Factual Television* (London: Routledge, 2005) 185.

12 Clifford G. Christians, Kim B. Rotzoll, Mark Fackler, Kathy Brittain McKee and Robert H. Woods, Jr, *Media Ethics: Cases and Moral Reasoning*, 7th edn (Boston: Pearson, 2005) 278.

13 Angela Cooke-Jackson and Elizabeth K. Hansen, "Appalachian Culture and Reality TV: The Ethical Dilemma of Stereotyping Others," *Journal of Mass Media Ethics* 23, no. 3 (2008): 183–200.

14 Ibid., 194.

15 Berrin A. Beasley, "Weight Watching: The Ethics of Commodifying Appearance for Profit," in *Ethics and Entertainment: Essays on Media Culture and Media Morality*, Howard Good and Sandra L. Borden (eds) (Jefferson, NC: McFarland and Company, 2010) 297–309.

16 Alan Wertheimer, *Exploitation* (Princeton, NJ: Princeton University Press, 1996).

17 Robert Goodin, *Protecting the Vulnerable: A Reanalysis of our Social Responsibilities* (Chicago: University of Chicago Press, 1985); and Robert Goodin, "Exploiting a Situation and Exploiting a Person," in *Modern Theories of Exploitation*, Andrew Reeve ed. (London: Sage Publications, 1987) 166–200.

18 Denis G. Arnold, review of *Exploitation: What It Is and Why It's Wrong*, by Ruth Sample, *Business Ethics Quarterly* 15, no. 4 (October 2005): 733.

19 Sample, Exploitation, xiii.

20 Ibid.

21 See Alan Wertheimer, review of *Exploitation: What It Is and Why It's Wrong* by Ruth Sample, *Utilitas: A Journal of Utilitarian Studies* 19, no. 2 (June 2007): 259–61; Jeremy C. Snyder, review of *Exploitation: What It Is and Why It's Wrong*, by Ruth Sample, *Journal of Value Inquiry* 40, no. 1 (2006): 115–21; Arnold, review of *Exploitation*.

22 Yusuf Has, review of *Exploitation: What It Is and Why It's Wrong* by Ruth Sample, *Ethics: An International Journal of Social, Political and Legal Philosophy* 115, no. 1 (October 2004): 190.

23 Cited in Sample, *Exploitation: What It Is and Why It's Wrong*, back cover material.

24 Wertheimer, review of *Exploitation*, 261.

25 I was fortunate to have the opportunity to test my application of Sample's theory with the author, who said she hadn't thought of applying it to reality TV but agreed with my assessment.

26 When I refer to producers of reality TV, I include anyone who has a hand in creating and constructing the product. I use "producer" as shorthand here.

27 Sample, *Exploitation*, 57.

28 Sample, *Exploitation*, 60–1.

29 Ibid., 68.

30 Sample, *Exploitation*, 57.

31 Sample, *Exploitation*, 74.

32 Rochelle Riley, "Reality TV Exploits Fame Seekers," *At Issue: Reality TV*, Karen F. Balkin ed. (San Diego: Greenhaven Press, 2004, 28.

33 Sample, *Exploitation*, 58.

34 Robert Bianco, "There's Nothing Beautiful About 'The Swan'," *USA Today*, 12 April 2004, 3D.

35 Ian Kilroy, "Knives Out in a Bid to be Beautiful; A US TV Series in Which 'Ugly Duckling' Women Try Cosmetic Surgery is Both Fascinating and Repellent," *The Irish Times*, 15 May 2004, 53.

36 Sample, *Exploitation*, 58.

37 Ibid., 61.

38 Mills, "Television and the Politics of Humiliation," 80–1.

39 Poniewozik, "Why Reality TV Is Good for Us."

40 Others have argued that reality TV inspires generosity. See Sara B. Miller and Amanda Paulson, "The Latest Buzz in TV Programming – Generosity," *Christian Science Monitor*, 16 September 2004, 01.

41 See Kira Cochrane, "A Misunderstood Democratic Triumph." www. newstatesman.com, 4 December 2006; Biressi and Nunn, *Reality TV: Realism and Revelation*; Murray and Oullette, *Reality TV: Remaking Television Culture*.

42 Biressi and Nunn, *Reality TV: Realism and Revelation*, 155.

43 Heather Havrilesky also argues for reality TV's community-building capabilities. See Heather Havrilesky, "Three Cheers for Reality TV," *Salon*, 13 September 2004. http:// dir.salon.com/story/ent/feature/2004/0-2/13/reality/index.html.

44 This argument is also made by Erik, "Keeping it Real; Gays and Lesbians Are Everywhere in Life, So Of Course They're on Reality TV. From Lance Loud to Chris Beckman and Brandon Quinton, the Diverse Bunch of Out Gays on These Shows Brings Viewers Face-to-Face with Our Queer Lives," *Advocate*, 30 April 2002, 38.

45 Sample, *Exploitation*, 86.

46 I've borrowed the "collaborative relationship" wording from Deni Elliott and David Ozar who were speaking specifically of the relationship between journalism and the public. I argue that the relationship should extend to all forms of media.

47 For a full discussion of the obligations of media consumers and a justification of those obligations, see Wendy Barger and Ralph Barney, "Media-Citizen Reciprocity as a Moral Mandate," *Journal of Mass Media*

Ethics 19, no. 3/4 (2004): 191–206; and Wendy Wyatt, "The Ethical
Obligations of News Consumers," in *Journalism Ethics: A Philosophical
Approach*, Christopher Meyers ed. (New York: Oxford University Press, 2010)
283–95.

Conclusion: Reality TV Conveys Responsibilities

Wendy N. Wyatt and Kristie Bunton

For those who, before reading this book, were ready to condemn reality TV for its lack of a moral compass, we hope the book has fostered some appreciation for the genre. For those who saw reality TV as simply entertainment and not something even to be considered in the ethical realm, we hope the book has helped develop an understanding of why exploring and critiquing the ethics of reality TV is essential. For those already convinced that reality TV is filled with ethical complexity and richness, we hope the book has offered some new ways of thinking about it.

When we take reality TV seriously and when we recognize the complexity of the reality genre, as this book does, we see that a simplistic approach to evaluating its ethics is unsatisfactory. We also begin to see that many of the typical charges made against reality TV are far less interesting than the ethical questions that arise when we examine it in more sophisticated ways. As just one example from this book, in Chapter 8, Edward Spence notes that it's interesting to ask whether reality TV producers give scripts to participants or edit those participants' conversations in a way that doesn't fully reflect "the truth." Far more intriguing, however, is the question Spence asks about whether reality TV constitutes axiological deception – whether it is "playing us false" by deceiving us in ways that corrode our values. In this book's Foreword, James Poniewozik suggests that the really important questions about reality TV's ethics are not those that relate to the producers' tactics, but instead are those questions that relate to audiences' reception of reality TV. How do viewers of reality TV interpret it? What kind of meaning are they making from it and what do they *do* with those meanings? As many chapters in this book have demonstrated, audiences aren't just passively consuming reality TV; they are actively engaging with it, and we think that's significant. Reality TV is powerful and complicated enough that it requires critical, media literate audiences. Most of us will never produce a reality TV show, but we'll be in the viewing audience for years. That conveys upon us as viewers the ethical obligation of media literacy.

The concept of "media literacy" has been around since at least the 1960s, and readers of this book from around the world will certainly have various experiences with it. For example, some countries such as the UK and Canada have mandated media education programs as part of their national school curricula. Other countries, such as the USA, have a far less comprehensive approach to media literacy; some schools teach it, while others don't. Although approaches to fostering media literacy vary, its core goals remain the same. Media literate audiences become sophisticated consumers of media. They understand media messages are constructions, which are the work of human beings. They take into consideration the people and organizations behind media messages. They recognize that all media have embedded values and points of view. They pay attention not only to what appears in the media, but to what's left out. They understand that different people make different meanings from the same message, and they know something about producing media, so if they end up being creators of reality TV shows someday, they are able to adopt a sophisticated approach to that creation.[1]

Media literate audiences are more discerning, but they're also more demanding. Therefore, we think media literate audiences can use reality shows to grapple with important ethical questions. But they can also use their collective power to say "no" to the most ethically troubling reality shows, those that bring unjustified harm to participants and audiences alike. What's more, as Christopher Meyers and Janie Harden Fritz point out in their chapters, media literate audiences can take the best reality shows as inspiration, as motivation and as stories that can help contribute to a life of flourishing. Too, because reality TV producers have ensured their audiences can interact with one another in online venues, media literate, ethically responsible audience members can take it upon themselves to congratulate programs that pose important questions about the reality of life in contemporary communities or to chide programs that exploit, stereotype or abuse reality participants.

While we think reality TV viewers have these sorts of ethical responsibilities, which should be taken seriously, that doesn't mean reality TV producers should be ethically free to do whatever they want, leaving the onus on viewers alone. The people who create reality TV – like all creators of entertainment – need to recognize they have ethical responsibilities, and they need to take those responsibilities seriously. Producers need to acknowledge that they can bring real harm to real people: As this book demonstrates, reality producers can exploit, they can stereotype, they can impose values, they can invade privacy and they can create communities based on fear. Yet, as veteran producer F. Miguel Valenti argued, many of the people behind entertainment products resist seeing their work as ethically laden, and they are uncomfortable serving in a role of "arbiter" of morals.[2] We agree with Valenti, however, that people who produce entertainment, including those who produce reality TV, must learn to become more comfortable with their ethical responsibilities and must act in ways that honor them. All shows are different, but we think all producers should refrain from treating participants as mere commodities and viewers as mere consumers. All producers should recognize the power of their programs not just to entertain but to inform and educate. All producers, to the greatest extent possible, should obtain informed consent from their participants. All producers should establish means through which audiences can engage in meaningful ways with their shows. We think reality TV producers can create products that are not only profitable and entertaining, but also ethical.

Perhaps more than any other current television genre, reality TV offers compelling messages that millions of viewers around the world regard as "real" – not to mention entertaining, shocking, troubling, amusing and exasperating. As this complex genre evolves, we believe the programs' producers and, most especially, their viewers should continue to take seriously reality TV and the ethical questions it never fails to raise.

Notes

1   These are skills widely recognized by scholars as those that are developed through training in media literacy. For additional information on the concept of media literacy, see: Center for Media Literacy, "Teacher's/Leader's Orientation Guide," *MediaLit Kit: A Framework for Learning and Teaching in a Media Age* (Santa Monica, CA: Center for Media Literacy, 2003).

2   F. Miguel Valenti, Les Brown and Laurie Trotta, *More Than a Movie: Ethics in Entertainment* (Boulder, CO: Westview Press, 2000) 4.

Bibliography

Aaronovitch, David. 'We Must Hate Kids to Put Them Through This: People Moan About Invasion of Privacy but are Happy to see Children Exploited for Their Own Sneering Entertainment'. *The Times* (London), 17 February 2009, 22.

Adams, Abigail. 'Quotes'. Goodreads Inc., 2001. http://www.goodreads.com/author/quotes/1479.Abigail_Adams.

Adams, Guy. 'Italian Americans Outraged at Reality TV "Slur"'. *The Independent* (London), 26 December 2009, 30.

Ahloowalia, S. B. *Invasion of the Genes: Genetic Heritage of India*. (New York: Strategic Book Publishing, 2009).

Althouse, Ann. '"What Not To Wear" Is Not the Kind of Reality Show I Would Normally Watch', 27 April 2008. http://althouse.blogspot.com.

Anderman, Joan. 'Critic's Corner'. *The Boston Globe*, 5 January 2009, G12.

Andrejevic, Mark. *Reality TV: The Work of Being Watched*. (Boulder, CO: Rowman & Littlefield, 2004).

Appiah, Kwame Anthony. *Cosmopolitanism: Ethics in a World of Strangers*. (New York: W. W. Norton, 2006).

—*Nicomachean Ethics*, translated by W. D. Ross. (Oxford: Clarendon Press, 1908). Available at The Internet Classics Archive (online).http://classics.mit.edu/Aristotle/nicomachaen.html.

—*The Nicomachean Ethics*, 5th edn, translated by F. H. Peters. (London: Kegan Paul, Trench, Truebner & Co., 1893).

Aristotle. *Politics*, translated by Benjamin Jowett. (Chelmsford, MA: Courier Dover Publications, 2000). Available at The Internet Classics Archive (online). http://classics.mit.edu/Aristotle/politics.html.

Arnett, Ronald C., Janie M. Harden Fritz and Leeanne M. Bell. *Communication Ethics Literacy: Dialogue and Difference*. (Thousand Oaks, CA: Sage, 2009).

Arnold, Denis G. Review of *Exploitation: What It Is and Why It's Wrong* by Ruth Sample. *Business Ethics Quarterly* 15, no. 4 (October 2005): 733.

Associated Press. '"Sister Wives" Stars Challenge Utah Bigamy Law', 14 July 2011. Available at First Amendment Center (online). http://www.firstamendmentcenter.org/sister-wives-stars-challenge-utah-bigamy-law.

Atkinson, Claire and Jon Fine. 'New Reality Dawns for TV Economics', *Advertising Age*, 27 September 2004, 75.

Bandura, Albert. 'Social Cognitive Theory of Mass Communication'. In *Media Effects: Advances in Theory and Research*, Jennings Bryant and Dolf Zillman (eds). (Mahwah, NJ: Lawrence Erlbaum, 2002) 43–67.

Barger Wendy and Ralph Barney. 'Media-Citizen Reciprocity as a Moral Mandate'. *Journal of Mass Media Ethics* 19, no. 3/4 (2004): 191–206.

Barnhart, Aaron. 'Reality TV Shows Find Success With Small Budgets, Strong Personalities'. *Kansas City Star*, 5 December 2010. http://www.kansascity. com/2010/12/05/2499791/biggest-loser-other-reality-shows.html.

BBC News online. 'Is Reality TV Harmful?' 1 September 2004. http://news.bbc. co.uk/2/hi/talking_point/3607482.stm.

Beasley, Berrin A. 'Weight Watching: The Ethics of Commodifying Appearance for Profit. In *Ethics and Entertainment: Essays on Media Culture and Media Morality*, Howard Good and Sandra L. Borden (eds). (Jefferson, NC: McFarland and Company, 2010) 297–309.

Bell, Christopher A. *American Idolatry: Celebrity, Commodity and Reality Television*. (Jefferson, NC and London: McFarland, 2010).

Bell-Jordan, Katrina E. 'Black. White. And a Survivor of The Real World: Constructions of Race on Reality TV'. *Critical Studies in Media Communications* 25, no. 4 (2008): 353–72.

Benn, Stanley. *A Theory of Freedom*. (New York: Cambridge University Press, 1988).

Bianco, Robert. 'There's Nothing Beautiful about 'The Swan."' *USA Today*, 12 April, 2004, 3D.

Bilteyst, Daniel. 'Media Audiences and the Game of Controversy: On Reality TV, Moral Panic and Controversial Media Stories'. In *European Culture and the Media*, Ib Bondebjerg and Peter Golding (eds). (Bristol, UK: Intellect Books, 2004) 117–37.

Bineham, Jeffery L. 'The Construction of Ethical Codes in the Discourse and Criticism of Popular Culture'. In *Communication Ethics, Media and Popular Culture*, Phyllis M. Japp, Mark Meister and Debra K. Japp (eds). (New York: Peter Lang, 2007) 13–39.

Biressi Anita and Heather Nunn. *Reality TV: Realism and Revelation*. (London: Wallflower Press, 2005).

Blauvelt, Christian. 'ABC's 'Secret Millionaire': Why it Sends the Wrong Message'. Entertainment Weekly.com, 6 March 2011. http://popwatch. ew.com/2011/03/06/secret-millionaire.

Bloustein, Edward. 'Privacy as an Aspect of Human Dignity: An Answer to Dean Prosser'. In *Philosophical Dimensions of Privacy: An Anthology*, Ferdinand Schoeman ed. (New York: Cambridge University Press, 1984.) 156–202.

Bok, Sissela. *Common Values*. (Columbia, MO: University of Missouri Press, 1995).

—*Lying: Moral Choice in Public and Private Life*. (New York: Vintage Books, 1999).

Booth, Wayne C. *The Rhetoric of Fiction*. (Chicago: University of Chicago Press, 1961).

Brenton, Sam and Reuben Cohen. *Shooting People: Adventures in Reality TV*. (London: Verso, 2003).

Bronzwaer, Stijn. 'Lachen! Je Bent Op TV!', *NRC. Next*, 17 March 2011, 1.

Brown, W. and A. Singhal. 'Ethical Dilemmas of Prosocial Televison'. *Communication Quarterly* 38, no. 3 (Summer 1990): 268–80.

Bruno, Luigino. 'The Happiness of Sociality. Economics and Eudaimonia: A Necessary Encounter'. *Rationality and Society* 22 (2010): 383–406.

Bruzzi, Stella. *New Documentary: A Critical Introduction*. (London: Routledge, 2000).

Bryant, Jennings and Dolf Zillmann. 'A Retrospective and Prospective Look at Media Effects'. In *The Sage Handbook of Media Processes and Effects*, Robin L. Nabi and Mary Beth Oliver (eds). (Thousand Oaks, CA, 2009) 9–17.

Calvert, Clay. *Voyeur Nation: Media, Privacy, and Peering in Modern Culture*. (Colorado: Westview Press, 2004).

Campbell, Shannon B., Steven S. Giannino, Chrystal R. China and Christopher S. Harris. 'I Love New York: Does New York Love Me?' *Journal of International Women's Studies* 10, no. 2 (2008): 20–8.

Cara Communications Corporation. 'AFV Release Forms', ABC. com. Last modified 20 November 2009. http://abc.go.com/shows/ americas-funniest-home-videos/release-forms.

Carey, James W. *Communication as Culture: Essays on Media and Society*, rev. edn. (New York: Routledge, 2009).

Carlson, Kathryn Blaze. 'Rise of Kidsploitation; They're in the Spotlight More Than Ever Before, but are the Children All Right?' *National Post*, 24 October 2009, A6.

Carter, Bill. 'Tired of Reality TV but Still Tuning In'. *The New York Times*, 13 September 2010, B4.

Cavender, Gray. 'In Search of Community on Reality TV'. In *Understanding Reality Television*, Su Holmes and Deborah Jermyn (eds). (London: Routledge, 2004) 154–72.

Celebitchy.com. 'Sister Wives Husand Kody Admits He Gets his Wives' Names Mixed Up,' 10 March 2011. http://www.celebitchy.com/145013/ sister_wives_husband_kody_admits_his_gets_his_wives_names_mixed_up/.

Center for Media Literacy. 'Teacher's/Leader's Orientation Guide'. *MediaLit Kit: A Framework for Learning and Teaching in a Media Age.* (Santa Monica, CA: Center for Media Literacy, 2003).

Chesebro, James. 'The Media Reality: Epistemological Functions of Media in Cultural Systems'. *Critical Studies in Mass Communication* 1 (June 1984): 111–30.

Chomsky, Noam, Peter Rounds Mitchell and John Schoeffel. *Understanding Power: The Indispensable Chomsky.* (New York: The New Press, 2002).

Christians, Clifford G., Kim B. Rotzoll, Mark Fackler, Kathy Brittain McKee and Robert H. Woods, Jr. *Media Ethics: Cases and Moral Reasoning*, 7th edn. (Boston: Pearson, 2005).

Cochrane, Kira'.A Misunderstood Democratic Triumph'. www.newstatesman. com, 4 December 2006.

Cooke-Jackson, Angela and Elizabeth K. Hansen. 'Appalachian Culture and Reality TV: The Ethical Dilemma of Stereotyping Others'. *Journal of Mass Media Ethics* 23, no. 3 (2008): 183–200.

Coontz, Stephanie. *The Way We Never Were: American Families and the Nostalgia Trap.* (New York: Basic Books, 2000).

Corner, John. *The Art of Record.* (Manchester: Manchester University Press, 1996).

Davis, Michael. 'Why Journalism is a Profession'. In *Journalism Ethics: A Philosophical Approach*, Christopher Meyers ed. (New York: Oxford University Press, 2010) 91–102

Debackere, Jan. 'EenFout en GevaarlijkProgramma'. *De Standaard*, 12 March 2005. http://www.standaard.be/artikel/detail.aspx?artikelid=GQFD8DAT

—'Op Zoeknaar de Cultuurclash'. *De Standaard*, 4 September 2006. http://www.standaard.be/artikel/detail.aspx?artikelid=G84113ET7

Deery, June. 'Reality TV as Advertainment'. *Popular Communication* 2, no. 1 (2004): 1–20.

Deggans, Eric. 'So-Called 'Reality TV' Really Just a Ploy to Grab Young Viewers'. *St Petersburg Times*, 10 December 2010, 2E.

Dehnart, Andy. 'ABC Rejects Golden Cage Because of Costs'. *Reality Blurred*, 8 May 2008. http://www.realityblurred.com/realitytv/archives/future_shows/2008_May_09_abc_rejects_golden_cage.

Deka, R. 'Mate Selection Criteria: Comparative Study of Parents and Youth'. Unpublished master's thesis, SNDT Women's University, Mumbai, India, 2011.

DeRose, Justin, Elfriede Fürsich and EkaterinaHaskins. 'Pop (Up) Goes the 'Blind Date': Supertextual Constraints on "Reality" Television'. *Journal of Communication Inquiry* 27 (2003): 171–89.

Desai, Mira K. and B. C. Agrawal. *Television and Cultural Change: Analysis of Transnational Television in India*. (New Delhi: Concept, 2009).

Descartes, René. *Meditations on First Philosophy*, John Cottingham ed. (Cambridge: Cambridge University Press, 1996).

Discovery Communications. 'OWN: The Oprah Winfrey Network Gives Sneak Peek of New Network Dedicated to Living Your Best Life,' 2 April 2009. http://corporate.discovery.com/discovery-news/own-the-oprah-winfrey-network-gives-sneak-peek-of-/.

Dnaindia.com. '"Our Marriage Will Last" Say Perfect Bride Winners'. 13 December 2009. http://www.dnaindia.com/entertainment/report_our-marriage-will-last-say-perfect-bride-winners_1323259.

Douglas, Susan J. *The Rise of Enlightened Sexism: How Pop Culture Took Us from Girl Power to Girls Gone Wild*. (New York: St Martin's Press, 2010).

Dovey, Jon. *Freakshow: First Person Media and Factual Television*. (London: Pluto, 2000).

Dubey, Bharati. 'An A-grade Idea'. *The Times of India*, 7 August 2011, 6.

Dubey, R. 'Who's Gearing for Swayamvar 3?' *Hindustan Times*, 20 March 2010. http://www.hindustantimes.com.

Dubrofsky, Rachel E. 'Fallen Women in Reality TV: A Pornography of Emotion'. *Feminist Media Studies* 9, no. 3 (2009): 353–68.

—'Therapeutics of the Self: Surveillance in the Service of the Therapeutic'. *Television and New Media* 8, no. 4 (2007): 263–84.

Durham, Gigi M. *The Lolita Effect*.(New York: The Overlook Press, 2008).

Etzioni, Amitai. *The Spirit of Community: Rights, Responsibilities and the Communitarian Agenda*. (New York: Crown, 1993).

Farhi, Paul. 'Reality TV Broadcasts "Bad Black Guy" Stereotype'. *The Washington Post*, 20 February 2001, C01.

Fisher, Walter R. 'Narration as a Human Communication Paradigm: The Case of Public Moral Argument'. *Communication Monographs* 51, no. 1 (1984): 1–22.

Garrison, Jim. 'Prophetic Epideictic Rhetoric: Poetic Education Beyond Good and Evil'. *Educational Theory* 53, no. 2 (2003): 221–41.

Gauthier, Candace Cummins. 'Privacy Invasion by the News Media: Three Ethical Models'. *Journal of Mass Media Ethics* 17, no. 1 (2002): 20–34.

Gicas, Peter. 'Michelle Obama to Guest Star on Extreme Makeover: Home Edition'. Eonline, 20 July 2011. http://www.eonline.com/news/michelle_obama

Godlewski, Lisa R. and Elizabeth M. Perse. 'Audience Activity and Reality Television: Identification, Online Activity, and Satisfaction'. *Communication Quarterly* 58, no. 2 (2010): 148–69.

Goffman, Erving. *The Presentation of Self in Everyday Life*. (New York: Doubleday, 1959.)

Goodin, Robert. 'Exploiting a Situation and Exploiting a Person'. In *Modern Theories of Exploitation* Andrew Reeve ed. (London: Sage Publications, 1987) 166–200

—*Protecting the Vulnerable: A Reanalysis of our Social Responsibilities*. (Chicago: University of Chicago Press, 1985).

Gray, Jonathan. 'Cinderella Burps: Gender, Performativity, and the Dating Show'. In *Reality TV: Remaking Television Culture*, 2nd edn, Susan Murray and Laurie Ouellette (eds). (New York: New York University Press, 2009) 260–77.

Gutman, Amy. *Democratic Education*, rev. edn. (Princeton, NJ: Princeton University Press, 1999).

Haack, Robin. 'Education and the Good Life'. *Philosophy* 56 (1981): 289–302.

Haggerty, Maryann. 'Reality TV: Is It Harmless Entertainment or a Cultural Threat?' *CQ Researcher* 20, no. 29 (2010): 677–700.

Halbert, Debora. 'Who Owns Your Personality: Reality TV and Publicity Rights'. In *Survivor Lessons*, Matt Smith and Andrew Wood (eds). (Jefferson, NC: McFarland, 2003) 37–56.

Hall, Alice. 'Perceptions of the Authenticity of Reality Programs and Their Relationships to Audience Involvement, Enjoyment, and Perceived Learning'. *Journal of Broadcasting & Electronic Media* 53, no. 4 (2009): 515–31.

—'Viewers' Perceptions of Reality Programs', *Communication Quarterly* 54, no. 2 (2006): 191–211.

Hall, Emma and Laurel Wentz. '"Space Cadets" Takes off without a Sponsor'. *Advertising Age*, 12 December 2005, 14.

Harden, Janie Marie. 'Rhetorical Example as Narrative: A Case Study of Selected Television Commercials'. Master's thesis, University of Georgia, 1984.

Harrison, Mary-Catherine. 'The Paradox of Fiction and the Ethics of Empathy: Reconceiving Dickens's Realism'. *Narrative* 15, no. 3 (2008): 256–79.

Has, Yusuf. 'Review of Exploitation: What It Is and Why It's Wrong by Ruth Sample'. *Ethics: An International Journal of Social, Political and Legal Philosophy* 115, no. 1 (October 2004): 189–90.

Havrilesky, Heather. 'Three Cheers for Reality TV'. *Salon*, 13 September 2004. http:// dir.salon.com/story/ent/feature/2004/0-2/13/reality/index.html.

'Heather'. *How to Look Good Naked*, season 2, episode 8. Directed by Becky Smith. Aired 9 September 2008 (Los Angeles: RDF USA).

Heffernan, Virginia. 'Mining Reality'. *The New York Times Opinionator*, 3 April 2011. http://opinionator.blogs.nytimes.com/2011/04/03/mining-reality/?pagemode=print.

Hendershot, Heather. 'Belabored Reality: Making It Work on The Simple Life and Project Runway'. In *Reality TV: Remaking Television Culture*, 2nd edn, Susan Murray and Laurie Ouellette (eds). (New York: New York University Press, 2009) 243–59.

Hill, Annette. 'Big Brother, the Real Audience,' *Television and New Media* 3, no. 3 (August 2002): 323–40.

—*Reality TV: Audiences and Popular Factual Television.* (London: Routledge, 2005).

—*Restyling Factual TV.* (London: Routledge, 2007).

Hopson, Mark C. '"Now Watch Me Dance": Responding to Critical Observations, Constructions, and Performances of Race on Reality Television'. *Critical Studies in Media Communication* 25, no. 4 (2008): 441–6.

Horkheimer, Max. 'Art and Mass Culture'. In *Critical Theory: Selected Essays*, translated by Matthew J. O'Connell. (New York: Continuum Publishing Company, 1999) 273–90.

India.gov.in. 'Sectors: Agriculture,' 29 April 2011. http://india.gov.in/sectors/agriculture/index.php.

India Ministry of Home Affairs. 'Census of India 2011: Gender Composition of the Population', 8 March 2011. http://www.censusindia.gov.in/2011-prov-results/data_files/india/Final%20PPT%202011_chapter5.pdf

—'Census of India 2011: Rural/Urban Distribution of Population', 15 July 2011. http://www.censusindia.gov.in/2011-prov-results/paper2/data_files/india/Rural_Urban_2011.pdf

Jermyn, Deborah. '"This Is About Real People!' Video Technology, Actuality and Affect in the Television Crime Appeal'. In *Understanding Reality Television*, Su Holmes and Deborah Jermyn (eds). (New York: Routledge, 2004) 173–90.

Juluri, Vamsee. 'Music Television and the Invention of Youth Culture in India'. *Television and New Media* 3, no. 4 (November 2002): 367–86.

Justin, Neal'.Reality TV Gets More Real'. Star Tribune, 17 April 2011, 1E.

Kant, Immanuel. *Groundwork on the Metaphysics of Morals*, translated by H. J. Patton. (New York: Harper Torchbooks, 1964).

—*Observations on the Beautiful and the Sublime*, translated by John T. Goldthwait. (Berkeley: University of California Press, 2004).

Kearney, Richard. *On Stories: Thinking in Action.* (New York: Routledge, 2002).

Kilroy, Ian. 'Knives Out in a Bid To Be Beautiful; A US TV Series in Which "Ugly Duckling" Women Try Cosmetic Surgery Is Both Fascinating and Repellent'. *The Irish Times*, 15 May 2004, 53.

Kraszewski, Jon. 'Country Hicks and Urban Cliques: Mediating Race, Reality, and Liberalism on MTV's The Real World'. In *Reality TV: Remaking Television Culture*, 2nd edn, Susan Murray and Laurie Ouellette (eds). (New York: New York University Press, 2009) 205–22.

Krijnen, Tonny, and Ed Tan. 'Reality TV as a Moral Laboratory: A Dramaturgical Analysis of *The Golden Cage*'. *Communications* 34 (2009): 449–72.

Kuehn, Manfred. *Kant: A Biography.* (Cambridge: Cambridge University Press, 2002).

Leonard, Tom. 'Thirsty Simon, or Are You Trying to Sell Us Something? How Product Placement Is about to Transform British TV'. *Mail Online*, 24 January 2011. http://www.dailymail.co.uk/news/article-1349936/Simon-Cowells-American-Idol-Coca-Cola-product-placement-transform-UK-TV.html.

Levinson, Jerrold. 'The Place of Real Emotion in Response to Fictions'. *The Journal of Aesthetics and Art Criticism* 48, no. 1 (1990): 79–80.

'Little People, Big World'. *TLC Family Guide: Monday Night Schedule.* http://tlc.discovery.com/guides/family/tlc-family-night/schedule.html

Lowry, Brian. 'Stereotypes: Reality TV's Dirty Little Secret'. *Variety*, 11–17 January 2010, 16.

Lundy, Lisa K., Amanda M. Ruth and Travis D. Park. 'Simply Irresistible: Reality TV Consumption Patterns'. *Communication Quarterly* 56, no. 2 (2008): 208–25.

Lury, Karen. 'For Crying Out Loud: The Repression of the Child's Subjectivity in "The House of Tiny Tearaways"'. *Semiotica*, 173, no.1 (2009): 491–507.

Lyall, Sarah. 'Squirming, but Watching a Dying Reality Star'. *The New York Times*, 20 February 2009, A1.

MacIntyre, Alasdair. *After Virtue*, 3rd edn. (Notre Dame, IN: Notre Dame University Press, 2007).

Magder, Ted. 'Television 2.0: The Business of American Television in Transition'. In *Reality TV, Remaking Television Culture*, 2nd edn, Susan Murray and Laurie Ouellette (eds). (New York: New York University Press, 2009) 141–64

Mahon, James Edwin. 'A Definition of Deceiving'. *International Journal of Applied Philosophy* 21, no. 2 (2007): 192.

Mansbridge, Jane. 'Everyday Talk in the Deliberative System'. In *Deliberative Politics, Essays on Democracy and Disagreement*, Steven Macedo ed. (New York: Oxford University Press, 1999) 210–21.

Manwaring-Wright, Sarah. *The Policing Revolution*. (London: Harvester Press, 1983).

Matheson, Sarah A. 'The Cultural Politics of Wife Swap: Taste, Lifestyle Media, and the American Family'. *Film & History* 37, no. 2 (2007): 33–47.

McIntosh, Fiona. 'Exploiting kids … just for the sake of TV viewing'. *Sunday Mirror*, 8 February 2009, 29.

McKay, Hollie. 'Wedding Themed Reality Shows Make a Mockery of Marriage?' *Fox News*, 14 March 2011. http://www.foxnews.com/entertainment/2011/03/14.

McKenzie, Robert. 'Audience Involvement in the Epideictic Discourse of Television Talk Shows. *Communication Quarterly* 48, no. 2 (2000): 190–203.

Meers, Erik. 'Keeping it Real; Gays and Lesbians are Everywhere in Life, So Of Course They're on Reality TV. From Lance Loud to Chris Beckman and Brandon Quinton, the Diverse Bunch of Out Gays on These Shows Brings Viewers Face-to-Face with Our Queer Lives'. *Advocate*, 30 April 2002, 38.

Meyers, Christopher. *Journalism Ethics: A Philosophical Approach*. (New York: Oxford University Press, 2010).

—'*Re*-Appreciating W. D Ross: Naturalizing Prima Facie Duties and a Proposed Method'. *Journal of Mass Media Ethics* 26, no. 4 (2011-forthcoming) [AQ].

Meyrowitz, Joshua. *No Sense of Place: The Impact of Electronic Media on Social Behavior*. (New York: Oxford University Press, 1985).

Mill, John Stuart. *Autobiography*. Bartleby.com: Harvard Classics (online).http://www.bartleby.com/25/1/.

—'On Liberty'. In *John Stuart Mill: On Liberty and Other Essays*, John Gray ed. (New York: Oxford University Press, 1859/1991).

—*On Liberty*, Currin V. Shields ed. (Indianapolis, IN: Bobbs-Merrill, 1956).

—*Principles of Political Economy*, 7th edn, William J. Ashley ed. (London: Longmans, Green and Co., 1909). http://www.econlib.org/library/Mill/mlP73.html.

—'Utilitarianism'. In *Classics of Political and Moral Philosophy*, Steven M. Cahn ed. (New York: Oxford University Press, 2002) 893–926.

Miller, Sara B. and Amanda Paulson. 'The Latest Buzz in TV Programming – Generosity'. *Christian Science Monitor*, 16 September 2004: 1.

Mills, Nicolaus. 'Television and the Politics of Humiliation'. *Dissent* (Summer 2004): 79–81.

Morgan, Michael. 'Cultivation Analysis and Media Effects. In *The Sage Handbook of Media Processes and Effects*, Robin L. Nabi and Mary Beth Oliver (eds). (Thousand Oaks, CA: Sage, 2009) 69–82

MTV. 'Message Board'. *Teen Mom – Your Story*, 2011. http://community.mtv.com/Content/Discussions/DiscussionResults.aspx?tcid=39738.

—'Season 2, Episode 212 Summary'. *Teen Mom*, 2011. http://www.mtv.com/shows/teen_mom/season_2/episode.jhtml?episodeID=170102#moreinfo.

Murphy, Kerrie. 'Irritating Regardless of Race, Colour or Creed'. *Weekend Australian,* 14 October 2006, 34.

Murray, Susan and Laurie Ouellette, (eds). *Reality TV: Remaking Television Culture*. (New York: New York University Press, 2004/2009).

Nabi, Robin L., Erica. N. Biely, Sara. J. Morgan and Carmen R. Stitt. 'Reality-based Television Programming and the Psychology of its Appeal'. *Media Psychology* 5 (2003): 303–30.

Natu, Nitasha. 'Mother Pushes 2 Kids, Leaps from 19th Floor'. *The Times of India*, 9 March 2011. http://articles.timesofindia.indiatimes.com/2011-03-09/mumbai/28672386_1_gaurav-malad-gupta-family.

NDTV. 'About The Show'. *The Big Fat Indian Wedding*, 2011.http://goodtimes.ndtv.com/GoodTimesShowPage.aspx?ShowID=14.

NDTV.com. 'Mumbai Woman Jumps to Death with 6 Year Old Son', 17 April 2011. http://www.ndtv.com/article/cities/mumbai-woman-jumps-to-death-with-6-year-old-son-99294.

Newell, Jay, Jeffrey Layne Blevins and Michael Bugeja. 'Tragedies of the Broadcast Commons: Consumer Perspectives on the Ethics of Product Placement and Video News Releases', *Journal of Mass Media Ethics* 24, no. 4 (October 2009): 201–19.

New York Post. 'Are Jon and Kate Gosselin Exploiting Their Children?' 28 May 2009. http://www.foxnews.com/entertainment/2009/05/28/jon-kate-gosselin-exploiting-children/.

Nichols, Bill. *Blurred Boundaries*. (Bloomington, IN: Indiana University Press, 1994).

Nielsen Research. 'Product Placements Rose 6% in First Quarter, Nielsen Reports', 5 May 2008. http://www.nielsen.com/us/en/insights/press-room/2008/product_placements1.html.

Nussbaum, Martha C. *Cultivating Humanity: A Classical Defense of Reform in Liberal Education*. (Cambridge, MA: Cambridge University Press, 1997).

—'"Finely Aware and Richly Responsible:" Moral Attention and the Moral Task of Literature'. *Journal of Philosophy* 82, no. 10 (1985): 516–29.

—*Love's Knowledge: Essays on Philosophy and Literature*. (New York: Oxford University Press, 1990).

Oprah.com. 'House Rules', 22 June 2011. http://www.oprah.com/oprahdotcom/House-Rules.

Orbe, Mark P. 'Representations of Race in Reality TV: Watch and Discuss'. *Critical Studies in Media Communication* 25, no. 4 (2008): 345–52.

Ouellette, Laurie. 'Reality TV Gives Back: On the Civic Functions of Reality Entertainment'. *Journal of Popular Film and Television* 68, no. 2 (2010): 66–71.

Ouellette, Laurie and James Hay. *Better Living Through Reality TV: Television and Post-Welfare Citizenship.* (Malden, MA: Blackwell, 2008).

Page, Clarence. 'Warped Reality on the Screen'. *The Washington Times*, 23 February 2001, A16.

Pal, Divya. 'Jasmeet, Inderpal's Expensive TV Wedding'. *The Times of India*, 17 March 2011. http://timesofindia.indiatimes.com/entertainment/tv/Jasmeet-Inderpals-expensive-TV-wedding/articleshow/7717533.cms.

Paoli-Lebailly, Pascale. 'Reality TV, Entertainment Viewing Surpasses Drama in 2010'. *Rapid TV News*, 28 March 2001, www.rapidtvnews.com.

Parker, James. 'Prison Porn'. *The Atlantic*, March 2010. http://www.theatlantic.com/magazine/archive/2010/03/prison-porn/7906/.

Pathak, Manish K. 'Harassed New Mother Jumps to Death; Husband, In-laws Arrested'. dailybhaskar.com, 11 May 2011. http://daily.bhaskar.com/article/MAH-MUM-harassed-new-mother-jumps-to-death-2094533.html.

Paton, H.J. *The Moral Law.* (London: Hutchinson and Co, 1972).

Pattanaik, Devdutt. 'Decoding a Hindu Marriage'. 6 February 2011. http://devdutt.com.

Plaisance, Patrick. *Media Ethics: Key Principles for Responsible Practice.* (Thousand Oaks, CA: Sage, 2009).

Plato. *The Republic,* translated by Benjamin Jowett. The Internet Classics Archive. http://classics.mit.edu/Plato/republic.html.

Poniewozik, James. 'How Reality TV Fakes It', *Time*, 29 January 2006. www.time.com.

—'Why Reality TV is Good for Us'. *Time*, 17 February 2003, 65-7.

Posner, Richard. 'An Economic Theory of Privacy'. In *Philosophical Dimensions of Privacy: An Anthology*, Ferdinand Schoeman ed. (New York: Cambridge University Press, 1984) 333–45.

Postman, Neil. *Amusing Ourselves to Death: Public Discourse in the Age of Show Business.* (New York: Penguin, 1985).

Pozner, Jennifer. *Reality Bites Back: The Troubling Truth about Guilty Pleasure TV.* (Berkeley: Seal Press, 2010).

Prosser, William. 'Privacy [A Legal Analysis]'. In *Philosophical Dimensions of Privacy: An Anthology*, Ferdinand Schoeman ed. (New York: Cambridge University Press, 1984) 104–55.

Pullen, Christopher. 'The Household, The Basement and the Real World'. In *Understanding Reality Television*, Su Holmes and Deborah Jermyn (eds). (London: Routledge, 2004). 211–32.

Putnam, Robert. *Bowling Alone: The Collapse and Revival of American Community.* (New York: Simon and Schuster, 2000).

Raphael, Chad. 'The Political Economic Origins of Reali-TV'. In *Reality TV: Remaking Television Culture*, 2nd edn, Susan Murray and Laurie Ouellette (eds). (New York: New York University Press, 2009) 123–40.

Rawls, John. *A Theory of Justice* rev. edn. (Cambridge, MA: Belknap Press, 1999).

Reality TV World. 'Guidelines'. *Message Board Forums*, 2011. http://community. realitytvworld.com/cgi-sys/cgiwrap/rtvw2/community/dcboard.cgi?

—'Message Board Forum'. *Super Nanny*, February 2005. http://community. realitytvworld.com/boards//DCForumID17/1171.shtml.

Redden, Guy. 'Making Over the Talent Show'. In *Exposing Lifestyle Television: The Big Reveal*, Gareth Palmer ed. (Manchester: Manchester University Press, 2008) 129–44.

Reisman, David. *The Lonely Crowd*. (New Haven, CT: Yale University Press, 1950).

Rice, Lynette. 'Jon & Kate Talk to EW about Life in the Fishbowl'. *Entertainment Weekly*, 13 May 2009. http://insidetv.ew.com/2009/05/13/kate-gosselin-o/.

—'Kids, Cameras, Controversy'. *Entertainment Weekly*, 22 May 2009. http:// www.ew.com/ew/article/0,,20278901,00.html.

Rich, Carole. *Writing and Reporting the News*, 6th edn. (New York: Cengage, 2010).

Riley, Rochelle. 'Reality TV Exploits Fame Seekers'. *At Issue: Reality TV*, Karen F. Balkin ed. (San Diego: Greenhaven Press, 2004).

Robertson, Denise. 'Bad Taste Reality TV? There's Worse to Come'. *Western Mail*, 13 December 2005, 20.

Rosen, Jeffrey. *The Unwanted Gaze: The Destruction of Privacy in America*. (New York: Random House, 2000).

Ross, William David Ross. *The Right and The Good*. (Indianapolis, IN: Hackett Publishing, 1988).

Russell, Bertrand. *Education and the Good Life*. (New York: W. W. Norton & Co, 1970).

Sample, Ruth J. *Exploitation: What It Is and Why It's Wrong*. (Lanham, MD: Rowman and Littlefield, 2003).

Sanneh, Kelefa. 'The Reality Principle, The Rise and Rise of a Television Genre'. *The New Yorker*, 9 May 2011, 72–7.

Saulny, Susan. 'Black? White? Asian? More Young Americans Choose All of the Above'. *The New York Times*, 30 January 2011, 1.

SBS Television. *Go Back to Where You Came From* (website), 2011. http://www. sbs.com.au/shows/goback.

Schejter, Amit M. 'Art Thou for Us, or for Our Adversaries? Communicative Action and the Regulation of Product Placement: A Comparative Study and a Tool for Analysis'. *Akron Law Review* 39 (2006): 207–42.

Scheufele, Dietram and David Tewksbury. 'Framing, Agenda Setting, and Priming: The Evolution of Three Media Effects Models'. *Journal of Communication* 57, no. 1 (2007): 9–20.

Schoeman, Ferdinand David ed. *Privacy and Social Freedom*. (New York: Cambridge University Press, 1992).

Shakespeare, William. *As You Like It*, Act 2, scene, 7. Lines 139–43. http://www. enotes.com/shakespeare-quotes/all-world-s-stage.

—*Hamlet*. William Shakespeare Literature (online). http://www.shakespeare-literature.com/Hamlet/index.html.

—*The Tempest*. The Complete Works of William Shakespeare (online). http:// shakespeare.mit.edu/tempest/.

Shields, David. *Reality Hunger: A Manifesto*. (New York: Alfred A. Knopf, 2010).

Simon, Caroline. *The Disciplined Heart: Love, Destiny, and Imagination.* (Grand Rapids, MI: Eerdmans, 1997).

Skeggs, Beverly and Helen Wood. 'The Labor of Transformation and Circuits of Value "Around" Reality Television'. *Continuum: Journal of Media & Cultural Studies* 22, no. 4 (2008): 559–72.

Smart, Ninian. *Worldviews: Cross-Cultural Explorations of Human Beliefs*, 3rd edn. (Upper Saddle River, NJ: Prentice-Hall, 2000).

Snyder, Jeremy C. Review of *Exploitation: What It Is and Why It's Wrong* by Ruth Sample. *Journal of Value Inquiry* 40, no. 1 (2006): 115–21.

Sonwalkar, P. 'India: Making of Little Cultural/Media Imperialism?' *Gazette* 63, no. 6 (2001): 505–19.

Spence, Edward H. 'A Universal Model for the Normative Evaluation of Internet Information'. *Ethics and Information Technology* 11, no. 4 (2009): 243–53.

Spence, Edward H. and Aaron Quinn. 'Information Ethics as a Guide for New Media'. *Journal of Mass Media Ethics* 23, no. 4 (2008): 264–79.

Stangor, Charles. 'The Study of Stereotyping, Prejudice, and Discrimination Within Social Psychology: A Quick History of Theory and Research'. In *Handbook of Prejudice, Stereotyping, and Discrimination*, Todd D. Nelson ed. (New York: Psychology Press, Taylor & Francis Group, 2009) 1–22.

Star India PVT. 'Exclusive Sneak Peak of the Show'. *Wife Bina Life*, 2011. http://starplus.startv.in/show/Wife_Bina_Life/publicopinion_0_163.aspx

Stelter, Brian. 'As Unknown Faces Become Stars, Reality Shows Fight Pay Escalation'. *The New York Times*, 27 July 2010, B1.

—'TV Viewing Continues to Edge Up'. *The New York Times*, 2 January 2011. www.nytimes.com.

Sur, A. K. *Sex and Marriage in India.* (Bombay: Allied Publishers, 1973).

Sweney, Mark. 'EU to Allow Product Placement on TV'. *The Guardian*, 23 November 2007. http://www.guardian.co.uk/media/2007/nov/30/advertising.television.

Taylor, Charles. *A Secular Age.* (Cambridge, MA: Belknap, 2007).

—*Sources of the Self: The Making of the Modern Identity.* (New York: Cambridge University Press, 1992).

Time/CNN. 'Time/CNN Poll: What Would You Do?' *Time*, 26 June 2000, 56.

The Times of India. 'Mass Marriage: 251 Couples to Wed in Ballia', 6 March 2011. http://articles.timesofindia.indiatimes.com/2011-03-06/varanasi/28659766_1_mass-marriage-hindu-couples-high-profile-wedding.

TLC. 'About the Show'.*Sister Wives*, 2011. http://tlc.howstuffworks.com/tv/sister-wives/about-sister-wives.htm.

Trigoboff, Dan. 'Whatcha Gonna Do? Sue'. *Broadcasting & Cable*, 8 June 1998, 32.

Tuchman, Gaye. *Making News: A Study in the Construction of Reality.* (New York: Free Press, 1978).

Turner, Graeme. *Ordinary People and the Media: The Demotic Turn.* (London: Sage, 2010).

TV.com. *Little People Big World, 2011.* .http://www.tv.com/little-people-big-world/show/61776/summary.html?tag=page_nav;main.

—'Show Overview'. *Queen for a Day*, 2011. http://www.tv.com/queen-for-a-day/show/20880/summary.html.

Tversky, Amos and Daniel Kahneman. 'Availability: A Heuristic for Judging Frequency and Probability'. *Cognitive Psychology* 5, no. 2 (1973): 207–32.

Twenge, Jean. *Generation Me: Why Today's Young Americans Are More Confident, Assertive, Entitled and More Miserable Than Ever Before*. (New York: Free Press, 2006).

Valenti, F. Miguel, Les Brown and Laurie Trotta. *More Than a Movie: Ethics in Entertainment*. (Boulder, CO: Westview Press, 2000).

Vande Berg, Leah R., Lawrence A. Wenner and Bruce E. Gronbeck (eds). *Critical Approaches to Television*, 2nd edn. (Boston: Houghton Mifflin, 2004).

Vasi, Nazia. 'KBC Makes Airtel a Crorepati'. *The Times of India*, 23 July 2005. http://articles.timesofindia.indiatimes.com/2005-07-23/india/27863981_1_sms-star-tv-indian-idol.

Wang, G., Jan Servaes and A. Goonasekera. *The Communications Landscape: Demystifying Media Globalisation*. (London: Routledge, 2000).

Ward,Stephen J. A. *Global Journalism Ethics*. (Montreal: McGill Queen's University Press, 2010).

Warren, Samuel D. and Louis D. Brandeis. 'The Right to Privacy [The Implicit Made Explicit]'. In *Philosophical Dimensions of Privacy: An Anthology*, Ferdinand Schoeman (ed). (New York: Cambridge University Press, 1984) 75–103.

Wasserman, Ed. 'The Ethics of Product Placement'. Presentation at the annual convention of the Association for Education in Mass Communication and Journalism, San Francisco, CA, 3 August 2006. http://ewasserman.com/2006/08/03/the-ethics-of-product-placement/.

Wasserstrom, Richard. 'Privacy: Some Arguments and Assumptions'. In *Philosophical Dimensions of Privacy: An Anthology*, Ferdinand Schoeman ed. (New York: Cambridge University Press, 1984) 317–32.

Weber, Brenda. *Makeover TV*. (Durham and London: Duke University Press, 2009).

We Live in Public, DVD, directed by Ondi Timoner. (Pasadena, CA: Interloper Films, 2009).

Wertheimer, Alan. *Exploitation*. Princeton. (NJ: Princeton University Press, 1996).

—Review of *Exploitation: What It Is and Why It's Wrong* by Ruth Sample. *Utilitas: A Journal of Utilitarian Studies* 19, no. 2 (June 2007): 259–61.

White, Robert A. 'Communitarian Ethic of Communication in a Postmodern Age'. *Ethical Perspectives*, 3–4 (December 1996): 207–18.

Wiltz, Teresa. 'The Evil Sista of Reality Television; Shows Trot Out Old Stereotypes to Spice Up Stagnant Story Lines'. *The Washington Post*, 25 February 2004, C01.

Wyatt, Wendy. 'Humiliation TV: A Philosophical Account of Exploitation in Reality Television'. Presentation at the Annual Convention of the Association for Education in Journalism and Mass Communication, Denver, CO, 4–7 August 2010.

—'The Ethical Obligations of News Consumers'. In *Journalism Ethics: A Philosophical Approach*, Christopher Meyers ed. (New York: Oxford University Press, 2010) 283–95.

Yang, Jeff,and Angelo Ragaza. 'The Beauty Machine'. In *Facing Difference: Race, Gender and Mass Media*, Shirley Biagi and Marilyn Kern-Foxworth (eds). (Thousand Oaks, CA: Pine Forge Press, 1997) 11–15.

Young, Iris. *Justice and the Politics of Difference*. (Princeton, NJ: Princeton University Press, 1990).

Contributors

Kristie Bunton is a communication ethics professor at Minnesota's University of St Thomas. She has published chapters in *The Ethics of Entertainment* (McFarland, 2010), *The Ethics of the Family* (Cambridge Scholars Publishing, 2010), *Handbook of Mass Media Ethics* (Lawrence Erlbaum, 2009), *Holding the Media Accountable* (Indiana University Press, 2000) and *Journalism Ethics: A Reference Handbook* (ABC-CLIO, 1997). Her work has appeared in journals including *American Journalism*, *Journalism and Mass Communication Quarterly*, *Journal of Mass Media Ethics*, *Journalism Educator* and *Public Integrity*, and she is lead author of *Writing Across the Media* (Bedford/St Martin's Press, 1999).

Mira K. Desai is an associate professor at SNDT Women's University in Mumbai, India. She has professional media experience in mainstream newspaper, television, internet, newsletter and documentary film-making environments. Before becoming an academician, she worked at Development Education Communication Unit-Indian Space Research Organisation, Educational Media Research Centre and the rural women's empowerment programme Mahila Samakhyain Gujarat. The 2002 recipient of the Government of India award for her book manuscript for neo-literates, she has a number of publications to her credit, including two books in Gujarati and two in English: *Television in India: Many Faces* (Authors Press, 2010) and *Television and Cultural Change: Analysis of Transnational Television in India* with Binod C. Agrawal (Concept, 2009). Her research interests are audiences, Indian television, research methodology, women's studies, gender and development, and the sociology of technology.

Deni Elliott holds the Eleanor Poynter Jamison Chair in Media Ethics and Press Policy at the University of South Florida. She is also the campus ombudsman and director of graduate studies for her department. She writes extensively across the fields of practical ethics, but with special attention to the roles of governmental officials, citizens, and the press in democracy.

Madeleine Shufeldt Esch is an assistant professor in the Department of English at Salve Regina University in Rhode Island, where she teaches courses in journalism and media studies. Her primary research focus is on issues of gender and consumption in lifestyle television, particularly the subgenre of home improvement programming. A portion of this research tracing explanations for the home improvement TV boom is published in *Exposing Lifestyle Television: The Big Reveal* (Ashgate, 2010). She is also the author of 'Rearticulating Ugliness, Repurposing Content: Ugly Betty Finds the Beauty in Ugly' in *Journal of Communication Inquiry*.

Janie Harden Fritz, who completed her PhD at the University of Wisconsin-Madison, is an associate professor of communication and rhetorical studies at Duquesne University in Pennsylvania. Her research focuses on communicative practices that constitute, sever and restore the ties that bind individuals to the institutions of which they are a part. She co-edited (with Becky L. Omdahl) *Problematic Relationships in the Workplace* (Peter Lang, 2006), co-authored (with Ronald C. Arnett and Leeanne M. Bell) *Communication Ethics Literacy: Dialogue and Difference* (Sage, 2009) and co-edited (with S. Alyssa Groom) *Communication Ethics and Crisis: Negotiating Differences in Public and Private Spheres* (forthcoming with Fairleigh Dickinson University Press). Her work appears in *Management Communication Quarterly*, *Communication Research Reports*, *Journal of Public Management and Social Policy*, *Communication Monographs*, *Journal of Business Communication*, *Journal of Business Ethics*, and in several edited volumes. Her current research project focuses on professional civility in the workplace.

Christopher Meyers is professor of philosophy and director of the Kegley Institute of Ethics at California State University-Bakersfield. Most of his research is in practical ethics, particularly bioethics and journalism ethics. Meyers is author of numerous publications, including *Journalism Ethics: A Philosophical Approach* (Oxford, 2010) and *A Practical Guide for Clinical Ethics Consulting: Expertise, Ethos and Power* (Rowman and Littlefield, 2007). Meyers is also the ethics consultant for most of the Bakersfield area hospitals, writes regular op-ed columns for *The Bakersfield Californian*, and is vice-president of the Board of Governors for Bakersfield Express, an online news source.

Gareth Palmer is a professor of media in the School of Media, Music and Performance at the University of Salford in the UK. He is widely published on reality television and surveillance. In 2003 he published *Discipline and Liberty* (Manchester University Press), one of the first books to look at the connections between surveillance and reality television. Recently, his focus has shifted to lifestyle television and the ways it forms moral and ethical issues for mass consumption. In 2008 he organized the first International Conference on Lifestyle Television. In 2010 he published a collection of papers on the subject, *Exposing Lifestyle Television* (Ashgate). Palmer has always combined his writing with practical work and has won external funding for media projects, most recently a grant from the Learning Technologies Fund to produce *New Mornings, Old Streets* about the people of Salford.

James Poniewozik joined *TIME* as media and television critic in 1999. He has written in-depth stories on subjects from reality TV to the *Sopranos*, and has written essays, features and reviews on subjects including international media coverage of the war in Iraq, the influence of 9/11 on popular culture, and the way Hollywood's portrayals of mobsters have affected the mafia itself. He's also written widely on books, movies, comic books, the news media and pop culture. Poniewozik was media critic and media section editor at Salon.com, has contributed to publications including *Fortune*, *Rolling Stone*, *New York*, *The New York Times Book Review*, Suck.com and *Talk*, and is a commentator for NPR's *On the Media* and *All Things Considered*. A native of Monroe, Michigan, Poniewozik graduated with a BA in English from the University of Michigan, and attended the graduate programme in fiction writing at New York University.

Edward H. Spence, BA (Honors, First Class), PhD (University of Sydney), is a senior research fellow at the ARC Research Special Centre for Applied Philosophy and Public Ethics (CAPPE) in Australia, and a research fellow at the 3TU Centre for Ethics and Technology, The Hague, Netherlands. He teaches media and new media ethics in the School of Communication and Creative Industries at Charles Sturt University. He is the lead author of *Advertising Ethics* (2005), co-author of *Corruption and Anti-Corruption: A Philosophical Approach* (2005), the author of *Ethics Within Reason: A Neo-Gewirthian Approach* (2006) and lead author of *Media, Markets and Morals*, Wiley-Blackwell (2011). He is also co-editor of *The Good Life in a Technological Age* (forthcoming from Routledge). He is the author of several papers in national and international journals in applied philosophy and applied ethics, including media and new media ethics and the ethics of information and technology. He is also the founder and producer of the *Philosophy Plays* project, which aims to introduce philosophy to the general public through drama and audience participation through discussion.

Bastiaan Vanacker is an assistant professor at Loyola University Chicago. His research focuses on media ethics and law. He holds an MA in philosophy from the University of Ghent in his native Belgium and a PhD in mass communication from the University of Minnesota. His book on hate speech regulation is titled *Global Medium, Local Laws: Regulating Cross-Border Cyberhate* (LFB Scholarly Publishing, 2009), and his ethics research has appeared in *The Journal of Mass Media Ethics*, *Ethics and Information Technology* and *Convergence*. He has recently taken up an interest in television studies, resulting in an article in the *Journal of Popular Film and Television* discussing the depiction of the mass media in *The Sopranos*.

Wendy N. Wyatt is an associate professor of communication ethics in the Department of Communication and Journalism at the University of St Thomas, Minnesota. Much of her research focuses on issues of media and democracy. In addition to interests in journalism ethics, citizen responsibilities to media, and media literacy, she has developed a theoretical perspective on press criticism that is introduced in her book, *Critical Conversations: A Theory of Press Criticism* (Hampton, 2007). Her work has appeared in such journals as *The Journal of Mass Media Ethics*, *Journalism and Mass Communication Quarterly*, and the *International Journal of Applied Philosophy*, as well as in several edited volumes. Wyatt has served on the Minnesota News Council and is currently book review editor for the *Journal of Mass Media Ethics*.

Index

Young, Iris 90
Your OWN Show: Oprah's Search for the Next TV Star 151–2
YouTube 99

Zamora, Pedro 29
Zeus 131

TE DUE